€ THE BOOK OF MONEY

**EVERYTHING YOU NEED TO KNOW
ABOUT HOW WORLD FINANCES WORK**

THE BOOK OF MONEY

EVERYTHING YOU NEED TO KNOW ABOUT HOW WORLD FINANCES WORK

DANIEL CONAGHAN & DAN SMITH

MITCHELL BEAZLEY

First published in Great Britain in 2013 by
Mitchell Beazley
A division of Octopus Publishing Group Limited
Endeavour House, 189 Shaftesbury Avenue, London WC2H 8JY
An Hachette UK company
www.octopusbooks.co.uk

A CIP catalogue record of this book is available from the
British Library.

ISBN: 978-1-84533-680-6

Editor and picture researcher: Julian Flanders
Designer: Craig Stevens
Infographics: Patrick Mulrey
Indexer: Nick Fawcett

10 9 8 7 6 5 4 3 2 1

Printed and bound in China

CONTENTS

The world has always been divided into the haves and have-nots, such as the people living side by side in this suburb of Buenos Aires. Today, as the rich become super-rich and poverty remains endemic, particularly in sub-Saharan Africa, many economists argue that the situation is worse than ever. However, the global financial downturn has prompted the world's financial institutions to look toward developing new systems to replace the outdated and discredited models that brought about the crisis in the first place.

It is hard to argue against the assertion that money is the single greatest invention of the human mind. In the 21st century it exists in all cultures, from tribes living in the rainforest to the cities of the planet's most powerful industrialized nations. Familiar, divisible and acceptable, money is the lifeblood of the world: oiling the wheels of business and commerce, acting as a store of value and standing as the essential gauge of relative value. Like all the great inventions, it is impossible to imagine what life was like before money came along.

INTRODUCTION

Throughout history the use of money has developed with astonishing speed. Today is no different. Advances in electronic technology and the Internet indicate that the days of coins and notes are numbered. First developed in the 1980s, the global customer base for online banking is set to reach over 650 million people by 2015, while the development of near-field technology has paved the way for "contactless purchasing" via a mobile device. Estimates are that by 2016 it will be possible to pay for everything in this way.

The global financial crisis

Only time will tell if the recent global financial crisis, which began in 2007, will be added to the list of major financial disasters. But, painful as it may be, the economic downturn has forced everyone to look again at the way the world's economy functions, something that may turn out to be the light at the end of a long tunnel.

As people turn their attention to the world of finance and banking, some see a world peopled by Masters of the Universe, quaffing champagne while planning on how to spend their bonuses. Others see gray-haired men in suits offering prudent advice to be thrifty and pay into your pension pot. The reality is, of course, somewhere in between. Whatever your viewpoint, most will agree that money is now housed in a bewildering and complex edifice. But help is at hand. *The Book of Money* is a window into that world, shining a light on all areas of finance and explaining apparently complicated systems in simple terms.

Macro- and microeconomics

The financial world works at two different levels: macroeconomics is the study of economics as a whole, evaluating the effectiveness of the economic policies of the world's government. At the other end of the scale, microeconomics is concerned with the economic behavior of an individual unit, maybe a person, a particular household or a particular firm. By examining both ends of the spectrum, *The Book of Money* explains the ways in which they are connected and how in the 21st century the collapse of a bank in Iceland, for example, can have serious consequences for a family living in Tokyo or Helsinki.

On a macro scale, the book looks at the various systems by which the world's governments manage their money, attempting, when all is said and done, to balance income and expenditure. It also examines the complexities of the relationship between government and the banks, which it does not control but upon which a nation's financial well-being depends. On a micro scale, the book looks at the importance of individual economic decisions and explains how they play out further down the line. In between the two are the world's financial markets, which, in today's global environment often appear to be stages on which the world's destiny is played out, 24/7. However, despite their reputation, they are nothing more than the name suggests, places to buy and sell. After all, despite its elaborate wrapping, there are surprisingly few things we can do with money: we can spend it, save it or give it away.

The great divide

In spite of its outstanding qualities, money is not without its problems. It has an array of characteristics and quirks that render it unpredictable, mysterious and unreliable. It is subject to force and to greed and can be at the heart of astonishing pain, both in its abundance and its scarcity. Of course, there have always been rich and poor, under every political system ever devised. But, in the second decade of the 21st century, statistics indicate that the rich are getting richer and the poor are getting poorer, indeed Barack Obama called financial inequality "the defining issue of our time."

The financial crisis has put this into sharp focus as the world's seven billion inhabitants look to find someone to blame. In turn, financial institutions and companies throughout the world are seeking to get their houses in order, accepting that financial accountability is increasingly required by their customers and knowing that if they are to survive they need to show a higher level of corporate social responsibility. When the world stood on the edge of the "fiscal cliff" and its governments announced their latest packages of austerity measures, it is heartening to think that they remembered the word's of Bill Gates, one of the world's richest men and its current greatest philanthropist, who said that "with great wealth comes great responsibility."

> **"THE IMPORTANCE OF MONEY FLOWS FROM IT BEING A LINK BETWEEN THE PRESENT AND THE FUTURE."**
> JOHN MAYNARD KEYNES (1883–1946), POLITICAL ECONOMIST

"MONEY MAY BE THE HUSK OF MANY THINGS
BUT NOT THE KERNEL. IT BRINGS YOU
FOOD, BUT NOT APPETITE; MEDICINE, BUT NOT
HEALTH; ACQUAINTANCE, BUT NOT FRIENDS;
SERVANTS, BUT NOT LOYALTY; DAYS OF JOY,
BUT NOT PEACE OR HAPPINESS."
HENRIK IBSEN (1828–1906), WRITER

1 A BRIEF HISTORY OF MONEY

↑
This clay tablet, dated between 3200–2300 B.C.E. and found on the site of the ancient Sumerian city of Susa (in present-day Iran), records economic transactions. It is believed that the Sumerians developed the world's first writing system in response to an increasingly complex society in which records needed to be kept on taxes, rations, agricultural products and tributes to keep society running smoothly.

It is not known exactly when money first appeared in the world, partly because it may well pre-date writing, but at least 5,000 years ago ancient civilizations, much concerned with agriculture, began to "need" some measure of value for the produce they wished to buy and sell. In other words, people required a currency, which had its foundations in the simple concept of trust.

The shekel facilitates commerce

The Mesopotamian civilization of around 3000 B.C.E. was the first to develop the idea of a currency and saw some of the first experiments with what we now call money. In Mesopotamia, the barter system, the exchange of one item for another of similar value, and the systems of gift economics, whereby items would be presented from one person to another, gradually gave way to commodity money, whose value derived from the material (such as gold or silver) of which it was made.

The Mesopotamians' *shekel* represented a specific quantity of barley and was both a unit of currency and of weight and was put to work to allow commerce – including the import and export of goods – to take place. The shekel made its way

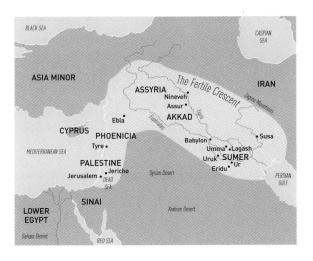

← Mesopotamia, the land that sits between the Euphrates and Tigris rivers, is known as the Fertile Crescent or the Cradle of Civilization, and corresponds roughly to modern-day Iraq. The area first attracted people because it offered food, turning the arid regions of western Asia into a fertile garden. The first people that laid claim to this area in around 3500 B.C.E. were the Sumerians.

MONEY TIMELINE

9000–6000 B.C.E. Domestication of livestock, particularly cattle, and the growing of plant products, particularly grain, leading to trade

6000–3000 B.C.E. Writing developed in Mesopotamia, probably for keeping accounts of barter exchanges. Use of the shekel – a quantity of barley – as currency Discovery of gold

3500 B.C.E. Bronze, an alloy of copper and tin, first produced, independently, in Middle East and Far East

3150 B.C.E. First Egyptian Dynasty

3000–2000 B.C.E. Banking invented in Babylonia, with the use of palaces and temples as safe places for the storage of valuable items, such as grain, livestock, agricultural implements and precious metals

2575 B.C.E. Construction of the Great Pyramid at Giza, a project requiring state planning and capital

c.1792–c.1750 B.C.E. Reign of King Hammurabi in Babylon; production of the Code of Hammurabi, which included laws governing banking operations

c.1200 B.C.E. First recorded use of cowrie shells as money in China

c.1100 B.C.E. Decline of Egyptian dynasties begins

into the Old Testament, which includes for example, the story of Joseph being sold to the Midianites for twenty shekels' weight in silver.

Ancient Egypt developed an economy that was centrally organized and strictly controlled. They used a type of barter system with standard weight sacks of grain and the *deben* – approximately 91 grams (3 oz) of copper or silver – as currency. Workers were paid in grain. Prices were fixed across the country and transactions were recorded to facilitate trade, in which grain was often used to "buy" other goods.

As such measures of value began to circulate, it was a natural progression for it to come under the rule of law. In ancient Babylon, King Hammurabi gave his name to the Code of Hammurabi, which was drawn up around 1760 B.C.E. and instituted laws governing interest on debt and the payment of fines for misdemeanors. Gradually, money became a tool for transacting business contracts and the sale and purchase of property.

↓ Hammurabi (standing), the sixth king of Babylon, is credited with issuing the first set of financial regulations. Known as the Code of Hammurabi they were written on stone tablets that stood in the city for all to see.

Shell money

Elsewhere in the ancient world there was use of shell money, with the cowrie shell making an appearance in Chinese accounts written up in the second millennium, in references to payments and treasure. Shell money, whose value was partly due to its decorative properties, was used as jewelry and currency across all the world's continents and endured, particularly in Africa, for many centuries. One shell even earned the nickname the "money cowrie" – from its Latin name *Monetaria moneta* – as it became synonymous with value exchange.

Once the first forms of money began to be circulated, the idea caught on quickly, spreading throughout the ancient world. It became the touchstone for the development of widespread commerce between countries and one of the foundation stones of organized and increasingly sophisticated societies, particularly in Italy and Greece.

THE DEVELOPMENT OF COINAGE

↓

The most widespread Roman coins (minted from the middle of the 3rd century B.C.E. to the middle of the 3rd century C.E.) included the aureus[1] (gold), the denarius[2] (silver), the sestertius[3] (brass), the as[4] (copper) and the dupondius[5] (brass). Inflation, lack of precious metals and the vagaries of politics and trade caused constant debasement of the Roman currency.

Money developed rapidly in the Greco-Roman world, which stretched from around the 8th century B.C.E. – (the first Olympic Games were held in Greece in 776 B.C.E.) while Rome was founded, according to legend, in 753 B.C.E. – until the middle of the first century C.E. It appeared in coin form around 600 B.C.E. when an uneven lump of gold and silver alloy was minted by King Alyattes in Sardis, Lydia (in present-day eastern Turkey). Now known as the Lydian Lion, this can reasonably claim to have been the world's first coin. Experts are divided as to its buying power: some historians believe it might have provided a month's living, others that it could buy only one sheep or three jars of wine.

One reason that King Alyattes produced the first coins might have been to pay Greek mercenaries in his armies who wanted their payment authenticated. In turn the Greek city-states began to issue their own coins, mainly made by hand out of silver from the mines at Laurium. As coin-producing technology developed so did the organization of mints. Some of the earliest were found on the island of Crete, which began to produce coins with a high level of technical and aesthetic quality.

The minting of money soon became widespread, as imperial governments sought to issue and control currency, literally stamping their authority on pieces of gold, silver and bronze.

Lifeblood of the Roman Empire

Ancient Rome was home to over a million people and, at its height, was the hub of a vast empire that spread out from the city and from Ostia, its major port. Trade – both by sea throughout the Mediterranean and the Black Sea and, famously, by the roads that the Romans built for both commercial and military purposes – was the Roman Empire's lifeblood.

AS RICH AS CROESUS

Born about 595 B.C.E., Croesus succeeded his father Alyattes as King of Lydia. Continuing his father's work, Croesus is now credited with issuing the first coins – made from electrum, an alloy of gold and silver – with a standardized level of purity. This important development, along with a great many tributes from the subjugated Lydian peasantry, allowed Croesus to amass enormous riches, some of which he translated into equally extravagant gifts for the god Apollo, at Delphi. In 546 B.C.E., Croesus' fortunes declined when he was defeated and captured by Cyrus the Great of Persia. Croesus' fate is unclear – one account has him being burned alive on a pyre, while another maintains that he was saved by the grateful Apollo, who sent a thunderstorm to extinguish the flames.

The Roman Empire ran with admirable efficiency, using a single currency and keeping customs dues to a minimum and suppressing pirates. It cost a vast amount of money to run, and trade provided much of the revenue needed. It was essential therefore for its armies to provide the necessary security under which trade could flourish. The Romans were huge exporters of all manner of goods, from basic foodstuffs such as corn, beef, olive oil and wine to wood and metal materials for construction to a plethora of luxury items such as papyrus, pottery, glass, silver and perfume. Its main trading partners were in Spain, France, the Middle East and North Africa.

↓

Trajan's Market sits at one end of the Forum in Rome opposite the Colosseum. Originally built as a marketplace in the center of the city, as it developed the area became the economic, political and religious hub of the city, and was regarded by many as the very center of the Roman Empire.

800 B.C.E. Approximate end of the Greek Dark Ages

776 B.C.E. First Olympic Games

753 B.C.E. Rome founded by Romulus

600 B.C.E. Forum built in Rome. Minting of the first coin, the Lydian Lion, by King Alyattes in Lydia (now eastern Turkey)

600–570 B.C.E. Use of coins spreads from Lydia to Greece

546 B.C.E. Use of coins spreads from Lydia to Persia. Persians mint first pure gold coins
First silver coins minted in Greece

500 B.C.E. Classical Greece

406–405 B.C.E. Greeks produce bronze coins

323 B.C.E. Classical Greece ends with death of Alexander the Great

300 B.C.E. Minting of the first Roman coins

269 B.C.E. Romans issue silver coins

146 B.C.E. End of Ancient Greece with defeat of Macedonia by the Romans

27 B.C.E. Expansion of the Roman Empire by Augustus, who reforms the monetary and taxation systems issuing new, almost pure gold and silver coins, and new brass and copper ones. He also introduces a general sales tax, a land tax and a flat-rate poll tax

27–29 C.E. Estimated date of biblical story of Christ chasing the money lenders from the temple in Jerusalem

476 C.E. Decline of the Western Roman Empire when Romulus Augustus is forced to abdicate

610 C.E. End of the Classical Roman state

The foundations of the banking system that we know today lie in the great cultural melting pot of the Renaissance in 15th-century Italy. While the Renaissance is mainly associated with art, science, literature and philosophy, money was, in many cases, the spur: wealth and patronage led to a flowering of art and architecture. More prosaically, it also gave birth to banks, which could accept deposits and – crucially – make loans.

THE EMERGENCE OF BANKING

Money went hand in hand with banking in Renaissance Italy. Indeed, we owe the word bank to the *banca* – the wooden bench used by Italian moneymen as desks and exchange counters. Italy's most famous banking family, the Medici, grew their eponymous bank to be the biggest and most trusted in Europe, partly because it dealt only in the *fiorino d'oro*, the gold florin, which took its name from the city of Florence. These coins – the equivalent of around $150 today – were of standard size and quality (54 grains of pure gold) and replaced silver as the principal currency for business transactions across Europe.

FIRST PRINCIPLES OF ACCOUNTING

A Renaissance mathematician – Luca Pacioli, born in Tuscany around 1450 – was one of the most important contributors to the development of accounting. His book *Summa de Arithmetica, Geometria Proportioni et Proportionalita*, published in 1494, was something of a bestseller. It taught principles of accounting that became widespread across Europe, the central tenet of which was that an inventory of possessions should be accompanied by accounts of debits and credits. The key to the system, which had its origins among Venetian merchants, was "double-entry," or making every record of a transaction in the books twice: any debit on the left-hand side had to be offset by a credit on the other. One of Pacioli's examples was: "Debit Featherbeds. Credit Capital for so much in feathers. Record number of beds, description as per Inventory, and value in Lire, Grossi, Picioli." By using this system of bookkeeping, a "balance" – or a snapshot of the state of the original inventory – could be seen at any time.

Noblemen in Italy and elsewhere, enriched by finance and trade, celebrated their success and perhaps assuaged their guilt (usury, or money lending, was still regarded as sinful) with lavish commissions to their finest artists and craftsmen. Trade guilds, which dominated Renaissance metropolitan society, acted as a further channel for money to find expression in beautiful objects. In Renaissance art, money is never far away, whether overtly or symbolically in the fine cloth and furs of costume and in allegorical depictions of the paying of tributes and gifts.

The world's oldest bank

While the Medici Bank was the most famous Italian bank of its day, Banca Monte dei Paschi di Siena, founded in 1472 to grant loans to "poor or miserable or needy persons" at an interest rate of 7.5 percent, can claim to be the world's oldest. Its name derives from the heap (*monte*) of money that was collected to lend to the poor of Siena, and from the region's state-owned pasturelands (*paschi*), which provided income for collateral against the loans. These revenues were divided into lots worth 100 *scudi* each and were issued as bonds guaranteeing a 5 percent annual return. The bank spent its first four hundred years growing steadily in the provinces of Siena and Grosseto, weathering economic storms, political reforms and a major earthquake in 1798, before branching out into the rest of Italy at the beginning of the 20th century. In 1999, the bank went public on the Borsa, the Milan stock exchange, and today, is Italy's third largest bank, with 3,000 branches serving 4.5 million customers.

↑
Masaccio's *Tribute Money* is a series of frescoes in the church of Santa Maria del Carmine in Florence, depicting a scene from St Matthew's gospel concerning Jesus and his apostles and the paying of a Roman tax collector. The frescoes, which pioneered the use of linear perspective, were painted around 1427 just as tax reforms were being debated in the city and, it is thought, may have been an encouragement to the citizenry to pay their dues.

806–821 C.E. A shortage of copper for coins leads Emperor of China Hien Tsung to issue paper money notes

1348–1350 C.E. The Black Death ravages Europe causing a collapse in economic growth

1397 C.E. Money-changer Giovanni Medici opens the first family bank in Florence

1400 C.E. Estimated date for the start of the European Renaissance, in Florence

1427 C.E. Masaccio paints *Tribute Money* frescoes in Florence

1450 C.E. Luca Pacioli born in Tuscany

1452 C.E. Leonardo da Vinci born in Tuscany

1454 C.E. Gutenberg invents the modern printing press, in Mainz, Germany, revolutionizing the dissemination of information

1472 C.E. Banca Monte dei Paschi di Siena founded

1494 C.E. *Summa de Arithmetica, Geometria Proportioni et Proportionalita* by Luca Pacioli establishes the principles of accounting

What is known as the Age of Discovery might also be called the Age of Greed. The years from the beginning of the 15th century until the 17th century saw European nations – particularly the Spanish, Portuguese, Dutch and English – build overseas empires.

BEGINNINGS OF GLOBALIZATION

They were driven partly by spiritual and strategic motives, but principally by the lust for gold, silver and other commodities. Rapidly expanding domestic economies caused shortages of money and of precious metals with which to mint it. At the same time, advances in navigation and boat-building technology allowed longer sea voyages – the stars aligned for audacious expeditions into new worlds.

The Portuguese were among the first to venture forth. They pressed south along the African coast until, in 1488, Bartolomeu Dias rounded the Cape of Good Hope, opening up vast opportunities in the Indian Ocean and beyond. Four years later, in 1492, his Spanish counterpart Cristobal Colon (Christopher Columbus) left the port of Palos, near Seville, and headed west across the Atlantic Ocean. Columbus' discoveries were somewhat accidental – in what we now know as the Caribbean he believed he had reached Asia – but admirably single-minded. Wherever he landed, he would show the local population gold coins and jewelry and ask them whether they had more of the same.

↓

By the 16th century, the Portuguese (purple) and the Spanish (pink) had developed significant trade routes to the east and west. Although the ships that plied the routes carried spices, tools, domestic animals, weapons, tobacco, potatoes and other crops, by far their most important cargo was gold and silver ... and lots of it. Between 1500 and 1540 an average of over 1,500 kg of gold arrived in Spain each year from the New World.

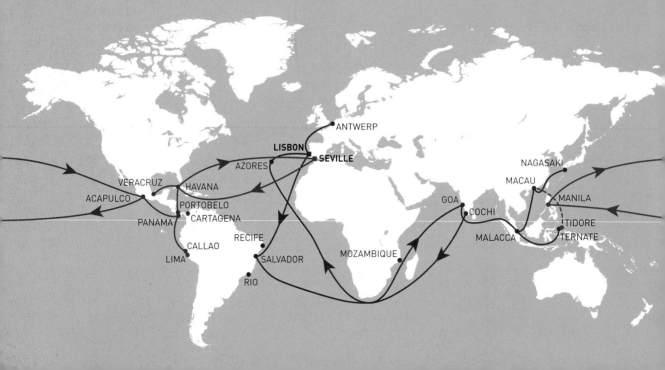

The commercial promise of adventure

The world, which was far bigger than these early explorers had first imagined, gradually shrank. Between 1519 and 1522, Portuguese explorer Ferdinand Magellan made his famous expedition from the Atlantic to the Pacific Ocean and it became clear that there were continents to be mapped, colonized and, to a large extent, plundered.

Money played its part from the beginning, both in financing expeditions by land and sea and then in the transfer of vast wealth from one part of the globe to another. These were bold, brutal and dangerous times, as trade routes were mapped out and appropriated, colonies defended and empires created, the likes of which had not been seen since classical times.

Fortunes were made – and lost. The 16th and 17th centuries continued the age of "adventuring," a word full of commercial promise. Expeditions from Europe to the new worlds of South and North America were financed by monarchs, their courtiers and wealthy merchants, who subscribed for shares in the companies of trusted sea captains and their crews. The spoils of such expeditions would be carefully divided up when – and if – they returned. All too often these perilous voyages ended in shipwreck, starvation and bloodthirsty encounters with natives.

↓

The trade in spices – particularly nutmeg, mace and cloves – from their only source in the Maluku and Banda Islands of Indonesia, became hugely important after their appropriation by the Portuguese in the early 16th century and later on by the Dutch. The trade in nutmeg was particularly fiercely fought over – a small bag of the precious spice, which was highly prized as an aphrodisiac and to ward off plague, could bring financial independence for life. The Dutch monopoly in the spice caused prices to rocket, exacerbated by the deliberate destruction of supplies.

1488 Portuguese explorer Bartolomeu Dias rounds the Cape of Good Hope

1492 Spanish explorer Cristobal Colon (Christopher Columbus) begins his discovery of the American continents

1498 Vasco da Gama arrives in Calicut, opening up the sea route from Europe to India

1500–1540 Huge quantities of New World gold, obtained by plunder from the Incas and the Aztecs, arrive in Spain

1519–1522 Portuguese explorer Ferdinand Magellan sails from the Atlantic to the Pacific

1540–1640 Due to the influx of gold and silver from the Americas, Europe experiences a prolonged period of inflation

1599 The spice trade, particularly in nutmeg and pepper, reaches its peak in Holland

1600 Foundation of the East India Company to develop foreign trade

1609 Foundation of the Bank of Amsterdam, a public bank intended to provide a superior and more controlled service than private banks

1619 Tobacco designated as the official currency of Virginia

1659 The first British cheque is issued: an order for the London goldsmiths Morris & Clayton to pay a Mr Delboe the sum of £400

1663 First British guineas produced: initially worth £1, they were coins milled using gold from West Africa, hence the name guinea

Money is an almost infinitely flexible tool, which can be used in a myriad of ways. Even the promise of it (English banknotes still carry the words "I promise to pay the bearer on demand ...") is a hugely powerful mechanism. Its protean character was not lost on clever financiers who, at the beginning of the 18th century, started to put money to work as never before. Their inventions, notably paper money and bills of credit and exchange, were much in demand – countries needed money to finance their domestic economies, their colonies abroad and their wars with each other.

THE BIRTH OF CREDIT

It was a man called John Law, a Scotsman with a knack for playing cards and charming monarchs and their distrustful finance ministers, who typified the spirit of the age. A financial buccaneer, he developed systems of credit and banking for Louis XV of France that were remarkably prescient (and whose descendants can be seen in the trading business (or divisions) of any modern financial institution). They were also highly volatile and, as it turned out, precarious. Law's most notorious creation, the Mississippi Company, which held trading rights for France's colonies in the West Indies and America, became bound up in the fortunes of Law's Banque Generale. There was wild speculation on the shares of the Mississippi Company, which promised enormous profits but delivered few, matched by an avalanche of printed paper money that ultimately became worthless. Law's audacious experiments with the French financial system illustrated the so-called madness of crowds, but also the dangers of credit.

ADVENTURER, GAMBLER, DUELIST, BANKER

John Law was an adventurer, gambler, duelist and an innovative thinker in the arena of finance and banking. He founded the first public bank in France, promoted the use of paper money and stabilized the bankrupt French economy. Unfortunately, his desire to exploit the apparently limitless resources of the Mississippi region of America prompted him to promise to pay off France's national debt. Share values soared, speculators decided to cash in, but when money was not forthcoming panic set in and the bank collapsed.

▼

1694 Bank of England founded, to raise money by taxation for war

1705 John Law suggests in his book *Money and Trade Considered* that banknotes should replace coinage

1716 John Law creates the Banque Generale, France's first public bank

1719–1720 The Mississippi Bubble and the South Sea Bubble – both speculative booms in the shares of companies with rights to trade in the colonies, which burst with dire consequences for investors and banks alike

1723 First notes issued in America by the Pennsylvania Land Bank

1727 Royal Bank of Scotland founded. It introduced a cash-credit system that allowed certain customers who had applied for loans to withdraw cash as required. Interest was paid only on the amount withdrawn – this is thought to be the origin of the overdraft

▼

Solid financial institutions

Other bankers learned from Law's mistakes. Although there were still many failures, the 18th century saw the foundations of solid financial institutions. In Britain, the Bank of England, founded in 1694 to raise money for William III's war with France, paved the way for scores of others so that there were 70 in London alone by 1800. Banks brought with them the first banknotes and cheques, but also the threat of forgery and of inflation. Gradually, institutions that were once the preserve of kings and the aristocracy became populist and the general public also put their faith in the new banking system. However, they learnt to trust only those that had enough gold in their vaults to balance the issue of their new-fangled paper notes.

↑
Mississippi Company shares were offered to the public in January 1719 at 500 *livres* (French currency at the time). Demand in Europe was immediate and huge, pushing the price up to 10,000 livres by December. Within a year the shares turned out to be worthless and instead of a promised fortune, many thousands of investors, such as these Dutch merchants in Amsterdam, were left with nothing.

THE 18TH CENTURY WAS THE AGE OF PAPER FORTUNES, STOCK MARKET "BUBBLES" AND, ULTIMATELY, SOBER REFLECTION

➔

The Industrial Revolution – depicted here by film director Danny Boyle during the opening ceremony of the London Olympics in 2012 – was a major turning point in history. The development of machinery driven by coal revolutionized manufacturing, mining, transportation and technology. As the price of machinery and factories climbed, the individual investors and financiers who had the ability to provide capital became increasingly important.

■ The 18th and 19th centuries witnessed not only the Industrial Revolution, but also a revolution in money, wealth and finance. In two hundred years, the world's average per capita income rose tenfold: as living standards rose, its population increased by a factor of six.

REVOLUTION

This mighty shift into the modern world was driven by technology, transport and thinking. Coal replaced wood as the primary fuel for powering machines and the invention of steam power revolutionized industrial processes. A boom in the manufacture of textiles was followed by advances in the steel, iron and machine tools industries as the industrialist replaced the merchant. Cities became more populous as workers – many of them women and children – flocked to the new mills, factories, blast furnaces and workshops.

The unequal flow of money

Where manufacture and trade occurred, money flowed, albeit unequally. Industrial entrepreneurism favored owners over workers and, although living standards rose overall, this age of innovation and industry also saw the rapid rise of urban slums in overcrowded cities. The divisions between employers and the employed, who often enjoyed little legal protection, frequently led to social unrest.

ROCKEFELLER

John Davison Rockefeller was born in Richford, New York State, on July 8, 1839, the son of a country doctor and farmer. Aged 14, he compared the $50 return he made from selling turkeys and lending out the cash at 7 percent to the $1.12 he received for three days' work digging potatoes and concluded that his future lay in finance.

At 16, he found his first job, as clerk and bookkeeper at the firm of Hewitt & Tuttle, in Cleveland, Ohio, which owned a wholesale warehouse. Having learned this trade, he set up a similar venture and set out to make his fortune. When oil was struck in Pennsylvania in 1859, Rockefeller was not far behind, investing in a small refinery and embarking on a series of acquisitions that eventually grew into Standard Oil. The company distributed an astonishing $751 million in dividends between 1882 and 1911, when it was dissolved by the US Supreme Court.

Rockefeller, who had also diversified into America's burgeoning railroad industry, retired at 56, having accumulated around $1.5 billion. Modest and unassuming, much of his later life was devoted to philanthropy, making donations of more than $500 million. His homespun wisdom on financial matters was much sought after by press and public: he maintained that hard work and living within one's means were the best foundations for life and business.

On a day-to-day basis, money was still local, with loans between family members a more common practice than personal banking. But the rise of capitalism also created new financial institutions and processes, which laid the foundations of modern finance. The Industrial Revolution was not all "boom" however. A long period of growth was followed by a slump at the end of the 19th century: overproduction and the double-edged sword of free trade provided a salutary lesson in the downside of a free-market economy.

The concept of capitalism

There have been many claims on the concept of capitalism – essentially, an economic system in which there is private ownership of the means of production in a competitive commercial environment or market economy – dating back to Classical times. But the concept was popularized in the mid-19th century by philosophers, historians and economists, such as Karl Marx and Friedrich Engels, not least in their three-volume *Das Kapital* (1867, 1885 and 1894). Capitalist economics was posited on the production of capital goods (industrial machines, vehicles, tools and factories) and consumer goods (a plethora of domestic items). Production could not take place without labor, land and capital goods, the last two being owned by capitalists.

In the 20th century, money took on further momentum, driven by unprecedented global conflicts in the form of two World Wars and by astonishing technological advances. At the beginning of the century, money was still being laboriously tallied up by hand, transactions were recorded in ledgers and wire transfers unheard of. By the end of it, banks and businesses routinely moved vast sums electronically, while individuals had begun to buy and sell goods – and pay and receive funds – on a worldwide network of computers called the Internet.

MODERN MONEY

Money joined what has been called the Great Acceleration – a phenomenon that saw numerous new inventions and processes reach so-called take-off points after the Second World War, and sharply accelerate. Notions of free trade

↓
As the economy has slowed down and fuel and food costs have soared in the last few years, many customers have taken advantage of new methods of payment in order to balance their budgets. Online shopping, paying credit cards off monthly, direct debit payments and price comparison websites are just some of the ways consumers can make the best of their household income.

WHERE THE MONEY GOES
Source: US Dept of Labor, 2010

TRANSPORT
Expenses and other transport
Fuel and motor oil
Vehicle purchases

INSURANCE AND PENSIONS

PERSONAL CARE

17.6%

1.2%

ALCOHOL

12.4%

AVERAGE US CONSUMER UNIT
Age: **48.8**
Number of vehicles owned: **1.9**

10.8%

Food away from home

Pensions, Social Security

FOOD

Food at home

Life, other personal insurance

0.9%

CLOTHING

3.8%

1.9%

3.7%

EDUCATION

CASH SPENDING

1.6%

Household furnishings and equipment

5.7%

5.4%

0.7%

0.7%

MISCELLANEOUS

Percent houseowner: **67%**
Number of persons in consumer unit: **2.5**
Number of earners: **1.3**
Income before taxes: **$63,091**
Annual average expenditure: **$49,638**

HEALTH CARE

ENTERTAINMENT

34.1%

TOBACCO

Accommodation

Utilities, fuels and public services

Household operations

Housekeeping supplies

READING

HOUSING

THE WORLD'S MOST VALUABLE COIN

Coins may seem quaint these days, but there is huge interest in rare examples. A 1933 double-eagle $20 piece appeared at auction in 2002, seventy years after it was minted in President Franklin Roosevelt's administration. Shortly afterwards, America was taken off the gold standard to help America weather the Depression and all the 1933 double eagles were melted down. Or almost all. Ten of the coins found their way into collectors' hands, and all but one were returned to the government because they had not been officially issued. The last surviving coin found its way to Cairo, in Egypt, where it was to be included in an auction of the legendary coin collection of King Farouk. The US authorities intervened and the coin disappeared. It popped up again in 1996, when a British collector tried to sell it to American Secret Service agents posing as dealers. Finally, a legal agreement was reached allowing it to remain in private ownership and it was auctioned in July 2002, realizing some $6 million. The US Treasury had the last word, however, requiring the new owner of the world's rarest coin to pay an additional $20 administration fee.

1914–1918 First World War: the British and French national debts rise hugely, inflation soars in Germany but the Japanese economy is greatly stimulated by the conflict. When the US joins the war in 1917, its national debt rises to $25 billion

1929 The Great Crash is followed by the Great Depression as the US economy slumps and its national product output falls by over 50 percent

1933 Roosevelt becomes president of the US and launches his New Deal, restoring confidence in the economy

1939–1945 Second World War: although national debts rise considerably, the major economies emerge with debts to be repaid at low rates of interest

1944–1971 Bretton Woods agreement establishes rules for commercial and financial relations between the world's major industrial states. The IMF and the IBRD are both established to help with global reconstruction

1974–1980 OPEC flexes its muscles controlling oil prices and affecting interest rates and inflation

1999 Euro adopted as the national currency of 11 member states of the EU

2007–2009 The subprime mortgage crisis prompts a collapse of the global credit system

2009– A global economic downturn sees recession as nations find it difficult to balance the books. Government intervention struggles to start significant recovery

areas and common monetary policies engendered phenomena such as a large-scale standardized currency: the birth of the euro in 1999 gave the world a new currency now used by 330 million Europeans and a further 175 million people worldwide (including 150 million Africans).

Electronic money

Toward the end of the century, money morphed dramatically into forms other than metal coins, cotton banknotes and paper cheques. Credit and debit cards combined with automated teller machines (ATMs), chip and PIN terminals and merchant services to allow people to withdraw, deposit and spend money without actually seeing it or handing it over. Trust placed in physical money, which had already partly migrated to bills of exchange and credit notes, moved further still, to reside in the electronic balances held in online bank accounts.

The century also saw the first widespread experiments in loyalty points and membership rewards, forms of synthetic money that have evolved into their own currency, allowing people to buy both more of the same goods, or entirely different ones. As these developments accelerated, not all of them successful, people began to talk about the end of money and imagine a world in which transactions are entirely coin- and banknote-free.

Money has certainly come a long way since the days when cowrie shells were exchanged – and it is still hurtling forward. In some ways, however, it has returned to its roots. After a long dalliance with coinage and paper money and the supremacy of electronic money, there is now an increasing interest in money-substitutes, which are not such a far cry from those precious cowrie shells. In fact, the coins in your pocket are soon going to be museum pieces.

MONEY AND YOU

Our relationship with the process of buying and selling is changing, too: increasingly, we may find ourselves bidding for things, rather than paying a fixed price for them (Google, which was founded at the turn of the century, bases its entire business model on a system of auctions whereby advertisers bid for its search result inventory). Loyalty points and membership rewards now play a large part in consumer spending decisions, which, in turn, drive economies around the world. Spending habits have also changed dramatically in this new century. In many Western countries one out of every ten units of currency is now spent online.

Collapse of the credit system

As money – and our relationship with it – reshapes, there are also dangers to contend with. The ballooning of easy money, debt that built up without due consideration as to how it would be repaid, characterized the opening years of the 21st century. The collapse in 2007–2009 of the credit system that

↓

The Chinese online retailer Dangdang went public in 2010 launching an IPO worth an estimated $1 billion. Since then it has profited from the country's strong economy and the popularity of online computer and mobile phone shopping among Chinese people. Some experts predict that the company will soon be competing with Amazon as the world's biggest online retailer.

THE STORY OF PAYPAL

The epitome of game-changing monetary technology, PayPal was born out of software developed by Confinity, a Californian start-up technology company, which enabled encrypted email payments to be made on handheld devices, turning them into the first electronic wallets. At PayPal's launch party, in July 1999, an investor "beamed" $3 million into the company's account via its founder Peter Thiel's Palm Pilot. In March 2000, Confinity merged with X.com, an Internet-based financial services company, and PayPal quickly began to dominate the nascent online transaction world, particularly for payments made by users of eBay. The online auctioneer acquired PayPal for $1.5 billion in October 2002 and made it an integral part of its service. Transactions using PayPal reached $71 billion in 2009 and it now operates in 190 countries, with more than 230 million accounts. The company now also allows users of other online retailers to make payments in the same way.

underpins borrowing by everyone from a credit card holder, a mortgagee or a large company, was a shock that will stand as one of history's greatest financial disasters. It was greatly exacerbated by a peculiarly present-day phenomenon: the interconnectedness of modern financial institutions around the world. In other words, when disaster struck in one place, it caused a domino effect elsewhere and, in some cases, everywhere.

This corporate and household debt crisis was swiftly followed by a sovereign debt crisis, in which countries weakened by the recession struggled to balance their books. Massive government interventions in the debt markets failed to resolve systemic weakness in weak economies. By 2011, huge fissures opened in the Eurozone group of 17 countries, which was plunged into disarray as Greece, Portugal, Spain and Italy showed signs of possible default on their governments' debt.

THE TOTAL GLOBAL MONEY SUPPLY FROM THE WORLD'S BIGGEST ECONOMIES (THE UNITED STATES, THE EUROPEAN UNION, CHINA AND JAPAN) IS THOUGHT TO BE AROUND $50 TRILLION

↓

In 2008 the imminent collapse of the credit system was illustrated in the media with pictures of bank employees leaving their places of work clutching their worldly possessions. The greatest shock to the world's economy since 1929 had serious repercussions: Lehman Brothers went bankrupt, while Merrill Lynch, AIG, Freddie Mac, Fannie Mae, HBOS, Royal Bank of Scotland and others all had to be rescued.

THE END OF CASH

1939 Experimental bankograph installed by City Bank of New York, accepting cheque and cash deposits only. Removed after six months due to lack of customer acceptance

1951 The first official credit card, the Diners Club card, introduced in New York City

1958 American Express card launched

1966 Visa and MasterCards launched

1972 First modern ATMs introduced into the UK

1990 Introduction of the debit card, where customers pre-paid any given amount and were able to use their cards for payment until their credit ran out

1997 Mobile phone commerce introduced via two Coca-Cola vending machines in Helsinki, Finland, with access via SMS text messaging

1998 PayPal founded in Palo Alto, California, which allowed payments and money transfers to be made via the Internet

2003 Oyster cards, which use "wave and pay" technology, issued by Transport for London

2004 Chip and pin system of payments introduced

2010 French government launches system of USB memory sticks for use in payment for bus and train journeys in Montpellier

2016 Analysts suggest that mobile devices will be used for most everyday purchases

2018 Projected end of the legal use of cheques as payment worldwide

2 RICH WORLD, POOR WORLD

↑
Shibuya Crossroads in Tokyo. Home to some 35 million people, Greater Tokyo is the world's most populous metropolitan area.

We live in an increasingly crowded world. By the end of 2011, according to the UN Population Fund, the world's population reached seven billion. It was not so much a cause for celebration as for anxiety. Forecasters reckon it could reach eight billion by 2025 and ten billion by 2083, depending on the availability of birth control, infant mortality rates and life expectancy, which has itself risen from a average of 48 in 1950 to 69 today.

What's more, the pace of growth is accelerating: it took until 1804 for the world's population to reach one billion, but only 123 years to reach two billion, in 1927. By 1959, a mere 32 years later, it was three billion and by 1974 it passed the four billion mark. Thereafter, the world has been growing by a further billion every twelve or thirteen years.

These very large numbers of people own, in aggregate, a great deal of what we loosely term wealth. The largest

THE RICHEST 10 PERCENT OF ADULTS OWN 85 PERCENT OF THE WORLD'S WEALTH, WHILE 50 PERCENT OWN LESS THAN 1 PERCENT OF IT

study to date, published by the World Institute for Development Economics Research of the United Nations in 2006 and using detailed data from 38 countries, showed that the principal elements of household wealth, including financial assets and debts, land, buildings and property, totalled $125 trillion.

The spiraling cost of living

Huge contradictions and inequalities have built up. Developed nations such as America and Japan contrast starkly with African countries and the poorer Asia-Pacific countries and the likes of North Korea.

Growing, longer-living populations bring with them pressing issues such as housing, food and other natural resources, energy, security and an ever-increasing gap between rich and poor. The poor look destined to get poorer: the current trend of demographic growth in sub-Saharan Africa, for example, will see its 900 million population double over the next forty years, mainly in its already overcrowded cities.

Such studies can be interpreted in different ways. The most common reaction to data showing such large disparities is to call for redistribution of the total pot of wealth. But many economists argue that wealth is a dynamic. The most important question is not how to separate the wealthy from their money, but how to help the poor become wealthy themselves.

In this chapter, we take a look at the whole spectrum of wealth in today's world, from the very rich to the very poor, not forgetting a very populous middle chunk that wields huge purchasing – and voting – power. Despite their very different relationships with money, all are subject to the rise in globalization and the mix of opportunities and threats it brings with it.

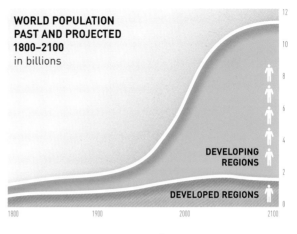

WORLD POPULATION PAST AND PROJECTED 1800–2100
in billions

DEVELOPING REGIONS

DEVELOPED REGIONS

1800   1900   2000   2100

↑
Though birth rates have dropped in the last half-century, estimates are that humanity will add another billion people to the planet in the next twelve years or so. Most of this will occur in developing countries in Asia, Africa and Latin America. The combined populations of Europe and North America will remain relatively stable, though some countries, such as Germany, Russia and Japan, are poised to edge downwards.

THE WORLD'S NEWEST COUNTRY

Southern Sudan, which won its independence and joined the other 192 UN members in July 2011, has one of the poorest populations in the world, despite having hugely valuable natural resources. Around 90 percent of its eight million people exist on the proverbial $1 a day, or less, suffer from chronic hunger, are largely illiterate and live in a war-torn land without proper roads and electricity. Ironically, the country has something in common with much richer countries: huge oil reserves. Southern Sudan boasts perhaps as much as seven billion barrels in proven reserves, which already produce revenues of $1 billion per annum. The key to this conundrum is a human, rather than financial, one: the country needs peace, education and a large helping of progressive economics if it is to bridge its own, yawning gap between rich and poor and live up to its national motto: "Justice, Liberty, Prosperity."

Globalization has been called the single biggest political, economic and social trend of the present day. What does it actually mean? Essentially, it is the ever-increasing integration of the world's trade and flow of people, goods, services and capital. It has been driven by the liberalization of trade and finance and improved – and cheaper – transport and communications. This has also led to a transformation in the way large companies operate and how their managers think about their customers and their suppliers.

GLOBALIZATION

↓
The global appeal of sport has seen a huge rise in the size of multinational sportswear companies in the last twenty years. Adidas and Nike have led the way, using golf, tennis and football stars to enhance their brand image. The German company Puma has joined the race using the Jamaican sprinter Usain Bolt as their figurehead.

In practical terms, globalization allows, for example, a sportswear company based in North America to use European designers, Asian manufacturers and global logistics companies to make and distribute its products in a seamless operation within multiple markets.

Equally, a financial institution in one country can route its customer enquiries through a call center in another and print its annual reports in yet another – decisions made based on competitive pricing, the best quality and the availability of the most skilled workforces.

While globalization has been underway since the 1950s, its pace has greatly accelerated in the last decade, and it shows no signs of slowing down. It has winners and losers, its supporters and its critics. While major multinational companies and their shareholders may have benefited hugely from outsourcing and cheap overseas labor, it could have come at a cost, not least in the exploitation of that cheap workforce.

Globalization has given rise to the multinational company, operating in multiple markets and currencies and employing staff from a multitude of countries and ethnic backgrounds.

GLOBALIZATION MEANS THAT A COMPANY BASED IN ONE PART OF THE WORLD CAN SOURCE GOODS AND SERVICES IN ANOTHER AND SELL THEM IN A THIRD

Truly global companies

According to *Fortune* magazine, which has tracked large multinationals for many years, leaders in the field are the likes of Walmart, the American supermarket chain, major oil producers such as Royal Dutch Shell, Exxon Mobil and BP, automobile manufacturers such as Toyota and Volkswagen and large financial companies like AXA and Fannie Mae.

In 2011, Walmart led the pack by revenues – $421 billion – and Nestlé by profits – $33 billion.

LOCAVESTING

Some people believe globalization has gone too far. A localization movement has sprung up to encourage investors (and consumers) to seek out smaller companies closer to home in preference to global multinationals. Local enterprises, they argue, are more often the catalysts for job creation in communities and encourage other entrepreneurial activity. Investing in such local businesses – locavesting – is often best achieved by neighborhood investor clubs and so-called business angels who provide mentoring as well as money. Of course, if they flourish there is always the possibility that these micro businesses will one day become global themselves...

Walmart is a chain of general merchandise retail stores started in 1962. Still controlled by its founders, the Walton family, it is based in Bentonville, Arkansas, and remains the biggest company in the world in terms of revenue.

Walmart now sells more food than any other store in the world

Walmart employs 1.6 million people and is the largest private employer

Walmart has approx 3,900 stores in the USA

This year, 7.2 billion different purchasing experiences will occur at a Walmart store (Earth's population is approximately 7 billion)

Walmart is the largest company in the history of the world

Americans spend $36,000,000 at Walmart every hour of every day

This works out to $20,928 profit every minute

90% of all Americans live within 15 miles of a Walmart

The ownership of land has been at the center of human progress and wealth accumulation since human beings first marked out territory for living, keeping cattle and cultivating crops. And wherever people have gathered together – in villages, towns or cities – land has swiftly been parcelled up, bought, sold and fought over.

THE IMPORTANCE OF LAND

↓

Land values have rocketed in the past decade and are following what investment managers call a straight-line trend – upward. While Western Europe, the USA, Canada, Australia and New Zealand remain the most valuable areas, central and Eastern Europe and South America are catching up fast, while land in sub-Saharan Africa is also attracting strong interest.

As the world shrinks as a result of globalization, land is becoming increasingly scarce and more valuable, driven by the age-old impetus of supply and demand. Tiny enclaves of particularly desirable property – often in sunny, tax-advantageous locations – command exorbitant prices.

While urban land is fought over with spiralling prices, farmland too is big business. Population growth and demographic change – in particular, a burgeoning middle class – means increasing demand for food and changing eating habits. The World Bank reckons that world food production must rise by 70 percent in the next thirty years to meet demand from growing populations and grain-based animal feeds to supply Asian countries with more meat.

In America, the tenant farms and smallholdings that characterized the first colonies have given way to huge agricultural concerns, which are often owned by pension funds, hedge funds and church organizations. The two

HOW MUCH DOES LAND COST?
APPROXIMATE LAND VALUES, 2011–2012
in US dollars, per hectare

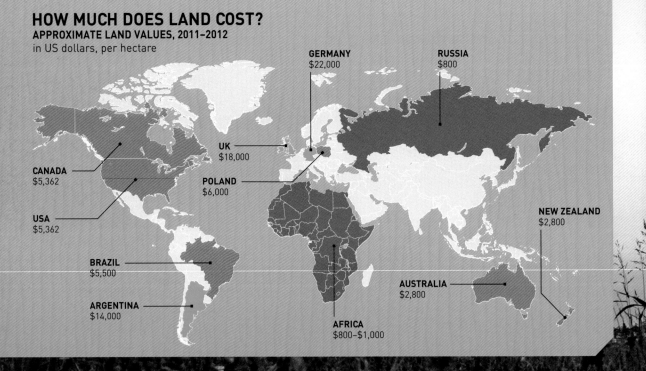

GERMANY
$22,000

RUSSIA
$800

UK
$18,000

CANADA
$5,362

POLAND
$6,000

USA
$5,362

NEW ZEALAND
$2,800

BRAZIL
$5,500

ARGENTINA
$14,000

AUSTRALIA
$2,800

AFRICA
$800–$1,000

biggest owners of American farmland are thought to be the Mormon Church and a $500 billion pension fund called TIAA-CREF, which own billions of dollars of land holdings. Such investments, which have all the reassuring characteristics of real assets in a world that has its doubts about complex and often synthetic financial products, have proved lucrative; in one year, at the end of the first decade of the 21st century land values in America rose by 20 percent, the largest single-year rise since the 1970s. The OECD estimates that $45 billion was invested in agricultural land in 2010 and that this figure will likely double or triple in future years.

Land grab

The land-grab has become a global phenomenon. As first-world territories have become ever more expensive, investors have turned their attentions to Second- and Third-World countries. In 2009, sovereign wealth funds acquired 45 million hectares of land (that's double the size of a country such as the UK) in developing countries, two-thirds of it in Africa.

Rising land values may be good for investors, but are potentially disastrous for the world's poor and hungry, particularly as some of the land being acquired is being banked rather than being actively farmed. Crops such as soya, sugar and maize – soft commodities traded on global exchanges – as well as grassland for beef cattle have seen dramatic price rises in the past decade, fuelling food poverty, which can, in turn, lead to social unrest.

None of this is good news for small, sustainable farming or for family-owned enterprises, which are increasingly being squeezed.

"BUY LAND, THEY'RE NOT MAKING IT ANYMORE"
MARK TWAIN (1835–1910), WRITER

↓

Darrell Stevenson (right), a cowboy from Montana, spotted a business opportunity on a visit to Russia – a trip ruined because he was unable to buy a steak. His response was to buy cheap land in the Voronezh region of southern Russia and transport his entire ranch, 1,400 cattle and its cowboys, from the US to set up the Stevenson Sputnik ranch to supply those missing steaks.

The world's very rich are growing both in number and in the amount of wealth they possess. In 2011, there were an estimated 10.9 million people classed as high net worth individuals (HNWIs), who have $1 million or more of investible assets, excluding their primary home. This fortunate group have combined wealth of $42.7 trillion (of which a third is held in equities). Despite recent economic shocks, the HNWI population is growing by about 10 percent per annum. They are scattered fairly evenly around the globe. Of the 10.9 million HNWIs, around 3.1 million live in the United States, while 3.3 million are spread across the Asia-Pacific region and 3.1 million in Europe.

↓

Although America still leads the way, the number of billionaires in China and Russia is increasing at a faster rate. There is rapid growth too in the success of entrepreneurs from the Asia-Pacific region, where wealth creation is based on healthy stock market trading.

THE VERY RICH

After the HNWIs, there are ultra high net worth individuals (UHNWIs), who comprise people, it is generally held, with $30 million or more in investible assets. From here it is another leap to the select group that is formed by the world's billionaires. At the last count, in 2011, there were some 1,210 billionaires, with a total net worth of $4.5 trillion. Those figures do not include world rulers (and the odd dictator), who form a very exclusive club of multi-billionaires (one such is the late Muammar Gaddafi, of Libya, who is said to have died after having amassed an illicit fortune of $200 billion).

The BRICs billionaires

The rise of Brazil, Russia, India and China – the so-called BRIC countries – has spawned a new generation of wealthy entrepreneurs. In many cases, they owe their financial success to a wave of internal political upheaval, as well as to business acumen and, of course, a little luck. While each tells a very different story, all have seen their respective countries embrace global capitalism with a vengeance. Brazil's new billionaires have often emerged as owners of agricultural businesses and commodities, while Russia's and China's have made fortunes from newly privatized heavy industry, oil and gas. In India, democracy and education have created wealth from technology and services businesses.

Often, wealth has flowed from political patronage. Russia's business oligarchs, as the word suggests, owe much of their great wealth to their proximity to the ruling class and, in particular to Russian presidents such as Boris Yeltsin and Vladimir Putin. In the 1990s, Russian politicians set in motion a wave of privatizations of state-owned enterprises, such as iron, steel, oil, gas and chemicals firms, which hugely enriched the businessmen in their inner circle. Many of these original industrial entrepreneurs –

NUMBER OF BILLIONAIRES
TOP TEN COUNTRIES

Country	Number
UNITED STATES	413
CHINA	115
RUSSIA	101
INDIA	55
GERMANY	52
TURKEY	38
HONG KONG	36
UNITED KINGDOM	32
BRAZIL	30
JAPAN	26

Mikhail Fridman, Oleg Deripaska, Roman Abramovich and Boris Berezovsky among them – have since diversified into a plethora of other sectors, including banking, property, art and sport. There are now over a hundred billionaires in Russia; their growing presence and conspicuous consumption highlighting a yawning gulf between the country's rich and poor.

The fastest-growing economies

Brazil has had a more modest trajectory – it is sometimes referred to as a junior BRIC – although it is also home to around 30 billionaires, concentrated in São Paulo and Rio de Janeiro. Brazil's natural resources and agricultural wealth has been augmented by a boom in finance, telecoms and media in the last few decades. It has duly attracted vast amounts of inward foreign investment, further enriching its burgeoning entrepreneurial class.

In Asia and the Far East, meanwhile, India and China jostle each other for the title of fastest-growing economy. Their new elites have started from very different places: democracy in India and communism in China. India has looked to the United States for a model of capitalism, which has seen fortunes made in industry, shipping and property, as well as in consumer-led sectors,

↓

The Lukoil petroleum refinery in Nizhny Novgorod. Lukoil is one of Russia's most successful oil companies. It was formed in 1991 when a decree issued by president Boris Yeltsin permitted the privatization and merger of three state-run companies. Using a Western-style business model, the company integrates the three branches of the oil industry – exploration, refining and distribution. In 2011 its revenue was $133.6 billion.

THE WORLD'S RICHEST MAN

Carlos Slim Helu, a 71-year-old, Cohiba cigar-smoking Mexican businessman with interests in telecoms, banking, airlines, mining, construction, retail and much more, has an estimated net worth of $74 billion. Slim's father Julian was a Lebanese immigrant who started a successful general store during the 1910 Mexican Revolution. By the age of 11, his son Carlos was investing his five pesos weekly pocket money in government savings bonds and a few years later he acquired shares in Mexico's largest bank. At 26, he was worth some $40 million, which allowed him to take advantage of bargain-priced businesses during Mexico's recession in the early 1980s. His rapidly growing conglomerate was crowned in 1990, when he acquired Telmex, Mexico's former national telecoms company, which now has the largest mobile phone network in Latin America. More recently, Slim has snapped up stakes in Citigroup, the American bank, and in Saks, the department store operator. A man of relatively modest personal tastes – his own home has only six bedrooms, albeit hung with world-class art – Slim is famous for running his companies parsimoniously. "Maintain austerity in prosperous times [in times when the cow is fat with milk]" – one of the mottoes he frequently fires out to his employees – continues to serve him well. Slim's three adult sons help their father run his sprawling business empire, gathering at home every Monday evening for a simple family dinner to discuss strategy – and how best to invest the estimated $30 million the Slim businesses earn each day.

TOGETHER THE BRICS (INCLUDING SOUTH AFRICA) ACCOUNT FOR 43 PERCENT OF THE WORLD'S POPULATION AND 40 PERCENT OF GLOBAL GDP

such as entertainment and information technology by people such as Lakshmi Mittal and the Ambani brothers. In China, wealth has come quickly to those who have led the transformation into a consumer society and embraced the capital markets. Stock market floatations and the rise of consumer goods empires has created over a hundred billionaires at the last count, led by Liang Wengen, a 55-year-old construction equipment magnate worth around $11 billion.

For all the BRIC countries, great wealth has highlighted the poverty endemic among the less fortunate. Many BRIC billionaires have become well-known for their lavish lifestyles; some have channelled their wealth into philanthropic projects. As they race toward ever-greater wealth and eye each other across the continents, they can probably agree on one thing, articulated by Bill Gates, one of their fellow-billionaires: "with great wealth comes great responsibility."

What's in a name?

When Goldman Sachs economist Jim O'Neill first coined the acronym BRIC in 2001, he might have guessed that other countries would also stake their claims. South Korea, one of Asia's economic powerhouses, was mooted as a possible participant in the group (providing a K to make BRICK). In 2010, South Africa, Africa's largest economy and regarded as an entry point to the vast untapped wealth of that continent, was formally admitted into the group, which became BRICS. Recently, sub-groups of emerging economies have also formed. South Africa has also been grouped with Colombia, Indonesia, Vietnam, Egypt and Turkey to form the CIVETS – high-growth countries with emerging democracies and increasingly educated and entrepreneurial populations.

CAN MONEY BUY HAPPINESS?

Economists have spent a long time pondering whether being rich makes you happy and, by extension, whether rich countries are happier than poor ones. The so-called Easterlin Paradox – Professor Richard Easterlin asked in a 1974 paper "Does Economic Growth Improve the Human Lot?" – suggests that there is no link between a society's economic development and its average level of happiness. Some disagree. One leading American study (the 2006 General Social Survey) showed that people tend to move from pretty happy to very happy the wealthier they get. But Nobel Prize-winning economist Daniel Kahneman and his colleague Alan Krueger say that although wealthy people are more likely to say "my life is happy" the reality is somewhat different: "People with above-average income are relatively satisfied with their lives, but are barely happier than others in moment-to-moment experience, tend to be more tense, and do not spend more time in particularly enjoyable activities." What do the rich themselves think? Taki Theodoracopulos, the wealthy author of a celebrated magazine column called "High Life," is clear on the matter: "Are the rich happy?" he asked. "Yes." Does money buy them more fun than you have? "You bet."

While the world's rich exercise a disproportionate fascination over the rest of its population, the fact is that most people are neither rich nor particularly poor. The vast majority of the world's population, at least in developed countries, leads a life that, in financial terms, is modest but comfortable. The French word *bourgeois*, first used to describe the wealthier members of France's pre-Revolutionary Third Estate (the common people) now captures a more universal class of aspirational consumers.

↓ Average middle-incomers they may be, but this group is the world's most populous and carries huge power with its money and its votes. Thousands of hours and millions of dollars are spent examining the demographics of a group that will mete out its justice at election time.

MIDDLE INCOME EARNERS

This enormous demographic group has, in modern times, become a vitally important one, as it makes both short- and long-term purchasing decisions that drive major consumer industries. It includes managers, professional workers, housewives and househusbands, students and, in rapidly increasing numbers, the retired. Endlessly segmented by research groups, the "average" shopper,

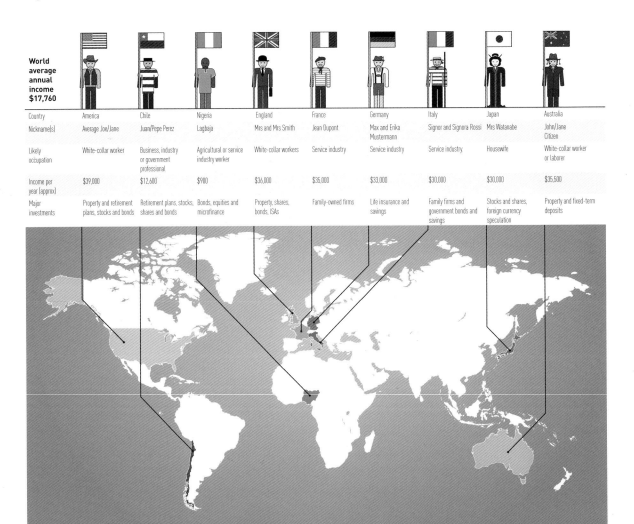

World average annual income $17,760	America	Chile	Nigeria	England	France	Germany	Italy	Japan	Australia
Country	America	Chile	Nigeria	England	France	Germany	Italy	Japan	Australia
Nickname(s)	Average Joe/Jane	Juan/Pepe Perez	Lagbaja	Mrs and Mrs Smith	Jean Dupont	Max and Erika Mustermann	Signor and Signora Rossi	Mrs Watanabe	John/Jane Citizen
Likely occupation	White-collar worker	Business, industry or government professional	Agricultural or service industry worker	White-collar workers	Service industry	Service industry	Service industry	Housewife	White-collar worker or laborer
Income per year (approx)	$39,000	$12,600	$900	$36,000	$35,000	$33,000	$30,000	$30,000	$35,500
Major investments	Property and retirement plans, stocks and bonds	Retirement plans, stocks, shares and bonds	Bonds, equities and microfinance	Property, shares, bonds, ISAs	Family-owned firms	Life insurance and savings	Family firms and government bonds and savings	Stocks and shares, foreign currency speculation	Property and fixed-term deposits

THE TYPICAL CITIZEN

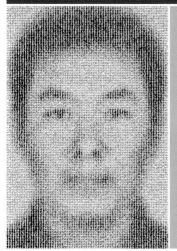

According to *National Geographic* magazine, the most typical person in the world is 28 years old, male, right-handed and of Han Chinese descent (until 2030, when they are more likely to be of South Asian origin). This picture is a composite image of 190,000 such individuals. From a financial point of view, this typical person earns less than $12,000 per annum, has a mobile telephone but no bank account (although the phone will very soon allow its user to interact with banking services). He is likely to be better educated than his parents and to have higher aspirations. This financially independent, technology savvy young man is also at the mercy of every global brand eager to part him from his $1,000 a month. But despite the relatively recent arrival of mass consumerism – and mass luxury in the form of global high-end brands – young men like our Chinese example are already showing signs of scepticism, trading brand for value as they make smarter spending decisions.

spender and saver is the marketing industry's holy grail. They are also much sought-after by political parties – in times of economic hardship, the middle layer of society may be relied on not to riot in the streets, but will exercise its vote at election time to oust governments it regards as having failed in its stewardship of the economy.

A quiet life is its own reward

Different countries have different stereotypes of this group. In Japan, it is personified by "Mrs Watanabe," a figure whose surname is one of the country's most common. In America, a hugely enthnically diverse country, the "Average Joe" or "Average Jane," is increasingly difficult to define, but will likely live a suburban existence on the outskirts of a large city and get by on a modest salary from a white-collar job. Salaries here, as elsewhere, tend to increase in proportion to the level of education and professional qualifications.

In Europe, "Mr and Mrs Smith," famous in Great Britain for their middle-market tastes and way of life, find reasonably common ground with the archetypal "Signor and Signora Rossi" in Italy, and their counterparts in France and Germany. These large, developed economies have broadly similar spending and saving habits. There are, however, very distinct regional differences. The British have a particularly strong culture of home ownership (some 14.5 million or 65 percent own their own homes), while many other Europeans prefer to rent and invest their money in other assets.

While it often seems that most people around the world aspire to great wealth, many are actually quite content being average, indeed, researchers often find that the latter brings stability and peace of mind, particularly in countries which have historically been scarred by war and upheaval. For many, a quiet, if not a particularly wealthy, life is, it seems, its own reward.

IN GERMANY, BEING AVERAGE IS KNOWN AS *NULL-ACHT-FUNFZEHN,* OR "08/15," AFTER A STANDARD-ISSUE ARMY MACHINE GUN

It is a sad truth that many of the world's people really do live on, or less than, the proverbial dollar a day, although the World Bank's official poverty line is now $1.25 per day. Around 10 percent currently exist at this level, while nearly half the world – 3.5 billion people – live on less than $2.50 and at least 80 percent survive on under $10 a day.

THE VERY POOR

The causes of such poverty are, more often than not, depressingly simple. Inadequate access to water and electricity, taken for granted in the developed world, remain two of the largest factors. Some 1.1 billion people have poor water supplies, 2.6 billion lack basic sanitation and 1.6 billion have no electricity.

Many of the world's poorest people struggle to leave a vicious circle whereby a disproportionate amount of their meager income goes on subsistence – food and shelter – and there is little chance of saving for capital items such as farming equipment, a fishing boat or higher education. Although extreme cases of food poverty exist in famine-struck countries, more food and better nutrition may not be the greatest challenges. In fact, there have been dramatic improvements in food supplies in Third-World countries in recent years. In many cases, the lack of regular income is a far greater problem and some charities now focus on encouraging entrepreneurism and microfinance initiatives to lift people out of poverty.

WHAT $1 BUYS AROUND THE WORLD

World Resources Institute research shows a startling disparity in the dollar's purchasing power:

Bangladesh (Chittagong)
1 DOZEN EGGS

Kenya
8 CUPS OF MILK

Ghana
4 1/3 BOTTLES OF COKE

Philippines
4/5 OF A BIG MAC

LIVING ON NOTHING AT ALL

Some people choose to live without money altogether. Daniel Suelo has lived in a cave in Moab, Utah, for more than ten years; a wartime refugee now living in Germany, Heidemarie Schwermer decided to live by exchanging things in 1994, giving up money completely two years later; and Tomi Astikainen, originally from Finland, lives life on the open road, relying on the goodness of the people he meets for food and shelter.

Mark Boyle, a business and economics graduate from the United Kingdom, gave up both cash and credit in 2008. In his book *The Moneyless Man*, Boyle describes how he found a home in the form of an unwanted caravan and installed a wood-burning stove to provide heat, solar panels for electricity and a compost toilet. He washes in a river or a solar shower and uses toothpaste made from cuttlefish bone and fennel seeds. As for food, he grows his own, forages in the wild, barters with others and finds waste food. Boyle maintains that his experiment – which he has continued – has brought him closer to nature and to his fellow human beings: "Where money once provided me with my primary sense of security, I now find it in friends and the local community."

	Uganda		Tanzania (Nzanza)		Colombia
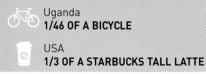	**1/46 OF A BICYCLE**		**1/3 LITRE OF PESTICIDE**		**COFFEE AND COOKIES**
	USA		India (Andhra Pradesh)		
	1/3 OF A STARBUCKS TALL LATTE		**1/2 UNIT OF BLOOD FOR TRANSFUSION**		

Burgernomics

The *Economist* newspaper has produced its Big Mac Index every year since 1986, using hamburger prices around the world to gauge whether currencies are at their correct level. Based on the theory that in the global marketplace a burger should cost roughly the same everywhere, the index measures discrepancies in purchasing-power-parity (PPP). This may indicate that one currency is over- or undervalued against another. In 2011, the ubiquitous Big Mac was 44 percent cheaper in China than in the US, indicating that the Chinese yuan was 44 percent undervalued against the dollar. However, because labor costs are cheaper in China, it is more accurate to align the index to GDP and average income. Tweaking the comparisons like this nevertheless shows that the Brazilian real is the world's most overvalued currency, closely followed by the euro, while the yuan is fairly valued against the dollar.

↑
Rocinha is one of Rio's de Janeiro's one thousand *favelas*. Estimates as to its population vary from 70,000 to 200,000 and the vast majority of families that make their homes in this small area live well below the World Bank's official poverty line of $1.25 per day.

Sometimes, small amounts of money can be more effective than large ones. In recent years, microfinance initiatives have revolutionized aid programs, allowing people in developing countries to borrow very small sums – typically, under $100 – to establish entrepreneurial businesses or to buy a telephone, livestock or machinery.

MICROFINANCE

↓

Funded by a local, community-owned lending cooperative, the basic idea of microfinance is to start a cycle of positive events that will, in turn, improve the local community. The system is aimed at asset-poor people who cannot get a bank loan. To apply you need to prove trustworthiness, a good work ethic and have a sound business idea. Loans can be as little as $40, enough for seed or stock, fertilzer or basic equipment, such as a sewing machine, which will be accompanied by basic business training.

More often than not, such loans are lent against no security, relying on trust between lender and borrower. Individual initiatives have frequently coalesced into lending-cooperatives – essentially, community-owned banks – that make small loans to their members.

Although microfinance has been around in various forms for many years, it gained new momentum from the work of Dr Muhammad Yunus, who set up micro-lending schemes for women in the village of Jobra, Bangladesh, while he was teaching economics at Chittagong University in the 1970s. In 1983, Yunus founded Grameen Bank, which now has more than eight million borrowers, 96 percent of whom are women, and branches in 80,000 villages. Since its inception, Grameen has disbursed $11.2 billion, of which $9.99 billion has been repaid. Yunus' pioneering work was formally recognized in 2006, when he was awarded the Nobel Peace Price for his efforts to create economic and social development from below.

How microfinance works

Microfinance projects vary, but many attempt to kick-start borrowing and lending with structures that eventually become self-financing. Based in New York, the Hunger Project is one charity whose Microfinance Programme has been operating in Africa since 1999. It now has a loan portfolio of around $2.4 million in countries such as Benin, Ethiopia, Malawi, Senegal and Uganda and 45,000 regular savers in its 21 rural banks. The program has three elements: first, training its rural "partners" to increase and manage their income; second, instilling the habit of saving (borrowers must save the first 10 percent of any

THE MICROFINANCE CYCLE

1 APPLIES FOR MICROLOAN
2 RECEIVES MICROLOAN TRAINING
3 RECEIVES MICROLOAN
4 CREATES/ EXPANDS BUSINESS
5 RECEIVES COACHING
6 BUSINESS THRIVES
7 FAMILY GAINS SELF-SUFFICIENCY
8 CHILDREN EDUCATED
9 REPAYS LOAN AND MONEY IS RECYCLED

Source: VisionFund

future loan); and third, credit. Loans are advanced only to groups of 5–15 people (to mitigate risk of non-repayment) and only on condition that all the borrowers enrol their children in school. To fund the loans, the charity typically makes an initial revolving loan fund of $20,000 to each epicenter and a local committee disburses it, collects the interest and disburses it again. In its fourth year, each scheme can apply to become a savings and credit cooperative – a government-sanctioned rural bank. And after a further two years, the bank should become operationally self-sufficient, allowing the charity to withdraw from the project.

CROWD FUNDING

As its name suggests, crowd funding involves aggregating the donations or investments of large numbers of people, each of whom provides a small amount of capital. The spread of the Internet, social media and micropayments have greatly increased such initiatives, which include charity fundraising and a multitude of entrepreneurial ventures, including low-budget films and even rock tours: in 1997, American fans of the rock group Marillion clubbed together $60,000 to fund a US tour for the band.

Peer-to-peer lending

Also known as person-to-person, or P2P, peer-to-peer lending (mostly) cuts out the middleman and allows loans – often of small amounts and over short periods – to be made between people themselves. Transacting on online platforms, a lender can choose a borrower, decide how much they wish to lend and on what terms. Equally, a borrower can set criteria they are comfortable with from the lender. A matchmaking process puts lenders and borrowers together. This democratization of lending, mostly in small amounts and for short periods of time, has spawned a marketplace with some 35 major players that have lent many hundreds of millions of dollars. One notable entrant into this market is Bitcoin, whose network allows for an amount specified in Bitcoins to be transferred between participants' addresses using digital signatures. Transactions are recorded in a publicly distributed database called the block chain. The block chain is built using a proof-of-work system that prevents double-spending and confirms transactions.

▶
See also Alternative Currencies (pages 72–3)

↓

Bangladeshi carpenter Anil Sutradhr, works at his backyard shop, which he opened with a small loan from the Grameen Bank microcredit project in Manikganj.

3

MONEY AND GOVERNMENT

↑

With money comes power. In the run up of the US Presidential election during the second half of 2012, the Democrats and the Republicans each spent up to $1 billion in their bids to take control of the White House. Campaign funds, most of which comes from private donations, are used for advertising (TV, posters, lawn signs), canvassing, campaign staff, polling and getting the vote out on election day among other things.

Money and power have become inextricably entwined. When a country elects a government, it is essentially tasking it to perform two very basic functions: to tax the populace and to spend the proceeds wisely, looking after it and helping it to develop. Governments' two key fiscal roles – to tax and to spend – have been at the cornerstone of every developed civilization. Without funds from taxation, governments and empires fall and societies disintegrate.

A third element – borrowing – has become an integral part of many government's modus operandi, particularly in modern times. These three preoccupations place an onerous burden on politicians and their civil servants, who must manage their countries' economies in a prudent way or risk popular discontent and worse – the wrath of the global stock and bond markets.

Politics is big business

On a more prosaic level, money and power have come together because of the way power is divided up, elections are managed and leaders are chosen. While

> **"WHEN OUR GOVERNMENT IS SPOKEN OF AS SOME MENACING, THREATENING, FOREIGN ENTITY, IT IGNORES THE FACT THAT IN OUR DEMOCRACY, GOVERNMENT IS US."**
> BARACK OBAMA (B.1961)

we tend to associate the idea of buying votes with unscrupulous dictators, there are echoes of it in the major First-World countries. In the United States' 2012 presidential election, for example, each of the main candidates spent up to $1 billion in campaigning. They invested huge sums in television advertising – over a million ads were shown by the two campaigns between June and October – social media engagement and by orchestrating networks of field offices around the country from which to reach out to voters.

Funds for political purposes do not, of course, come from a country's Treasury, but from private donations and, in large part, from corporate donors. Some make their donations for altruistic reasons, but many do so because a particular political party may favor a policy that has commercial implications. So, politics – and, by extension, government – is big business.

↓

Despite appearances, a nation's government is really owned by its people. Employees earn money from employers. This money is then spent on goods and services provided by companies who use them to create more jobs. Every time money changes hands the government takes a proportion of the transaction in taxes, the revenue from which is, in turn, used to fund the government.

HOW THE ECONOMY WORKS

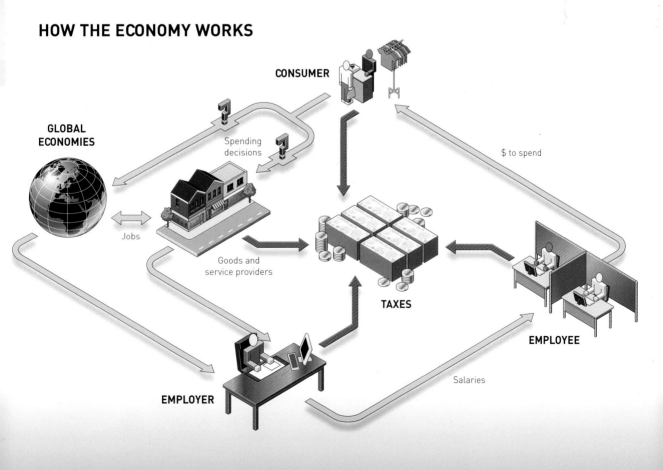

CONSUMER

GLOBAL ECONOMIES

Spending decisions

$ to spend

Jobs

Goods and service providers

TAXES

EMPLOYEE

EMPLOYER

Salaries

What exactly is an economy? The word itself derives from the Greek *oikonomia* meaning "the management of a household" and that remains a useful analogy. A busy, productive "household" is one that perhaps grows crops, tends livestock or makes things and this is its economic activity. It can either consume these goods and services itself or sell them on to other households. This, in a nutshell, is what a country does, too.

THE ECONOMY

On an annual basis, the total of this activity is called a country's gross domestic product, or GDP, and it is the growth (or lack of growth) of GDP that is the main barometer of economic health. Technically, it can be calculated in three principal ways: from total output, from income and from expenditure. (Occasionally, gross national product, or GNP, raises its head, but this includes production owned by a country's citizens, which may occur outside that country's borders.)

GDP and its sprawling family tree of other inputs and outputs keep politicians and their Treasury officials on their toes. They have their hands on the levers not only of power, but also of money: they can slow an economy down or speed it up. This is the great balancing act that occupies their every waking moment.

The great balancing act

In times when borrowing has grown too big, a government can embark on a program of austerity, retrenching and recalibrating by raising taxes or cutting spending. If, on the other hand, a government fears growth is stalling and its citizens are heading for a recession it can try to stimulate the economy by cutting taxes, raising spending and, often, borrowing to fund the attempt.

These initiatives may seem remote from our daily lives, but the devil is in the details. A slight raise in a tax such as Value Added Tax on everyday goods can soon make its presence felt in a family's budget. And as it does so, it affects

→

Global economic activity and growth is measured in a number of ways. One increasingly useful gauge is car sales as it encompasses consumer confidence, industrial production and demand for oil all at once and therefore tends to indicate which way the economy is heading.

PRINTING MONEY – THE LAST RESORT

In times of severe financial crisis, a Treasury or, more usually, a central bank, may be tempted to dust off its printing presses to print more money. Pumping this newly created money – hundreds of billions of dollars of it – into the system acts as a stimulus, encouraging cautious investors out of hibernation and getting money circulating in an economy. In the jargon, Quantitative Easing – or QE – has been rolled out by ailing economies such as Japan in the 1980s and, more recently, by a recession-bound United States and the United Kingdom.

QE is not a universal panacea, however. It is inherently inflationary, pushing prices up. And because it often uses government debt securities as its transmission mechanism, it can have a negative domino effect on other assets that are pegged to such debt securities (in the UK, pension annuity rates have fallen dramatically as a result of QE). Although it has become widely accepted, QE is essentially an emergency measure, so the counterfactual – what might happen without it – probably does not bear thinking about.

confidence. In an economic slowdown, people may put off buying large items – a new car or kitchen appliances – or simply stop spending altogether. This can spell disaster (and deflation or price falls), as people hoard money in their bank accounts and it stops flowing around the system. As a last resort to stem deflation, a country's central bank may have to print new money and inject it into the economy, in the hope that it will encourage demand for goods and services.

↓

Economists study trade, production and consumption decisions, such as those that occur in a traditional marketplace. A market might deal with a product (such as the wheat being collected by these Palestinian farmers), or with services as a factor of production (e.g. brick-laying, book printing, food packaging). Together, all this activity makes up a nation's economy.

It is the role of a Treasury to balance a government's books. As the name suggests, they are the repositories of a nation's treasure – the "public purse" – which in today's world largely means its tax receipts. Having gathered in such taxes, the Treasury, sometimes called the Ministry of Finance, must then disburse them again, as directed by lawmakers, politicians and civil servants. The ebb and flow of these public finances is a Treasury's lifeblood.

TREASURIES

As a general rule, most Treasuries' starting position is that they should not spend more on government projects (for example, defence, education, health and social security) than the tax revenues they collect. Often, this proves difficult, if not impossible, and many spendthrift governments that spend more than they collect therefore run a deficit. (A deficit differs from a structural deficit, which, as its name suggests, is more persistent and exists even when an economy is performing well.) Running a deficit is not necessarily a bad thing, however, as it allows for flexibility in the economy. If a government can borrow funds cheaply (i.e., if the bond markets can see future growth and economic stability), it probably should. This debt funding can be used to initiate large infrastructure projects – building roads, railways, power stations and the like – in order to stimulate growth and create jobs in the great chain of contractors and suppliers.

Funding a deficit

It is a key part of a Treasury's role to address a budget deficit and to fund it, usually by borrowing from domestic and international markets. To do this, Treasuries will issue securities – essentially, government debt – in the form of bonds, which offer interest and the promise to repay the principal amount at a given future date. Because a government itself stands behind these bonds, they are – depending on the government, of course – regarded as being one of the safest investments. The likelihood of the government not paying the interest or the principal is thought unlikely and therefore such bonds are often regarded as being safe-haven investments. Unlikely, but not impossible. When things go really badly, governments are unable to meet their obligations on these bonds – the interest payments or the repayment of the principal – and are then in default. In recent times, Argentina famously defaulted in 2001 and Russia in 1998. Nigeria has defaulted

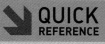

QUICK REFERENCE

Although spending differs in countries across the globe, the chances are that your taxes will be spent on some or all of the following:

- Defence
- Healthcare
- Benefits and pensions
- Public protection
- Government
- Transport
- Industry and the economy
- Housing
- Recreation, sport and culture
- Waste and the environment
- Overseas aid
- Debt interest

no fewer than five times since 1960. Further back in history, the list of defaulters contains such monster economies as China (twice, in 1929 and 1939).

When a country defaults on its debt, drastic action is required. Often, its creditors will agree to reschedule or restructure what they are owed, although they will invariably lose money in any case, known as "a haircut." Worse, however, is the fact that a country that has defaulted will find it very difficult to sell more of its debt to investors. This can create a vicious circle – or "death spiral" – that can be very difficult to get out of. The predicament that Greece has found itself in since 2009, over-extended borrowing exacerbated by a chronic inability to collect taxes, has made it almost entirely dependent on the largesse of its Eurozone neighbors, Germany in particular.

> **"WHICHEVER PARTY IS IN OFFICE, THE TREASURY IS IN POWER."**
> HAROLD WILSON, BRITISH PRIME MINISTER, 1964–70, 1974–76

US BUDGET: 2011
$3,818,000,000,000

Source: kleptocracy.us

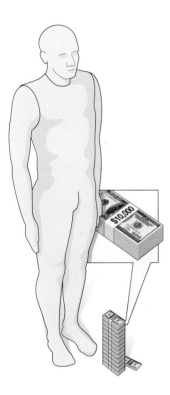

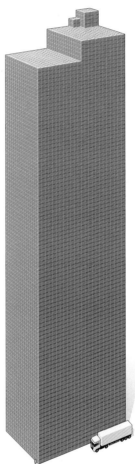

SPENT PER SECOND

The US Government spent $121,067 per second.

Of the total money spent per second, the government borrowed $52,162.

SPENT PER DAY

The US Government spent $10,460,188,800 ($10 billion, 460 million) per day.

Of the total money spent each day, the government borrowed $4,506,849,315 ($4 billion, 506 million).

SPENT PER YEAR

The US Government's budget for 2011 was $3,818,000,000,000 ($3 trillion, 818 million).

Of the total money spent in 2011, $1,645,000,000,000 ($1 trillion, 645 million or approximately 40 percent) was borrowed money.

The nations of the world have never been more in debt to each other. The Economist Intelligence Unit's debt calculator – modelled on the famous clock on New York's Sixth Avenue, which serves as a constant, grim reminder of the United States' burgeoning national debt – puts total global government debt at some $46.7 trillion and counting. The most indebted nations are those in North America and Europe and the least in Asia and the Far East.

NATIONAL DEBT

↓

The National Debt clock on Sixth Avenue in Manhattan in New York City constantly updates to show the US' gross national debt and each American family's share of it. The idea came from real-estate developer Seymour Durst, who wanted to draw attention to the rising debt, and he installed the first clock in Times Square in 1989. In 2004 a new clock was installed in its current location.

As the EIU helpfully points out, world governments owe this gargantuan amount to their own citizens, not to Martians who might come calling, and we are, therefore, all in it together. Nevertheless, there is a downside: burgeoning public debt often leads to higher taxes, political upheaval and social unrest – destabilizing effects that keep politicians and economists alike awake at night.

Government debt manifests itself as bonds, often described as being IOUs, which are sold to investors (whether private individuals, financial institutions or, indeed, other governments) and pay regular interest until they are redeemed by the issuer at a given date. These bonds vary considerably from country to country and their relative attractions to investors are measured by the stability and creditworthiness of the issuing country.

The debt curse – here to stay?

National debt figures for individual countries each tell a different story. In Europe, some countries such as Germany, the Netherlands and Luxembourg have relatively modest debt levels (and better-than-average records of investing in growth), but others such as Greece, Portugal and Italy have almost buckled under both their debt levels and the crisis of confidence in their investors. The bulk of Japan's national debt has been acquired by internal investors; by contrast, nearly half of America's huge debt is foreign-owned, much of it by China, and the United Kingdom has also sold vast quantities of its debt to overseas investors. Elsewhere, the historically heavily indebted nations such as Brazil, India and Russia, all of whom suffered debt crises in recent times, have emerged as stronger relative to their peers.

WHO OWES WHAT?

National debt as percentage of GDP
(in US dollars)

Source: Economist global debt clock and other sources, 2013

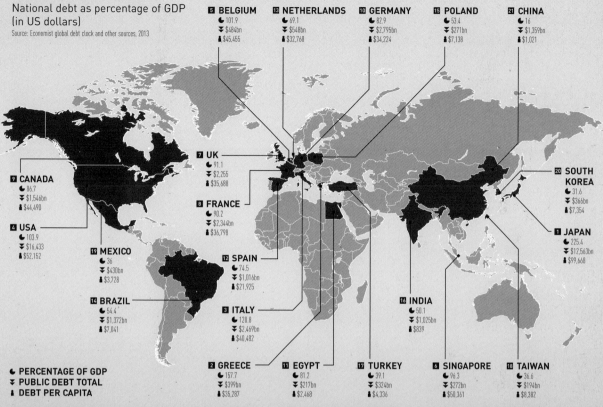

5 BELGIUM
- 101.9
- $484bn
- $45,455

13 NETHERLANDS
- 69.1
- $548bn
- $32,768

10 GERMANY
- 82.9
- $2,795bn
- $34,224

15 POLAND
- 53.4
- $271bn
- $7,138

21 CHINA
- 16
- $1,359bn
- $1,021

7 UK
- 91.1
- $2,255
- $35,688

9 CANADA
- 86.7
- $1,546bn
- $44,490

4 USA
- 103.9
- $16,433
- $52,152

8 FRANCE
- 90.2
- $2,344bn
- $36,798

19 MEXICO
- 36
- $430bn
- $3,728

12 SPAIN
- 74.5
- $1,016bn
- $21,925

14 BRAZIL
- 54.4
- $1,372bn
- $7,041

3 ITALY
- 120.8
- $2,469bn
- $40,482

16 INDIA
- 50.1
- $1,025bn
- $839

20 SOUTH KOREA
- 31.6
- $366bn
- $7,354

1 JAPAN
- 225.4
- $12,563bn
- $99,668

2 GREECE
- 157.7
- $399bn
- $35,287

11 EGYPT
- 81.2
- $217bn
- $2,468

17 TURKEY
- 39.1
- $324bn
- $4,336

6 SINGAPORE
- 96.3
- $272bn
- $50,361

18 TAIWAN
- 36.6
- $194bn
- $8,382

- PERCENTAGE OF GDP
- PUBLIC DEBT TOTAL
- DEBT PER CAPITA

While national debt is now commonplace – national surpluses have existed but are even frowned on by many economists – some predict that the biggest industrialized nations may have to endure a so-called debt curse for many years to come, as they struggle to rebalance their economies and bring their debts down to sustainable – around 60 percent of GDP – levels.

▶
See also The Bond Markets (pages 92–3) and Bonds (pages 120–1)

RATING GOVERNMENT DEBT

Just as companies receive ratings of their creditworthiness, so do countries. The three big ratings agencies – Standard & Poor's, Moody's and Fitch – keep a gimlet eye on individual sovereign governments' debt piles and, more importantly, their ability to pay interest, refinance and repay them. The likelihood of default – missing such repayments – is a specter which haunts the debt markets and even modest downgrades make it more expensive for governments to raise further debt as investors demand more of a risk premium. In recent times (August 2011), Greece has been given an unenviably low credit rating – CCC – by S&P, while even the US has seen its long-term rating downgraded from gold-plated AAA to AA+ (the joke was that this was a downgrade from standard to poor). Bottom of the pile is North Korea, which has around $12.5 billion in outstanding debt, but shows little inclination to repay it and gets a D for default from the ratings agencies.

Tax has attracted more jokes, cartoons and comic turns than almost any other piece of the money puzzle. It is, of course, gallows humor. Taxes, along with death, are proverbially the only two certainties in life and so we must make the best of them. But tax is deadly serious. Without them, governments and their economies, which rely so heavily on tax revenues, would fail.

TAX

↓

Tax is the lifeblood of every national economy. The money is collected by a specialist government department and then handed over to the Treasury for distribution to a huge array of government departments. This graphic indicates how a modern European government might divide up its annual expenditure.

There is a bewildering array of taxes, including tax on income, sales, property, fuel, alcohol and tobacco, estates and inheritance. Historically, tax has been levied on such oddball items as windows and hearths (a form of property tax), wigs and powder (in 18th-century England), text messages (a short-lived tax in the Philippines, scuppered by a text messaging campaign) and even freedom (10 percent paid by freed Roman slaves to their former masters).

WHERE THE MONEY GOES

Source: The Guardian

TOTAL SPEND
US $600bn

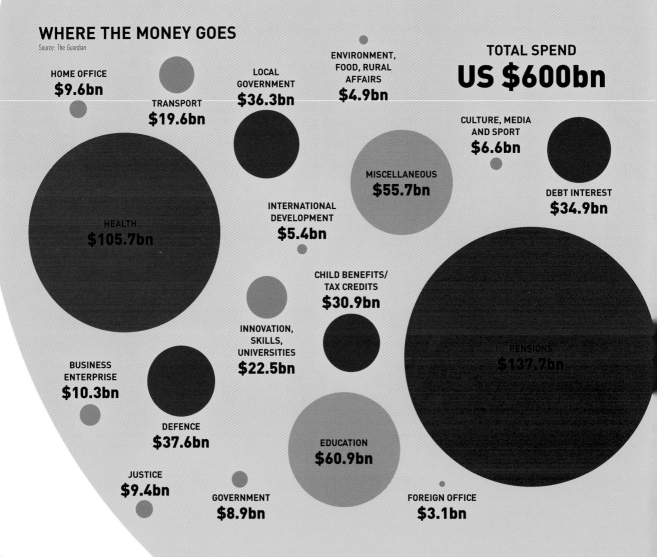

HOME OFFICE
$9.6bn

TRANSPORT
$19.6bn

LOCAL GOVERNMENT
$36.3bn

ENVIRONMENT, FOOD, RURAL AFFAIRS
$4.9bn

CULTURE, MEDIA AND SPORT
$6.6bn

MISCELLANEOUS
$55.7bn

DEBT INTEREST
$34.9bn

HEALTH
$105.7bn

INTERNATIONAL DEVELOPMENT
$5.4bn

CHILD BENEFITS/ TAX CREDITS
$30.9bn

INNOVATION, SKILLS, UNIVERSITIES
$22.5bn

PENSIONS
$137.7bn

BUSINESS ENTERPRISE
$10.3bn

DEFENCE
$37.6bn

EDUCATION
$60.9bn

JUSTICE
$9.4bn

GOVERNMENT
$8.9bn

FOREIGN OFFICE
$3.1bn

THE TAX-FREE LIFE

Is it possible to be tax resident nowhere and pay no taxes at all? Yes, but although it may be in theory, you might have to buy a boat, preferably registered in a suitably tax-friendly country such as Liberia or Panama. You may also be required to hire some locals to act as crew. Secondly, you may have to keep afloat and spend only short periods in any one port so that you might therefore avoid the attentions of the local tax authorities who may regard you as having taken up residency for tax purposes. Should you tire of this nomadic life and wish to return home, you might find that you do not qualify for any of the benefits that accrue for normal taxpayers (such as state pensions and the like).

Creative accounting

In many developed countries, the rich pay the most tax (in the UK for example, the top 1 percent of earners pay nearly a quarter of the total income tax bill and the top 10 percent pay more than half), but while this may seem fair, it also presents problems. Tax these people too much and they may leave the country and seek more benign fiscal environments, creating an added burden for the poor. Those who leave are unlikely to head for Belgium or Denmark, who have the highest personal income tax rates, but they might head for Japan or the US where rates are more favorable.

Naturally, people who have taxes forced upon them will quickly try to find ways to avoid paying them for as long as possible – or at all. Although tax evasion is, in most jurisdictions, a criminal offence, many tax authorities tolerate a certain amount of creative accounting.

The possibility of deducting, or offsetting, expenses from tax bills has stretched human ingenuity, with claims being made for all manner of business expenses, including cat food, cosmetic surgery, swimming pools and free beer for garage customers. Equally, many people overpay tax and do not claim all their entitlements (if you are dealing in satellites, space stations and spacecraft – including launch vehicles – for example, these are qualifying assets for roll-over tax relief in Britain).

> **"GOVERNMENT'S VIEW OF THE ECONOMY COULD BE SUMMED UP IN A FEW SHORT PHRASES: IF IT MOVES, TAX IT. IF IT KEEPS MOVING, REGULATE IT. AND IF IT STOPS MOVING, SUBSIDIZE IT."**
> RONALD REAGAN (1911–2004), PRESIDENT OF THE UNITED STATES, 1981–89

Lotteries promise instant wealth and freedom from financial worry. For their operators – which are often governments – they are an excellent way of raising funds for both good causes and, occasionally, nefarious ones (war, historically, is a favorite). They are, therefore, a "win-win" – assuming you win. Unfortunately, millions of punters do not. Like any other form of gambling, lotteries are predicated on odds that will always favor the lottery operator.

LOTTERIES

Critics of lotteries claim they are a form of regressive tax (although arguably a voluntary one), encouraging poorer people to spend proportionately more of their incomes on schemes that have little chance of giving them a good return.

Nothing new

Lotteries are not new. The Great Wall of China was partly financed by the proceeds of the sale of Keno slips during the Chinese Han Dynasty between 205 and 187 BC. They were employed by the Romans and throughout medieval times, often for the purposes of raising funds to fortify a town. Queen Elizabeth I sanctioned a lottery in England in 1569 to fund "publique good workes," which employed sales agents, essentially the first stockbrokers, and allowed speculators to purchase shares of individual tickets.

In modern times, lotteries have become more widespread, more sophisticated and richer, so that prizes running into the multi-millions are seen as the norm. Many millions of people play on a regular basis, spending an average $4–$5 per week. Often, however, winners do not receive the huge lump sums they see advertised as a jackpot. It is increasingly common for winners to receive annuity payments for a specified term, sometimes with a balloon payment in

↓
Sun Bae (left), owner of the Times Market in Bishop, Texas, sells lottery tickets to a customer. In June 2010, Bishop native Joan Ginther won $10 million from a ticket purchased in Bae's store. Two years before Ginther had won on another ticket bought in the same shop.

LUCK OR JUDGMENT?

One in eighteen septillion (18, with 24 zeros) – those are the odds that Joan Ginther, a 63-year-old former maths professor from Las Vegas, Nevada, beat when she won $5.4 million in 1993, $2 million ten years later, $3 million two years after that and, finally, in 2010, a further $10 million. Ginther bought the last two winning tickets, both $50 scratchcards, from the same mini-supermarket in the small town of Bishop, Texas, where she grew up. The Texas Lottery Commission doesn't suspect any wrongdoing on Ginther's part. She may have figured out the algorithm that picked the winning numbers and somehow identified where the tickets were to be sold, but on the other hand she may just have been very, very lucky.

the final year. And while many countries' tax authorities regard lottery winnings as tax-free, others, including the United States, do not: a jackpot can suddenly seem rather less life-changing.

Olympic innovation

Hosting the Olympics is spectacularly expensive. Since the Los Angeles games in 1984 (which was paid for entirely from funds raised through sponsorship) rising costs have been met with funds raised through a combination of public and private money and sponsorship. (Beijing 2008 was an anomaly as the Chinese government, which paid the whole bill, has never released figures. Some estimates put the cost of those games at $43 billion!). But the official record for the most expensive games goes to London 2012, which cost an estimated $14.8 billion.

In an innovative move these latest games introduced a new funding stream as the UK's National Lottery is said to have contributed $6 billion for the Olympic and Paralympic Games. This money included support for 1,200 athletes and grants for the construction of the various venues. In return, the lottery will share in the profits made from land and property sales in the future, which it will use to provide a legacy for the people of east London and the wider UK.

Rio 2016 intends to go back down the now traditional private-public partnership route and the search for sponsors is already underway. It remains to be seen whether the use of lottery funds has worked, but with bids normally underestimating sharply escalating costs, it seems a highly effective instrument.

THERE ARE PUBLICLY OPERATED LOTTERIES IN AT LEAST 100 COUNTRIES WORLDWIDE WITH SALES OF OVER $250 BILLION

THE ESCALATING COSTS OF HOSTING THE GAMES

Year	Host city	Estimated cost in billions of US dollars
1984	Los Angeles	1.2
1988	Seoul	4
1992	Barcelona	7.5
1996	Atlanta	1.8
2000	Sydney	4.1
2004	Athens	15
2008	Beijing	43*
2012	London	14.8

*Figures were never officially released

Politics and money make uneasy bedfellows. Nevertheless, as the world's largest economies rely ever more heavily on each other, governments spend an increasing amount of time negotiating with one another about money. This manifests itself as trade tariffs (who can sell what to whom and at what price) and finance treaties such as the Basel agreements on banking, named after the Swiss city where central bankers gather. (Basel III, for example, which is the latest edict to be put into effect, will focus on strengthening banks' balance sheets against unforeseen shocks.)

POLITICS

Politicians and their officials have much to discuss, therefore. This has led to the formation of groups that reflect the size, influence and economic wealth of their respective nations:

→

The leaders of the world's major industrial economies (G8) meeting at Camp David in May 2012 to discuss their response to the possibility of a full-blown financial crisis in Europe.

- **G7:** the seven major industrialized economies, comprising the US, UK, France, Germany, Italy, Canada and Japan.
- **G8:** the G7 and Russia.
- **G20:** the G8 and developing countries like China, India, Brazil and Saudi Arabia. It gained in significance after leaders agreed how to tackle the 2008–09 financial crisis and recession at G20 gatherings.

The interconnectedness of banking

Each of these groups descends regularly on a designated capital city. In fact, most of the negotiating will have been done already and these showy events are really about public relations and to reassure the world that politicians are addressing the issues of the day. Many of those issues are about money and, in recent times, how to address financial crises. The interconnectedness of the world's banking system means that the failure of an institution in a small city in the United States can have serious ramifications in Tokyo or Frankfurt.

So politicians need to take a global view of money and how it is flowing. They also need to understand the strengths and weaknesses of other economies, not least because this quickly affects the currency markets. Equally, when governments issue debt, much of it may end up in foreign hands. (Of the United States' debt of $16.4 trillion, foreigners own $4.45 trillion, some 32 percent. China alone owns 8 percent of the total.) In other words, one country may actually become another's bank manager. And if you subscribe to the idea that it pays to be polite to your bank manager, you can see how important money has become in the great chess game of national and international politics.

↓

Since the late 1990s G8/ G20 summits have become the focus of a worldwide protest movement, under the banner of anti-globalization. Rioting has occurred at some protests, for instance in Seattle, London, and Genoa, in Italy, where one man died and extensive damage was done to buildings including McDonald's and Starbucks.

↓

It is estimated that the cost of the conflict in the Middle East between 1991 and 2010 was $12 trillion. The figure is calculated by comparing the current GDP to the potential GDP in times of peace. Had there been peace and cooperation between Israel and Arab League nations since 1991, the average Israeli citizen would have been earning over $44,000 instead of $23,000 in 2010. In terms of the human cost, it is estimated that the conflict has taken 92,000 lives (74,000 military and 18,000 civilian between 1945 and 1995).

Wars are mightily expensive. They have a disproportionate effect on governments' finances, yet rarely does the cost of war, at least in modern times, stop a government from pursuing it. War can also act as a catalyst for change (in 1694, the Bank of England was founded by a group of British financiers to raise funds for the war against the French), but they are rarely anything but a huge drain on the public purse.

WAR

Ultimately, wars are financed by raising taxes, selling government debt and increasing the money supply. Aside from the often terrible human cost, wars tend to lead to inflation, lower living standards and the redirection of resources into the war effort.

The costs of war

In the 20th century, war wreaked havoc with the global economy. The economic cost of the First World War is put at around $500 billion, while the Second World

War has been estimated at $1.5 trillion. Of this, the US spent 21 percent, Britain 20 percent, Germany 18 percent and the USSR 13 percent. Ironically, such costs can turn into a grim merry-go-round: the massive reparations demanded of Germany by the terms of the Treaty of Versailles after the First World War, for example, were indirectly financed by the United States, which lent prodigious sums to Germany in the years after 1918. In doing so, some historians argue, they also paid for Germany to re-build its economy and to re-arm itself.

In the late 20th and early 21st centuries, the costs of modern warfare have risen exponentially – Brown University's 'Costs of War' project reckons the total cost for wars in Iraq, Afghanistan and Pakistan is at least $3.2–$4 trillion.

Taxpayer dollars aside, there are many other costs to war. The human costs are felt not only in the loss of manpower, but also in those of caring for the wounded, for veterans and for those who have been displaced. Countries affected by war must account for similar displacement, as well as huge environmental and health costs and the costs of rebuilding their physical infrastructure. Sometimes, of course, war brings benefits – the overturning of tyranny and the establishment of democracy has been a common theme – but invariably at huge financial cost.

> **"TO CARRY ON WAR, THREE THINGS ARE NECESSARY: MONEY, MONEY, AND YET MORE MONEY."**
> GIAN JACOPO TRIVULZIO (1440–1518), ITALIAN GENERAL

CIGARETTE MONEY

War engenders both black market entrepreneurism and ingenious opportunism. During the Second World War, an Allied soldier called Robert Radford was incarcerated for several years in a German prisoner of war camp. Radford observed how his 50,000 fellow prisoners traded clothing, food and swapped items for services such as a haircut, creating the camp's own micro economy. Without paper money, the prisoners used the cigarettes donated by the Red Cross as a form of currency.

In 1945, Radford wrote a much-praised article "The Economic Organization of a POW Camp" in which he described how simple barter gave way to rough scales of exchange values: ("It was realized that a tin of jam was worth ½ lb of margarine plus something else; that a cigarette issue was worth several chocolate issues, and a tin of diced carrots was worth practically nothing"). Soon, the prisoners' tobacco became the standard of value, with goods measured in numbers of cigarettes (a shirt, for example, could be bought for 80 to 120 cigarettes, depending on its condition; and tea, coffee or cocoa were two cigarettes a cup). The system became a mirror of a cash economy, with its own inflation, deflation and feverish trading in times of cigarette shortage. It ended in April 1945 with the prisoners' liberation by the 30th US Infantry Division. Radford concluded drily: "the ushering in of an age of plenty demonstrated the hypothesis that with infinite means economic organization and activity would be redundant, as every want could be satisfied without effort."

Do governments lead the markets, or do markets lead governments? In times of financial crisis, it is often difficult to tell. So powerful have the bond and, to a lesser extent, equity markets become that it often looks like the tail is wagging the dog.

CRISIS

Ultimately, however, only governments have the heavy lifting gear – whether legislation, monetary stimulus or swingeing taxes – to sort out financial crises. Central banks and regulators keep a watchful eye – though not always as watchful as it should be – on stresses and strains in the financial markets. They are, essentially, trying to identify idiosyncratic risk (risk confined to one financial institution or instrument) and systemic risk (risk that can affect the entire financial system) and to prepare accordingly.

Crisis in the financial markets can be triggered by any number of events – one-off natural disasters, terrorist attacks or the long drawn-out death spirals, which can affect an entire part of say, the credit market. Financial institutions' size and interconnectedness – their reliance on each other as counterparties and as syndicate partners – means modern crises can escalate very quickly and dangerously.

Finding solutions

Governments tend to have short, medium and long-term approaches to crises. In the short term, governments invariably have to respond to financial crisis by supplying increased liquidity – cash – into the markets and by relaxing their rules on, for example, overnight lending between banks which oils the wheels of their balance sheets. In the medium term, their

←

The current economic downturn has seen a number of European governments putting severe austerity measures in place. The colossal debts and rock-bottom growth of Greece, Italy and Spain, for example, have hammered market confidence. The interest rates on their sovereign bonds have soared, making it difficult for them to borrow in international markets. Protests have become a common sight on the streets of Europe's cities as these austerity measures bite.

RECESSION AND DEPRESSION

A recession is usually defined as two consecutive quarters of negative growth in the rate of economic output. There is no real consensus on what constitutes a depression, although it is essentially a prolonged recession. Some have suggested that it represents a decline in real GDP of more than 10 percent, or that it is a recession lasting two years or more. The Great Depression took its worst toll in the four years following the Wall Street Crash of October 1929, but affected both the United States and other countries for most of the 1930s. Global industrial production, wholesale prices and foreign trade tumbled, while unemployment soared to as much as 33 percent in some countries. Economists differ on how the Great Depression ended, but many believe increased spending by governments during the Second World War kick-started their economies again.

priority is often to address the solvency of financial institutions – to work out whether they are still viable, need propping up or, as a last resort, bringing on to the government's own books by nationalization. Finally, in the longer term, a government will likely strengthen rules and regulations to try to ensure a particular crisis does not happen again. Often, however, there is another one brewing to take its place.

Volatility creates opportunity

While there are many losers in financial crises, there are also some winners. In the early days of the so-called credit crunch of 2007 to 2009, for example, some investors made huge profits by betting that debt markets would seize up and that banks would suffer calamitous losses from their exposures. While the majority of the financial community dreads such events, some financial speculators, including some hedge funds, thrive on crisis situations: they create volatility, which in turn creates opportunity in the markets.

↑

The Great Depression was the most widespread and deepest depression of the 20th century. In the US unemployment ran at 25 percent for almost a decade as heavy industry, construction and farming virtually collapsed. This picture sees a long line of jobless men waiting to receive cabbage and potatoes from a federal relief agency in Cleveland, Ohio.

While the interaction between governments and the economy can often seem like dark arts, nationalization and privatization are two practical examples of how a government can influence a company or an entire industry.

NATIONALIZATION AND PRIVATIZATION

Nationalization brings a company or a set of assets under state control and throughout history has been one of the principal strategies pursued by countries favoring socialism over capitalism (after the end of the Second World War, for example, Poland nationalized all companies with over 50 employees).

Equally, a state-owned entity can be sold off by a government to generate funds or to create private-sector competition in a particular industry and this privatization – literally taking private – has been the hallmark of countries making the transition to a capitalist society. The vast privatizations of former state-owned commodities companies in Russia and Ukraine in the 1990s are just one example.

Historically, large systemically important companies and industries have been those subject to this governmental tug of war: postal services, broadcasters, electricity and gas producers, railways, mines and oil producers have been particular targets. Often, the driver is ideological: left-leaning politicians have long argued that systemically important industries should be owned by everyone, rather than just by a handful of private shareholders. The political right, conversely, maintains that companies flourish in a market free of the dead hand of government.

↓

Belief in the policies of nationalization and privatization normally falls along political lines, and socialist politicians, such as former president Hugo Chavez of Venezuela and Cristina Kirchner, president of Argentina, have used nationalization of a wide range of businesses, such as energy, banks and state pensions, to help their economies during the current global downturn.

Profit and control

While politics has often played its part in both nationalizations and privatizations, so too has the desire for profit and control. Nationalizations mostly involve compensation to an owner, although expropriation, where no recompense is made and a government simply seizes assets, is not uncommon. If a company – or bank – is failing and there is a risk that by doing so, there will be a domino effect that could cause widespread instability, nationalization is a way of containing risk.

Privatizations, for their part, can generate vast fortunes for the state (and large fees for investment banks handling the process) and, ultimately, for their new owners, by the sale and purchase of shares. If such a sale is conducted on the public markets, small retail investors can often participate, allowing them to become investors in, for example, the postal service or electricity company they may use in their daily lives.

Opinions differ as to whether companies do better with or without state control. Many state-owned entities thrive in the private sector, but others struggle to compete with existing rivals and end up being re-nationalized.

HEALING THE WOUNDS

One of privatization's greatest success stories comes from Rwanda in central Africa. In the late 1980s global coffee prices plummeted. Economic devastation followed as the nation's economy depended on subsistence farming with coffee and tea as its principal exports. The consequences were rapid and dramatic, coffee trees were uprooted and replaced with quick-growing food crops needed to overcome an escalating famine. A savage civil war, with its roots in poverty, began, culminating in the 1994 genocide in which 800,000 people died. In 1998 the Tutsi-led government embarked on a major program of privatization by lowering trade barriers, which included the coffee industry. The move signaled the resurgence of economic activity and an annual rise in GDP. The industry has since created jobs, boosted small farmer expenditure and consumption, and fostered social reconciliation by reducing ethnic distance among the Hutus and Tutsis who work together harvesting the beans.

"OVER THE LONG TERM, THE STOCK MARKET NEWS WILL BE GOOD. IN THE 20TH CENTURY, THE UNITED STATES ENDURED TWO WORLD WARS AND OTHER TRAUMATIC AND EXPENSIVE MILITARY CONFLICTS; THE DEPRESSION; A DOZEN OR SO RECESSIONS AND FINANCIAL PANICS; OIL SHOCKS; A FLU EPIDEMIC; AND THE RESIGNATION OF A DISGRACED PRESIDENT. YET THE DOW ROSE FROM 66 TO 11,497."

WARREN BUFFETT, QUOTED IN *THE NEW YORK TIMES*, OCTOBER 2008

4 BANKS AND BANKING

↑
The Eccles Building in Washington, DC is the headquarters of the Federal Reserve System, which was established in 1913. The Fed, as it is known informally, is the gatekeeper of the US economy. It is the central bank of the United States – the bank of banks and the bank of the US government. It regulates financial institutions, manages the nation's money and influences the economy.

Ask a child to draw a picture of a bank and he or she will probably still describe a grand stone edifice with pillars and a portico. This classical bank has its roots in antiquity and in the pictures of the Federal Reserve or the Bank of England that we see on television. These days, however, a bank may just as easily be an anonymous office block in a big city, a sprawling call center in an out-of-town office park or even on the mobile phone belonging to someone running a 'community bank' in sub-Saharan Africa.

What all these examples – including the grand classical bank – have in common is the element of trust. They are, variously, trusted by their customers, whether they are individuals, businesses or entire nations, to look after their money. Their common characteristic is that they are perceived as a safer place to put money than under the proverbial mattress. In return for this trust, banks offer a variety of financial incentives and services, ranging from paying interest on deposits to making available loans and mortgages.

A vital cog in the money machine

Banks and banking are nothing new, but the majority of the world's population still does not have a bank account. Gradually this is changing. New recruits will find that their relationship with a bank is heading rapidly toward being an online one, albeit with support from a branch network and a call center, possibly thousands of miles away. Most will, however, never meet a bank manager, the patriarchal figure who once opened the bank in the morning, welcomed customers and offered friendly, but prudent, advice.

Although the macro picture suggests they are still catching on, as well as changing dramatically, banks have become very much part of everyday life for billions of people. In the commercial world, they are also the cornerstones of business transactions and vital nodes on the enormous, interconnected network that forms the international financial markets. They remain a very important cog in the global money machine.

AT THE LAST COUNT, THE COLLECTIVE ASSETS OF THE WORLD'S LARGEST THOUSAND BANKS TOTALLED $96.4 TRILLION

↓

The bank that most embodies the image of an impressive stone building complete with pillars and a grand portico is the Bank of England. Established in 1694, (it is the second oldest central bank in the world, the oldest being the Bank of Sweden), it moved to its current headquarters in Threadneedle Street in 1793. This engraving, by Rowlandson, shows the main business room in 1808.

At the top of the banking tree are so-called supranational banks, which are institutions often formed – and funded – by groups of countries to be responsible for global financial stability and liquidity. Stability means that the financial system is robust and can withstand shocks, such as stock market falls; liquidity means that there is enough cash to honor payments, settle trades and, ultimately, that banks lower down the food chain can repay depositors when they want their money back.

SUPRANATIONAL BANKS

With more or less limitless capacity, they may truly be said to be "too big to fail." Fundamentally, these banks stand as the world's so-called Lender of Last Resort. In extremis, countries can turn to them for help, which is offered, subject to stringent conditions, in the form of emergency short- and long-term loans – or bailouts – to tide them over.

→

Economist John Maynard Keynes (1883–1946), (center), represented the United Kingdom at the United Nations International Monetary and Financial Conference at Bretton Woods, New Hampshire in July 1944. The conference established the rules for commercial and financial relations among the world's major industrial states toward the end of the Second World War. Setting up a system of rules, institutions, and procedures to regulate the international monetary system, the planners at Bretton Woods also established the International Monetary Fund (IMF).

The International Monetary Fund (IMF)

Best known among these giants is the International Monetary Fund, which was mooted by a group of 45 countries in 1944 to engender economic cooperation and lend money after the Second World War. It is now owned and financed by no less than 187 member countries.

The IMF welcomed its first customer – France – in 1947. Since then there have been sporadic calls on its services. In 1976, for example, the United Kingdom negotiated a £2.3 billion loan when inflation reached record levels and the pound slumped dramatically. During the recent financial crisis, the IMF has provided rescue loans to the likes of Iceland, Greece, the Irish Republic and Portugal.

Development banks

While the IMF acts as something of a global financier, the World Bank has a more developmental role, focusing on poorer countries that need financial help to combat poverty, malnutrition and lack of communications and infrastructure. The World Bank has a staff of more than 10,000 and a huge program: in 2010 alone, it provided $47 billion for 300 projects in developing countries around the world. Current initiatives range from AIDS-prevention in Guinea and school programs in Bangladesh to healthcare in Mexico and earthquake relief efforts in Gujarat.

Similar to the World Bank, but devoted to European economies, is the European Bank for Reconstruction and Development (EBRD), which was established by the European Union and its member countries to promote East-West economic integration following the fall of the Berlin Wall.

↓

The EBRD is the major funder of a new sarcophagus to be built over the Chernobyl nuclear reactor, scene of the world's worst nuclear accident in 1986. Workers confirmed that the current structure, built in the immediate aftermath of the accident to confine radioactive leaks, is now crumbling. It is estimated that the new construction will cost some $2 billion.

Leading supranational banks

IMF: The IMF's fundamental mission is to help ensure the stability of the international economic system. It does so in three ways: keeping track of the global economy and the economies of member countries, lending to countries with balance of payments difficulties and by giving practical help to its members.
Founded: 1944
Who owns it? It has 187 member countries
Key Player: Christine Lagarde

WORLD BANK: The World Bank is a source of financial and technical assistance to developing countries around the world. It helps governments in these countries reduce poverty by providing them with the money and technical expertise they need for a wide range of projects – such as education, health, infrastructure, communications and government reforms.
Founded: 1944
Who owns it? All 193 members of the United Nations, plus Kosovo
Key Player: Jim Yong Kim

EUROPEAN BANK FOR RECONSTRUCTION AND DEVELOPMENT: The EBRD provides project financing for banks, industries and businesses in central Europe, the western Balkans and central Asia. By bearing risk on behalf of its clients, it helps countries in the region become open market economies.
Founded: 1991
Who owns it? It has 63 member countries, the European Union and the European Investment Bank
Key Player: Sir Suma Chakrabarti

However dependent they may be on the world's supranational banks, most countries also have their own central bank, which acts both as a government's banker and the guardian of monetary policy, financial stability and money supply. In times of crisis, central banks also invariably assume the role of a nation's Lender of Last Resort, providing liquidity, guarantees and a safe haven to troubled financial institutions.

CENTRAL BANKS

↓

Bob Bernanke (left) former Chairman of the Federal Reserve, and Sir Mervyn King, his counterpart at the Bank of England, and perhaps the two most famous faces in world banking. Central bankers – a very different breed from investment bankers – like to say they have influence rather than power, but their forecasts and decisions undoubtedly move financial markets. Because of this, they tend to be secretive and to pick their words with infinite care. Historically, at the Bank of England, one of the world's oldest central banks, even the governor's eyebrows, occasionally raised in disapproval, have been interpreted as a barometer of monetary policy.

Many central banks are technically independent from their governments, although most are still nominally owned by them. In practice, this means they are free of political interference to set monetary policy, which might otherwise be used to influence public opinion and win votes.

The balance of risks

Monetary policy, largely directed at controlling inflation (and deflation), is at the core of a central bank's role. Most have an army of economists and an arsenal of economic models to inform their decisions. Central banks must constantly gauge the balance of risks when setting interest rates and managing the money supply (by issuing or removing banknotes and coins from circulation). In theory, a central bank has unlimited capacity to create new money and to inject it into the economy.

Central banks try to use these diverse levers to control inflation and maintain price stability in the wider economy. Their actions are carefully calibrated, but nevertheless often have immediate and dramatic effects on stock and bond markets, as well as on general investors and consumer sentiment.

If central banks rarely sleep, it is because they are often preoccupied with the fluctuations of the so-called overnight rate, the interest rate at which central banks lend to commercial banks, most of which will have accounts at the central bank. This wholesale rate, in turn, influences the rate at which banks lend to each other – the so-called interbank rate. It is important that this rate does not deviate too much from the core interest rates that are used in the wider, retail economy, for commercial loans, homeowners' mortgages, credit cards and so on.

Besides keeping the economy on track, central banks are often the custodian of a country's foreign exchange and gold reserves (collectively known as reserves). A country's gold, often stored in vaults in a central bank, is seen as a reassuring presence, particularly when most currencies are "fiat currencies," with no intrinsic value (worth nothing if not used as money). Foreign exchange reserves are mostly held in US dollars – the world's pre-eminent reserve currency – but central banks also hold large quantities of sterling, euros, yen and Swiss francs.

Unconventional measures

In times of severe economic hardship, central banks such as the US Federal Reserve, the Bank of England and the European Central Bank have added what they call unconventional measures to their monetary policy toolkit to stimulate growth and avoid deflation. Known as Quantitative Easing (see page 45) and pioneered by the Bank of Japan in the 1990s, this involves buying their government's own debt (or long-term "repos" in the case of the ECB, since it is not allowed to buy government debt). And lots of it. The Fed has bought over $2 trillion, while the Bank of England has purchased $520 billion since 2009.

To do this, the central banks print money and inject it into the economy by buying government debt from financial institutions such as pension funds. In theory, these financial institutions will use the cash to buy riskier assets, boosting prices and encouraging demand. At the same time, the amount of money circulating in the financial system increases. QE initiatives have been so large that they also engender a feel-good factor in the financial markets. But they are strong medicine, with some side effects that can bend the bond markets out of shape. At some point, too, central bank governors will have to decide how to exit their positions, thereby tightening (as opposed to easing) policy, by selling their bonds back into the markets.

▶

See also The Money Markets (pages 90–1)

QUICK REFERENCE

The world's leading central banks

US Federal Reserve (The Fed)
European Central Bank (ECB)
Bank of England (BoE)
Bank of Japan (BoJ)
Swiss National Bank (SNB)
Bank of Canada (BoC)
Reserve Bank of Australia (RBA)
Reserve Bank of New Zealand (RBNZ)

Standard duties include: setting monetary policy, maintaining adequate reserve backing for a nation's commercial banks, acting as custodian of its reserves and regulating the exchange rate of its currency.

THE GLOBAL BANKING POLICEMAN

Many of the world's central banks have responsibility for overseeing the financial stability of commercial banks, brokers and fund managers. In a world in which many such firms have become inextricably interconnected, there are tough international standards to follow.

BIS – the Bank for International Settlements – in Basel, Switzerland, acts as something of a global policeman. This international association of central banks, which also has the distinction of being a bank for central banks, was set up in 1930. These days it sets levels for the capital adequacy of banks, the minimum

buffer they must maintain in case of financial shocks, and for their liquidity. The powerful Basel Committee on Banking Supervision created a set of rules called Basel II, followed by Basel 2.5, and, in response to the global financial crisis, has now created Basel III, which aims to improve banks' ability to withstand sudden financial shocks (such as the collapse of Lehman Brothers in September 2008, which had a domino effect on countless other banks and brokerages), to improve their risk management and strengthen their transparency so that there are fewer potential systemic threats lurking in the shadows.

Despite the increasing number of electronic transactions, banknotes and coins are still produced in vast quantities, mostly at the direction of a country's central bank. Physical production takes place at a mint, the ancient forerunner of a treasury, which nowadays works with third-party manufacturers such as De La Rue, a British company that prints banknotes for around 150 countries.

COINS AND COINAGE

In Europe, where 17 countries share a single currency, the euro, banknotes are produced jointly by the national central banks, which share the costs and the burden of forecasting how many notes will be needed across the entire Eurozone. (Coins, on the other hand, are the responsibility of individual national governments.) It is an enormous task: at the last count, there were nearly 8.5 billion euro notes, from €5 to €500, in circulation (worth a total of €184.5 billion) and 52.5 billion coins, from the ¢1 to the €2 coin.

→

Production of euro coins is the responsibility of member countries, here a worker examines €1 coins at the mint in Rome. On January 1, 1999, the euro became the official currency in 11 countries, including Italy. In its first issue, Italy produced almost seven billion coins. Prior to this the Italians had not used many coins, the smallest banknote was worth L.1,000, which was equivalent to ¢50. For Christmas 1998, the most popular present for Italians was ... a purse.

Combating the counterfeiters

When the Bank of England was designing its latest £50 note, it incorporated a groundbreaking security feature in the form of a motion thread, containing holograms of the £ symbol and the number 50, which move up and down and from side to side. That's not all. An ultraviolet test shows a scattering of red, blue and green images which appear only under ultraviolet light; the number 50 and the words "Bank of England" are in hard-to-reproduce embossed print; hidden inside the Queen's portrait is microlettering, which is barely visible to the naked eye; there is a see-through register of irregular shapes, which combine to the £ symbol; finally there is a watermark of the Queen's head and a metallic thread,

M IS FOR MONEY

Keeping track of notes and coins is no easy task. Central banks typically use a system of Ms to classify different types of money. Typically, the Ms range from M0 (narrowest) to M3 (broadest), although there are regional variations.
- **M0:** includes bank reserves, so is referred to as the monetary base, or narrow money.
- **MB:** is referred to as the monetary base or total currency – the base from which other forms of money are created and is traditionally the most liquid measure of the money supply.
- **M1:** equivalent to M0 but without bank reserves.
- **M2:** money and close substitutes; this is a key economic indicator, often used to forecast inflation.
- **M3:** M2 plus large and long-term deposits.

which runs from the top to the bottom of the banknote. This sort of technology, combined with a three-stage printing process to give real notes a high-quality sheen, is gradually reducing banknote counterfeiting, but there are still around 500,000 counterfeit notes (principally of the £20 denomination) in the UK alone.

Banknotes are a paper version of Fort Knox. This €100 note has dozens of security features, including holograms, watermarks and microprinting, as well as some that are kept secret by the European Central Bank. The note's country of origin is included in a coded serial number, rather than being part of the overall design.

SERIAL NUMBER: beginning with a letter, the long serial number on the reverse is its own mini code, which is broken by a divisibility rule using the number 9, where the remainder is 0.

WATERMARKS: each euro note contains at least three watermarks (visible when held up to the light): a standard, digital "digimarc" watermark and infrared/ultraviolet watermarks.

SECURITY THREAD: a black magnetic thread runs through the note, top to bottom.

VARIABLE COLOR INK: if the reverse of the note is viewed from different angles, the colors in the lower right-hand-side corner will appear to change.

HOLOGRAMS: holographic bands contain the note's denomination, note-specific illustrations and microprinting.

BAR CODE: metallic bars, which vary according to the note's value, are visible when held up to the light. The bar code is converted to Manchester Code, a secure identifier, on scanning.

Some people have experimented with money and localization by setting up their own currency. That is what Christian Gelleri, an economics schoolteacher from Prien am Chiemsee in Bavaria, Germany, did in 2003. Devising a classroom project for his 16-year-old pupils, he named his currency the *chiemgauer* (after the Chiemgau region) and encouraged local people and businesses to start using its 1, 2, 5, 10, 20, and 50 banknotes, with one chiemgauer equalling one euro. The project, which initially had the schoolchildren designing and distributing vouchers, started slowly – the currency had a turnover of €75,000 in its first year.

ALTERNATIVE CURRENCIES: THE CHIEMGAUER

Nearly a decade on, the currency's turnover has grown to some €5 million, with nearly 500,000 chiemgauer in circulation, making it one of the world's most successful alternative currencies. But what is its purpose exactly? Firstly, it is designed to encourage consumers to use the local businesses, which accept the currency (and which pay a small charge to join the scheme), and to keep currency within the locality. For 200-odd local non-profit organizations, there is an added bonus: they can buy 100 chiemgauer for €97 and resell them for €100, retaining the difference. Other profit-making businesses pay a small commission, which covers the cost of administrating the currency, but which may be offset by attracting locals to buy their goods and services.

→

A woman uses a chiemgauer note to buy cheese in the market in Rosenheim, Bavaria. More than 600 businesses and 2,500 people in the Rosenheim-Traunstein area of Upper Bavaria currently use it for daily transactions.

←

Although it started as a school project and was initially slow to catch on, with a turnover of €5.1 million in 2010, the chiemgauer is now the most successful alternative currency in the world.

Ingenious twist

The chiemgauer has another characteristic, which is that it loses value if it is not spent, thereby accelerating its circulation. Users can 'renew' their notes at a charge of 2 percent of their face value every three months (so, effectively, it depreciates at a rate of 8 percent per annum). This ingenious twist, which Gelleri conceived after studying the work of economists John Maynard Keynes and Irving Fisher, who had pondered the liquidity-inducing effects of a rapidly depreciating currency, might not work in a large-scale economy, but it has proved a success in Bavaria. Even local banks have joined in, providing the means to transact and exchange chiemgauer.

While the currency has spawned some 65 other regional currencies in Germany, collectively they remain local rather than national and rely on the euro as their peg. Nevertheless, given the problems that have afflicted the Eurozone in recent years, there may come a time when collective currencies such as the euro fall out of favor and local currencies find a much wider audience.

The success of the chiemgauer and its cousins prompted the Bundesbank, Germany's mighty central bank (which is responsible for issuing around €146 billion or a third of the continent's notes) to ask in 2007 whether such regional currencies were "competition for the euro?" The answer was no, not yet, but they are certainly giving the central bankers pause for thought.

ALTERNATIVE ALTERNATIVES

Alternative forms of money have a long history and appear to be growing in popularity. It seems likely that the financial downturn in recent years has prompted this development. Some of these systems use actual currency, others take the form of mutual credit, others still are simply exchange systems. Here are some of the most effective:

Bitcoin: Started in the USA in 2009, this is an encrypted, peer-to-peer digital currency.

Flattr: Developed in Sweden, this system requires users to pay a monthly fee of their choosing. The user accesses (or flatters) certain services and the fee is then divided between them at the end of the month.

Ithaca hours: A local currency system in use in Ithaca, New York, since 1991 and intended to promote local economic strength. Notes are available in several denominations but one hour is said to be worth $10 or one hour's work.

Metacurrency: Claims to be the next economy, intended to be a decentralized, peer-to-peer information technology that operates by mutual agreement by allowing people to decide what they value and how that will be measured and acknowledged.

Payswarm: Allows people who create digital content, such as films, music, photos, virtual goods, to distribute it through a website and receive direct payment from their fans and/or customers.

Ripple: A monetary system that makes simple obligations between friends as useful for making payments as regular money.

Timebank: A platform where groups and individuals can pool and trade time and skills, bypassing money as a measure of value.

Although they now offer a bewildering array of services, most banks still rely heavily on the fundamentals from which they were originally conceived: deposits and loans. At its simplest level, their business model depends on charging higher rates of interest on the loans they make than the rates they pay depositors.

COMMERCIAL BANKS

Unlike most commercial companies selling goods and services, banks' assets are predominantly debts owed to the banks, such as mortgages. Liabilities in banking are money they owe to clients, such as to deposit account holders.

A familiar presence

Banks depend on a good deal of trust from their depositors. If they get into trouble, it does not take long for their customers to demand their money back; since the majority of their funds are lent out at any one time, a sudden rush of withdrawals can be fatal. This run on the bank often results in a bank having to be rescued by a central bank, or at worst being allowed to go bankrupt. History is littered with scenes of angry depositors besieging their banks' branches, desperate to salvage their savings.

Thankfully, banks are subject to increasingly tight regulations, which are designed to protect them and their customers. A prime example is the amount of core capital – known as Tier 1 Capital – they are required to hold (a mixture of ordinary share capital, reserves and retained profits) as a buffer against crises of liquidity or of solvency.

Commercial banks are continually looking to expand their customer base with innovative ideas. One of the latest is the introduction of smart banking, launched by Citibank in Hong Kong in 2010. Typically, a smart bank will feature high-tech digital equipment to allow customers to speak to advisers via videoconferencing facilities and Wi-Fi, conduct online banking and keep up-to-date with the latest financial information on giant screens.

Banks remain an integral feature of the global money machine. Despite the rise in Internet banking, banks' physical branches are still a familiar presence. The United States boasts around 82,000, China 67,000 and Japan 12,000. In Europe, Germany, France and Italy have around 30,000, while the United Kingdom has around 15,000.

QUICK REFERENCE

Main functions of commercial banks

1. Accepting deposits from the public for reasons of security, savings and the convenience of payment.
2. Advancing loans to the public, both secured and unsecured.
3. Advancing loans in the form of overdrafts.
4. Discounting of bills of exchange: a system used for advancing money to financial traders for short-term purposes.
5. Investment: a bank will invest its surplus funds in securities.
6. Banks will also act as an agency under instruction from its customers: such as collecting cheques, dividends, making payments, buying and selling securities and sending money from one place to another.
7. Other functions include: safety deposits, providing references, buying and selling foreign exchange, providing financial advice, issuing letters of credit and providing small loans for consumer durables.

THE WORLD'S TOP 20 BANKS

Source: *The Banker* magazine

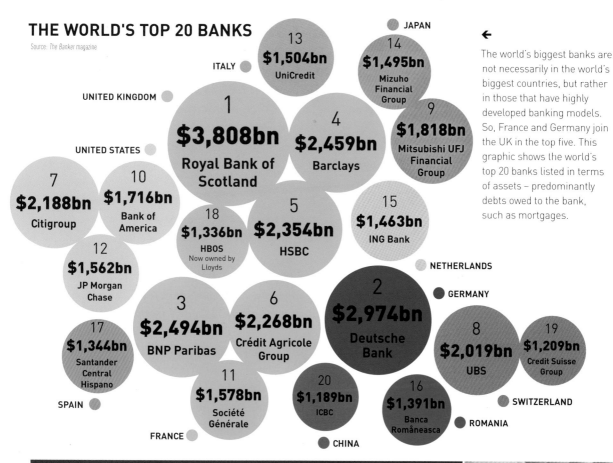

13 **$1,504bn** UniCredit

ITALY

JAPAN

14 **$1,495bn** Mizuho Financial Group

UNITED KINGDOM

1 **$3,808bn** Royal Bank of Scotland

4 **$2,459bn** Barclays

9 **$1,818bn** Mitsubishi UFJ Financial Group

UNITED STATES

7 **$2,188bn** Citigroup

10 **$1,716bn** Bank of America

18 **$1,336bn** HBOS Now owned by Lloyds

5 **$2,354bn** HSBC

15 **$1,463bn** ING Bank

12 **$1,562bn** JP Morgan Chase

NETHERLANDS

GERMANY

2 **$2,974bn** Deutsche Bank

17 **$1,344bn** Santander Central Hispano

3 **$2,494bn** BNP Paribas

6 **$2,268bn** Crédit Agricole Group

8 **$2,019bn** UBS

19 **$1,209bn** Credit Suisse Group

SPAIN

11 **$1,578bn** Société Générale

20 **$1,189bn** ICBC

16 **$1,391bn** Banca Româneasca

SWITZERLAND

ROMANIA

FRANCE

CHINA

The world's biggest banks are not necessarily in the world's biggest countries, but rather in those that have highly developed banking models. So, France and Germany join the UK in the top five. This graphic shows the world's top 20 banks listed in terms of assets – predominantly debts owed to the bank, such as mortgages.

UP AND ATM

Consider the humble cash dispenser – we take this ungainly metal and plastic box entirely for granted as the easiest way to withdraw cash from our bank accounts. There are now over two million of them around the world (including one for polar researchers at McMurdo Station in Antarctica). Credit for inventing the ATM is claimed by many. An inventor called Luther George Simjian trialled a hole-in-the-wall machine with an American bank as early as 1939, but found little enthusiasm for it among the public. There was a flurry of further activity in the late 1960s, when John Sheppard-Brown, managing director of De La Rue, the banknote printers, persuaded Barclays Bank to install an ATM in a branch in north London in 1967. In the same decade another British businessman called James Goodfellow filed patents (including one for the first PIN, or Personal Identification Number). Their American counterparts, including John D. White who created the Credit Card Automatic Currency Dispenser in 1970, also joined the race to popularize the machine. But it was not until the late 1970s that they began to appear on main streets.

Where next for the ATM? Although they have been adapted to dispense everything from postage stamps to gold ingots, ATMs are probably ultimately destined for the scrapheap. Just as LPs gave way to CDs, which in turn have bowed to electronic downloads, so cash may eventually move entirely online.

Investment banks – essentially, banks with corporate rather than retail customers – are popularly imagined to be hugely powerful money machines peopled by "Masters of the Universe" – financial geniuses, who work 24 hours a day and think lunch is for wimps. The truth is more prosaic. Investment banks are often rather fragile institutions, with relatively weak balance sheets. And while there are certainly many talented traders and dealmakers in the front office, there are many more employees in the banks' administrative departments, whose job it is to ensure regulatory compliance, settle trades and keep track of complex transactions.

INVESTMENT BANKS

↓

This statue, which stands in Bowling Green Park near Wall Street in New York, has become the city's financial district's unofficial mascot. The oversize, 3,200 kg bronze sculpture, depicts a bull, the symbol of aggressive financial optimism and prosperity, leaning back on its haunches with its head lowered as if ready to charge.

Investment banks still pride themselves on their core mergers and acquisitions (M&A) advisory work, helping corporate clients initiate, finance and complete transactions. Investment bankers tend not to sit around waiting for the phone to ring. They will be out pitching ideas, suggesting Company A restructures itself, raises debt or equity finance, buys Company B, C and D and so on. When large transactions between companies happen, an army of investment bankers will invariably be involved. Some favored bankers get hired by one side simply so that the other side cannot hire them. In return for their deal-making skills, as well as their ability to endure interminable meetings and many late nights, bankers get well paid if a transaction is successful, less so if it is not.

The Gate Library
24hr Tel: 0333 3704 700

Returned Items 15/04/2017 14:00

Item Title

Book of Money: Everything You Need to
Know About

Thank you for returning items

www.newham.gov.uk
thegatelibrary@newham.gov.uk
Free library catalogue app available - see
staff for details
To register for the free E-mail pre-overdue
service see a member of staff
Thank you - The Gate Library

The Gate Library
24hr Tel: 0333 3704 700

Returned Items 15/04/2017 14:00

Item Title

Book of Money: Everything You Need to Know About

Thank you for returning items

www.newham.gov.uk

thegatelibrary@newham.gov.uk

Free library catalogue app available - see staff for details.

To register for the free E-mail pre-overdu service see a member of staff

Thank you - The Gate Library

INSIDE AN INVESTMENT BANK

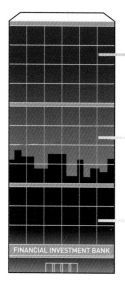

FINANCIAL INVESTMENT BANK

Back Office
OPERATIONS: making sure the bank runs smoothly by submitting trades, maintaining databases, and transacting required money transfers

Technology: the information technology department

Middle Office
RISK MANAGEMENT: analyzing credit and market risk for the bank

Compliance: making sure operations are complying with regulations

Finance: responsible for capital management and risk monitoring

Front Office
INVESTMENT BANKING/M&A

INSTITUTIONAL CLIENT SERVICES (inc. Fixed Income, Commodities and Currencies; Equities)

ASSET/WEALTH MANAGEMENT

Structuring and origination: creating and marketing financial products

Research: into industries companies and products

↑

The standard makeup of a modern investment bank.

Besides this corporate deal-making activity, investment banks have vast operations that trade in the world's financial markets both for their clients and for themselves. Many have divisions known as FICC – Fixed Income, Commodities and Currencies – which trade in bonds, all manner of commodities from gold, silver and tin to oil, soya beans and energy, and the world's key currencies, whether the US dollar, Japanese yen, British pound, Brazilian real or Norwegian krone. Besides their corporate client accounts, many banks have large Proprietary Trading operations, in which traders use the bank's own balance sheet to take bets on these and other markets.

The third leg of the investment-banking stool is commonly that of Asset Management and, where this is undertaken for high net-worth private clients, Wealth Management. These activities may cross over with their other divisions, as they seek to build and manage investment portfolios and distribute financial services products. In some cases, investment banks have gone retail, dispensing credit cards to their clients and offering them loans and mortgages.

Risky business

Investment banking is a high-stakes business, which makes governments and the banks' regulators and shareholders uneasy. Various proposals have been made to limit their riskier activities and to separate retail operations from so-called "casino" banking activities. Among the proposals are the so-called Volcker Rule, put forward by former US Federal Reserve chairman Paul Volcker, that American banks be prohibited from activities such as proprietary trading (trading using their own balance sheets) and making investments in hedge funds. The Volcker Rule echoed the Glass-Steagall Act and the Dodd-Frank Financial Regulatory Reform Bill, which was passed following the 2007–2009 financial crisis.

✳ JARGON BUSTER

The key principle when one company buys another is to increase the shareholder value over that of the sum of the two companies. A **merger** is when two companies combine to make another; an **acquisition** is the purchase of one company by another in which no new company is formed.

Technically, a private bank is simply a bank that is not incorporated. In other words, it may be owned by an individual, a family or a partnership. This structure provides some comfort for the bank's depositors, in that they have recourse to both the bank's assets and the owner's. For the owner, this means they often have so-called "unlimited liability" for any losses the bank may incur.

PRIVATE BANKS

↓

Originally formed in 1692, Coutts Bank is one of the heavyweights of the English private banking system. Since 2000 it has been owned by the Royal Bank of Scotland, which is currently preparing to grow the brand internationally, opening an office in Dubai in order to target high net-worth individuals in the Middle East, Eastern Europe and Asia.

This banking model has a long history, dating back to the 17th century. In the United Kingdom, the Bank of England began life as a private bank, in 1649, closely followed by C. Hoare & Co, which has retained this status since 1672 (along with such idiosyncrasies as its own interest rate, based on the approximate percentage growth rate of the trees on its founder's country estate).

Switzerland has many similarly historic private banks – such as Wegelin & Co, Landolt & Cie and Morgue d'Algue & Cie – which are still family-owned and maintain their independent stance, despite many changes in the banking industry that have seen many smaller players swallowed up.

Banking for the aristocracy

These private banks, characterized by an air of exclusivity, discretion and often boasting an aristocratic clientele, have, at least in part, inspired a vast industry of what is also now called private banking: this is essentially a personal banking service, often with preferential borrowing rates and bespoke financial services, accompanied by all the paraphernalia of exclusive credit cards and fancy brochures, but unfortunately without the unlimited liability.

Swiss cities such as Geneva and Zurich remain centers for such activity – not least because the country offers certain tax advantages – but private banking has, in the last few decades, gone global. While it owes much to skilful marketing and not a little schmoozing, it has also become increasingly sophisticated and a multi-billion dollar industry in its own right. Professional private bankers, often attached to large, multinational investment banks, are proficient in advising on tax, investments and inheritance matters for their clients. Often, they act as a switchboard, plugging wealthy individuals and their families into other parts of a bank's financial services armory.

Discretion is the watchword

A numbered Swiss bank account is often associated with shady tycoons or James Bond villains. In fact, it is simply an account identified by a number rather than a name. Although a bank must, in most cases, name its customers, it is not always obliged to link those customers to their accounts. Only a few countries, such as Switzerland and Austria, allow this level of secrecy, and there are increasingly strict regulations to encourage disclosure and to prevent money laundering. But discretion is still Swiss banks' watchword – most will not reveal account information unless there is proof of deliberate fraud. In 2009, however, a one-off agreement between the USA and Switzerland forced UBS, a global bank with Swiss roots, to reveal the identities of a large number of private clients, a move that may well be repeated in the future.

→

Private banking developed in 17th-century Europe, catering for the extremely wealthy. Switzerland's neutrality, established at the Congress of Vienna in 1815 and still maintained today, has provided a stable political environment that continues to make it an attractive destination for wealthy people's assets.

BUILDING SOCIETIES

If private banks are often associated with Switzerland, building societies are a peculiarly British invention. The industrial city of Birmingham, Britain's second largest city, can claim to be the birthplace of "mutual societies" – financial institutions owned by their members.

The first building society was founded by a pub landlord, Richard Ketley, as Ketley's Building Society, which took members' subscriptions and used it as collateral to raise further funding, all with the aim of building houses for its members. Eventually, when all the society's members were housed, the society was terminated. This model continued, although increasingly without the termination, and soon most towns in Britain had at least one such society.

Gradually, such societies began to resemble banks, particularly after legislation in 1986 allowed them to demutualize, giving members shares in a limited company. In the early years of demutualization, so-called carpet baggers – investors who would deposit a minimal sum in a society in the hope of profiting from a demutualization – became the scourge of the societies, many of which were forced to change their membership rules, and the flurry of demutualizations ended in 2000.

In many developed countries, online or Internet banking use has now surpassed that of real-world branch banking. What began in the 1980s as a basic suite of account-checking, bill payments and money transfer services using telephony and the first home computers has now become a whole world of banking and financial services on both desktop PCs and mobile devices.

ONLINE BANKS

Many banks have actively encouraged their customers to move online by offering better interest rates and other incentives than in their bricks-and-mortar outlets, thus keeping their own costs down. Some banks have moved entirely online.

Early days

New York witnessed the birth of online banking in 1981, when four banks – Citibank, Chemical, Chase Manhattan and Manufacturers Hanover – began to offer customers a system called Videotex, which used modems to send information back and forth to a television monitor. The UK followed with Prestel (which was also

"CONTACTLESS" PURCHASING

It is only a small step from banking online to banking and transacting on your mobile device. After several false starts and many years of development, mobile wallets have now become a reality, allowing a seamless transaction between a customer, their bank and a retailer. Already, the global value of transactions made using mobile devices is put at $240 billion (Jupiter Research) – a figure that looks likely to rocket. As soon as 2016, according to analysts, it may be possible to use a mobile device to pay for most everyday goods and services, with consumers using contactless chip technology called near-field communications or NFC. Users simply wave their handsets at a terminal, which completes the transaction with the customer's bank (or mobile operator) and beams a receipt back to the handset.

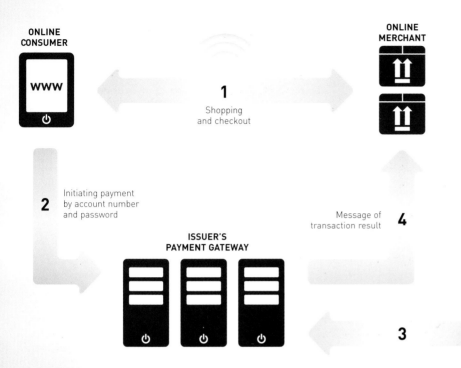

ONLINE CONSUMER

WWW

1
Shopping
and checkout

ONLINE MERCHANT

2
Initiating payment
by account number
and password

ISSUER'S
PAYMENT GATEWAY

Message of
transaction result

4

3

ISSUING BANK

Standard online financial transactions work in a very simple way. Payment is triggered by the issuing bank's server (or payment gateway) on receipt of the customer's account number and password. The bank, or banks, involved are informed of the debit/credit transaction and the server will then alert the customer and the seller when the transaction has taken place.

taken up by Sweden, the Netherlands, Finland and West Germany), while France added simple banking services to its long-established Minitel system.

Since these first steps in online banking, the explosion in Internet usage has encouraged banks to invest heavily in new platforms and the integration of suites of new services, including online brokerages, mortgage and loans distribution and pension fund management.

Although there are a number of reasons for the extraordinary expansion of this sector of the industry the global economic downturn must take center stage as both sides have seen benefits. By developing the online services they offer the banks have attracted new customers, cut costs and enhanced profit margins. For their part, customers find the online systems more cost and time-effective, enabling them to feel more in control of their finances just when they need to. Customers in the US and the UK remain the largest users of Internet banking services around the world.

The key issue

Security remains a key issue, however. The most common current security system is known as PIN/TAN – PIN being a Personal Identification Number, a numeric password, and TAN being a Transaction Authentication Number. The latter is now often generated randomly from a small device like a key fob, which is sent by a bank to its online customers. These TANs are generated using two-factor authentication (2FA). In addition, banks often utilize SSL secured connections in web browsers.

EXPERTS ARE PREDICTING THAT THE GLOBAL CUSTOMER BASE FOR INTERNET BANKING WILL REACH 657.2 MILLION BY 2015

Capitalism, not to mention Darwinism, may be said to have found its ultimate expression in the banking world, which encourages fierce competition, the free market and the survival of the fittest. But not all banks exist just to make money. Some are managed according to social and environmental criteria, making investments in sustainable and ethical businesses and giving shares in their profits to charity.

ETHICAL BANKS

The Norwegian Cultura Sparebank – known as Cultura Bank – is one such institution. Headquartered in Oslo, Cultura was first conceived in 1982 by an enlightened group of academics who took inspiration from GLS, the leading ethical bank in Germany (which in turn has it roots in the anthroposophy philosophy of Rudolf Steiner, the Austrian philosopher and social reformer).

Positive banking

Having secured a full banking license in 1997, Cultura now offers a range of ethical products to savers and borrowers. These include loans where a portion of the interest rate is redirected to charities such as the World Wildlife Fund and Save the Children.

↓
Occupy New York protestors gather in Zucotti Park before marching southwards to Wall Street. The Occupy movement began in the US in September 2011 but spread quickly to some 95 cities across 82 countries. Although its aims are widespread and disparate, it is mainly a vehicle for people to express their dissatisfaction with the economic and social inequality brought to a head by the global economic downturn and the lack of accountability of those who allegedly caused it. Its slogan, "We are the 99%" refers to the concentration of wealth among the top 1 percent of earners compared to the other 99 percent.

BANKS – GOD'S WORK OR VAMPIRE SQUIDS?

Banks and other financial institutions contribute huge sums to the global economy but, some argue, at a high cost when it comes to ethical behavior. Banks – and bankers – found themselves facing criticism following the financial crisis of 2007–2009, when many of them had to be bailed out by governments. Accused of recklessly endangering the financial system by making risky bets, giving irresponsible advice to investors and being rewarded for failure, banks were heaped with opprobrium by the media. *Rolling Stone* magazine famously described Goldman Sachs, one of the Wall Street's most illustrious institutions, as "a great vampire squid wrapped around the face of humanity." In contrast, Goldman Sachs boss Lloyd Blankfein told a journalist that he was doing "God's work."

Activists from the Occupy movement took to the streets of the financial districts of New York, London and many other cities to protest at what they saw as a concentration of greed in the industry. For their part, banks have had to rebuild their reputations brick-by-brick. Many have separated their retail banking arms from the so-called "casino" investment banking to restore investor confidence and have started paying bonuses (a particularly contentious issue) in the form of deferred shares rather than cash to their executives. Convincing the public they have changed for the better may be more difficult, but many banks still contribute to society at large through charitable foundations and arts sponsorship programs.

The bank concentrates its commercial lending activity in sectors such as organic agriculture, healthcare and education, where it believes can make a positive difference to people's lives. Equally, it will consider investing in entrepreneurial businesses that might be turned away by more traditional banks and has a strong track record of providing microfinance.

There are now many other ethical banks in Europe, North America and Oceania.

↙

Concern about the ethics of banks in the Netherlands has led to the development of the Dutch Fair Bank Guide, a dynamic database that rates the top 10 consumer banks on various social, economic and environmental issues such as climate change, transparency in its investments, human rights, the arms trade and so on. The purpose of the website is not just to allow customers to make informed judgments about where they put their money but also to inform the banks about where they should or should not invest their profits.

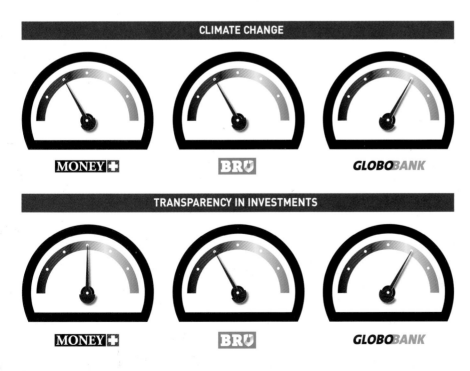

● GOOD
◓ ADEQUATE
◕ MODERATE
● LESS THAN ADEQUATE
● POOR

Islamic banking, which dominates the Middle East and the oil-rich Gulf states, has become a major force in world finance, with assets controlled by Islamic banks estimated to be $200–$500 billion and growing at 10–15 percent per year. The banking system, which has its roots in ancient times but blossomed in the 1970s, is founded on Shari'ah law, as laid out in the Koran.

ISLAMIC BANKING

At its heart is the principle that all forms of interest – known as *riba* – are forbidden. Acknowledging that money itself has no intrinsic value, as a matter of faith a Muslim cannot lend money to, or receive money from someone and expect to benefit. Instead, a bank and its customer share the risk of any transaction, dividing profits and losses alike. Equally, Islamic banks are not allowed to lend to each other and charge interest.

Islamic banking products

While these strictures are widely observed, Islamic banks use a variety of products, often based on the principle of partnership, to work with counterparties.

A *murabahah*, in that a commodity such as a metal traded on an exchange, is used for interbank lending. The transaction is essentially a loan and any price increase in the commodity is booked as a profit – instead of interest – to the lender. The *murabahah* is widely used for making loans where a bank might buy goods for a borrower, add a margin and sell the goods to the borrower in instalments.

UNDER SHARI'AH LAW ISLAMIC BANKS NEVER KNOWINGLY INVEST IN COMPANIES INVOLVED IN GAMBLING, ALCOHOLIC BEVERAGES, OR PORCINE FOOD PRODUCTS

➔

One of the fastest-growing centers of Islamic banking is the city of Doha, capital of Qatar. Although Islamic banking is often thought to be a recent phenomenon, its basic principles date back to the 7th century; in fact, many believe that its ability to adhere to both ancient and modern economic principles is one of its core strengths.

SHARI'AH ADVISORY BOARDS

Islamic banks are required to set up advisory boards, also known as religious boards, to advise and ensure that they maintain adherence to Shari'ah law – making sure that investors' profits are legitimate and that complex financial transactions are compliant with the concept of PLS, or profit-and-loss-sharing. The committee must certify every account and service provided by the bank and it cannot introduce a new product or service without the committee's approval.

Similarly, a leasing agreement known as *ijara* enables the financing of so-called Islamic mortgages, where the bank might buy a property and sell it to its customer, who can make capital or rental payments, gradually transferring ownership of the property from the bank to themselves. A further variation is the widespread practice of *musawamah*, in which seller and buyer may negotiate a sale of goods but without the seller being required to disclose the costs of the items or indeed the asking price.

Interface with international banking

The growth of Islamic banking – Iran, Saudi Arabia, Qatar and Malaysia have become the largest hubs – has given rise to an entire banking and fund management sector that has embraced Shari'ah-compliant products: *sukuk*, or Islamic bonds, which are widely traded internationally; *takaful*, a form of insurance; and *wadiah*, the concept of safekeeping by a bank, akin to its acting as trustee. Recognized indices, agreements with international financial regulators and its own school of economic thought have given Islamic banking a key role in the financial markets.

JARGON BUSTER

Ijara: a hire purchase, leasing or rental arrangement.
Murabahah: commodity trading, involves client in cost-plus sale.
Musawamah: a negotiated sale in which the seller does not have to disclose the original price.
Riba: literally excess; generally refers to interest.
Sukuk: Islamic bonds.
Takaful: Islamic insurance, based on the concept of mutual support.
Wadiah: the acceptance of a sum of money for safekeeping and a guarantee on its return.

5 THE MARKETS

↑

Traders at work on the floor of the New York Stock Exchange (NYSE). The world's largest equities exchange in the world, situated on Wall Street in Lower Manhattan, sees daily trading of around 1.6 billion shares with a value of more than $45 billion – more than one-third of the daily global total.

The world's financial markets are just that: places in which to buy and sell, to exchange news and information, to gossip and, ultimately, to trade and make money. Despite their immense scale and the extraordinary amount of technology employed in them, in the end the markets are still remarkably human. They are concerned with the fortunes of companies' equity and debt, the relative values of currencies and the supply of the world's commodities.

In this chapter, we'll take a look at some of the world's main markets and how they operate in an increasingly global environment, without borders and, often, 24 hours a day. Trading is the lifeblood of the exchange of securities. Frequent trading generates liquidity, which in plain terms, means buy and sell prices that are reasonable close together (known as the spread) so that a buyer can be assured that he is buying something at a correct price and one at which he can, if necessary, sell again. Pretty much anything that can be traded is traded and, increasingly, as much by individuals sitting at a home computer as by

24/7 TRADING

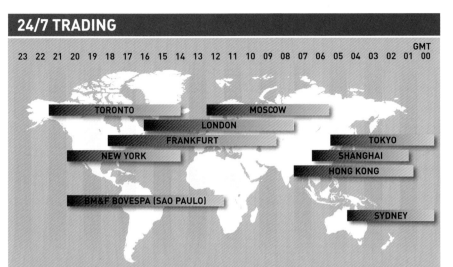

| | | | | | | | | | | | | | | | | | | | | | | | GMT |
|23|22|21|20|19|18|17|16|15|14|13|12|11|10|09|08|07|06|05|04|03|02|01|00|

TORONTO
MOSCOW
LONDON
FRANKFURT
NEW YORK
TOKYO
SHANGHAI
HONG KONG
BM&F BOVESPA (SAO PAULO)
SYDNEY

Since the mid-1980s, when stock markets opened up to non-indigenous players, exchanges have gone global. Screen-based trading, which replaced old-fashioned telephone broking and paper-based orders, allowed exchange participants to see their peers' and counterparties' trades and positions. A decade on, in the mid-1990s, the Internet hastened an even greater degree of transparency and, indeed, democracy, as individuals (retail in the trade) were able to access similar data and to trade on multiple exchanges just as easily as the big broking houses and banks (institutional). These days, both groups can trade around the clock, as the world's exchanges open, close and overlap. The boom in so-called stock futures also blurs the time zones, giving traders an indication of whether a market will trade up or down as the opening bell nears.

← Exchanges open and close according to their trading hours, but the global marketplace with multiple time zones and trading platforms means that the business of buying and selling securities continues on a more or less 24/7 basis. Nowadays a trading desk at an investment bank in, say, London will simply hand over its position to colleagues in New York or Tokyo at closing time. The Internet and dedicated trading technology, including high-frequency algorithms managed entirely by computers, mean that trading (although not regulatory supervision) now operates largely without geographic boundaries.

large financial institutions with sophisticated dealing rooms. So, the markets are becoming more democratic, more transparent and more liquid – although arguably more volatile and fickle.

The principal markets

There are two principal types of market – Over the Counter and Exchange. For the former, where securities such as bonds or foreign currencies are not listed on a centralized exchange, transactions take place between two counterparties (two banks for example) often via an intermediary called an interdealer broker.

Stocks and shares and futures are, however, listed on exchanges, which provide a platform for trading and, crucially, liquidity in what is called the secondary market (i.e. the market that develops after the initial, or primary, listing of a security). Such exchanges are available to both institutional and retail investors to deal on and, by and large, they are remarkably efficient (although some economists argue otherwise) at allowing buyers and sellers to trade, thereby fixing a value – known as market capitalization for a security.

✳ JARGON BUSTER

Equity and debt: the debt/equity ratio is seen as a measure of a company's financial leverage. It is equal to the company's long-term debt divided by common shareholders' equity.
Futures: a financial contract that requires the buyer to purchase an asset (or the seller to sell an asset), such as a physical commodity or a financial instrument, at a specific price on a predetermined date in the future.

Trying to navigate the world's stock, bond and commodities markets can be confusing even for the most experienced trader. Hence investors' reliance on the financial world's equivalent of a map – the index. The sheer number of stocks, shares, bonds, units of currency, commodities and a multiplicity of derivative financial products requires a set of measurements to keep track of them. Hence indices.

INDICES

An index allows us to get an overview of a basket of similar financial products, grouping them by genre, sector or geography (once you have a few indices you can even create an index of the indices and use that to measure – and trade – the global market). In all cases, they are useful tools to calibrate and compare how the constituents of a particular financial market behave.

↓

A trader in the VIX pit holds his head. The VIX Volatility Index is quoted in percentage points and translates the expected movement (or implied volatility) in the S&P 500 index over the upcoming 30-day period.

Snapshots

Indices have become an indispensible shorthand for financial markets' performance. In the case of stocks, the Dow Jones Industrial Average (United States), the Nikkei (Japan), the FTSE – or "Footsie" (United Kingdom),

THE VIX – 'THE FEAR INDEX'

The Chicago Board Options Exchange's Volatility Index, known as the VIX, has been based on the S&P 500 stock index option prices since 1993. Volatility is, to some extent, an indication of nervousness in the market. It means that large numbers of securities are changing hands and the prices are moving frequently and, often, in large jumps. This, in turn, makes investors nervous. The VIX is, therefore, seen as a barometer of 'fear' or, conversely, of investor confidence. It is, by its very nature, volatile and adventurous investors often place calls and puts – buys if they are bearish on stocks and sells if they are bullish – on the VIX.

the BOVESPA (Brazil) and many other indices allow us to get an instant overview of an entire economy. Because stock markets have many thousands of companies listed, indices are often produced showing snapshots of themselves: such as the FTSE-100 (the largest 100 companies, by market capitalization, listed in London) or, in France, the CAC-40 (the largest 40).

Equally, the bond and commodity markets have their own indices, each tailored to the peculiarities of their securities. Bonds, for example, unlike shares, are partly defined by their duration, so indices sometimes adjust for maturity dates to give a fair comparison between them. Each index has its own calculation methodology. It is usually expressed in terms of a change from a base value – so the percentage change is more important than the actual numeric value.

↓

An electronic stock market index board in Kuala Lumpur. A stock market index is a method of measuring a section of the market. Many indices are cited by news or financial services firms and are used as benchmarks to indicate the state of a nation's economy or the global economic situation.

KEY INDICES

FTSE-100 – the 100 largest (by market capitalization) companies listed in London. Base value of 1,000 set in 1984.

CAC-40 – (*Cotation Assistée en Continu*, or Continuous Assisted Quotation) – the 40 largest companies listed on the Paris Bourse (now Euronext). Base value of 1,000 set in 1987.

DAX – (*Deutscher Aktien IndeX*, or German Stock Index) – 30 major blue-chip German companies listed in Frankfurt. Base value of 1,000 set in 1987.

NIKKEI 225 – (named after *Nihon Keizai Shimbun* newspaper) – the 225 largest companies on the Tokyo Stock Exchange. Founded in 1950.

DOW – (Dow Jones Industrial Average, named after co-founder Charles Dow) – 30 major US corporations, founded in 1896.

S&P 500 – (founded by Standard & Poor's) – large-cap US equities (companies with a market capitalization value of more than $10 billion). Published since 1957.

IBOVESPA – (*Indice Bovespa*, the index of the *Bolsa de Valores, Mercadorias & Futuros de São Paulo*) – index of around 50 companies listed in São Paulo. Base value of 100 set in 1968.

The money market is essentially the market for short-term lending and borrowing. It is a vitally important part of the great body politic of the financial system, and is relied on by its participants for liquidity and to balance their books on a daily and overnight basis.

THE MONEY MARKETS

Private investors can access the money market (for example, if they have a large amount of cash on deposit for only a few days – perhaps during a house sale and purchase – and want to earn interest but also have instant access), but by far the largest users are institutional.

The money market comprises the trading of a wide variety of instruments, collectively known as "paper," including government debt securities (in the United States, Treasury bills), certificates of deposit and borrowing/lending securities known as repurchase agreements or repos.

In most cases, such paper is short-dated, in other words it matures in under one year with the date fixed at issuance. So, this market is highly liquid and fast moving. It is also low-margin, in that banks that access the money market tend to use it as a utility rather than to make money.

Interbank lending

While central banks – where financial institutions tend to have their own current accounts – are the hub of the money market, the real business takes place between commercial banks themselves, in interbank lending, which is, in turn, calibrated by reference to LIBOR – the London Interbank Offered Rate.

At the moment LIBOR is fixed at 11 a.m. each weekday in London by the British Bankers' Association, published around 11:45 a.m. and, as its name suggests, sets the benchmark for banks to lend to each other. Ultimately, the LIBOR fix flows down to the public, in the form of interest rates set for mortgages, corporate loans and credit cards. After all, LIBOR is essentially the wholesale market for money, which has a direct domino effect into the retail market: you and me.

↓

These Treasury bills represent money bought from and guaranteed by the US government. Valued at $1,000 each, up to a maximum of $5 million, they mature either in one month, three months or six months. They are sold at a negotiated discount and bought back at maturity for their full value – therefore the bigger the discount, the greater the return to the investor.

THE LIBOR CALCULATION

EXAMPLE

BANK	3-MONTH RATE %
HBOS	2.75000
CREDIT SUISSE	2.74000
BANK OF AMERICA	2.73000
J.P. MORGAN CHASE	2.72000
HSBC	2.72000
BANK OF TOKYO-MITSUBISHI	2.72000
BARCLAYS	2.72000
NORINCHUKIN BANK	2.72000
ROYAL BANK OF CANADA	2.71750
LLOYDS	2.71000
WESTDEUTSCHE LANDESBANK	2.71000
RABOBANK	2.71000
UBS AG	2.71000
ROYAL BANK OF SCOTLAND	2.70500
DEUTSCHE BANK	2.70000
CITIGROUP	2.70000

Between 11 and 11:10 a.m. London time, the 16 banks listed here report the rates at which they borrow money from other banks.

The two center quartiles are averaged to calculate the day's LIBOR rate.

The rate is published at about 11:45 a.m. GMT.

The 3-month LIBOR rate in US dollars is:

2.71594%

Source: British Bankers' Association; Reuters

←

Banks lend money to each other all the time – the majority of these loans are short-dated, sometimes less than a week and often overnight. All banks are required to hold an adequate amount of liquid assets to meet any potential payouts. If a bank cannot meet this requirement then it needs to borrow the money to cover the shortfall; conversely some banks may have an excess of liquid assets and will make it available on the money market. LIBOR, the interbank lending rate, is the average interest rate that would be charged if one bank borrowed money from another.

LIBOR's influence has grown hugely since it was first established in 1986 and it is now used as the benchmark for $350 trillion of financial products. It also helped establish London as a major global financial center, so that now over 20 percent of all interbank lending takes place in the city. It has some equally influential overseas cousins, in the form of TIBOR, the Tokyo equivalent for yen, and EURIBOR, the Brussels version for euros.

THE $350 TRILLION QUESTION ASKED EACH DAY OF DEALERS AT MAJOR BANKS, TO GAUGE LIBOR, IS: "AT WHAT RATE COULD YOU BORROW FUNDS WERE YOU TO DO SO BY ASKING FOR AND THEN ACCEPTING INTERBANK OFFERS IN A REASONABLE MARKET SIZE, JUST PRIOR TO 11 A.M.?"

Just as debt ranks ahead of equity in a company, so the bond markets tower over the equities markets in the global financial system. Their sheer size – recent estimates put total bond issuance at around $50 trillion – and the fact that they include many hundreds of billions of government debt securities mean that they exercise a profound influence. Indeed, in recent times, as sovereign governments (which can issue only debt rather than equity) have struggled to finance themselves, the bond markets have seemed to dictate political policy rather than follow it.

THE BOND MARKETS

Bonds come in all shapes, sizes and, most importantly, risk levels. Historically, government bonds, which have a country's Treasury standing behind them, have been considered safe and often highly liquid, so that investors can buy and sell them easily. Of course, this depends on the country and its Treasury. Corporate bonds will have the issuing company's guarantee but, equally, this will devolve to its ability to pay coupons – from its cash flow – and, eventually repay the principal (often by refinancing).

Although government bonds comprise a disproportionate chunk of the bond markets, corporate debt also figures large. Large companies issue bonds to raise money for acquisitions and working capital; institutional investors are drawn to them as sources of regular income – bonds pay six-monthly or annual interest – and because, if they avoid default, they preserve the original principal investment, which is repaid at the end of the bond's term. That term depends on the issuer and on investor appetite, but is typically five to ten years.

How bonds work

Bonds trade much like any other security, with a bid and offer price and, in inverse relation, a yield (the value of the interest). Invariably issued at an interest rate of 100 percent (known as par), bonds' prices can – and do – fluctuate during their lifetime, which in turn affects both their "running yield" (the interest yield on a day-to-day basis) and their "yield to maturity" (the yield calculated relative to their maturity date). A bond's interest rate is known as the coupon. It is usually paid annually or semi-annually and is, in most cases, unchanging. The original loan amount of a bond, the principal, is repayable in full to the investor at the end of its term (the redemption).

QUICK REFERENCE

Bonds: a 'loan' from an investor that pays a fixed rate of interest to the investor and is then repaid at the end of a term.

Corporate bonds: issued by companies in a variety of tranches, either secured on the company's assets, or unsecured.

Government bonds: issued by governments to investors; government bonds are comprised of a country's national debt.

Financial bonds: issued by banks and other financial institutions – make up the biggest proportion of the global bond market.

Fixed-rate bonds: bonds that pay a fixed rate of interest to an investor, normally annually or semi-annually.

Floating-rate bonds: bonds that pay a varying rate of interest, normally pegged to an industry rate such as LIBOR.

Retail bonds: bonds available to retail investors in small amounts.

Inflation-linked bonds: bonds that pay interest rates that are pegged to inflation (and pay an interest rate higher than inflation).

```
DES
VODAFONE GROUP    VOD8 ⅛  11/26/18    134.107/134.880    (2.13/2.02) RBSM
VOD 8 ⅛ 11/26/18 Corp    99) Feedback                Page 1/1 Description: Bon
                              94) Notes  ▾    95) Buy    96) Sell    97) Settings  ▾
21) Bond Description    22) Issuer Description
Pages            Issuer Information              Identifiers
1) Bond Info     Name   VODAFONE GROUP PLC       BB Number  EH6299497
2) Addtl Info    Type   Cellular Telecom         ISIN       XS0400780960
3) Covenants     Security Information            BBGID      BBG0000X0DS7
4) Guarantors    Mkt of Issu Euro MTN            Bond Ratings
5) Bond Ratings  Country    GB      Currency GBP Moody's    A3
6) Identifiers   Rank    Sr Unsecured Series EMTN S&P        A-
7) Exchanges     Coupon 8.125       Type   Fixed Fitch      A-
8) Inv Parties   Cpn Fre Annual                  Composite  A-
9) Fees, Restrict Day Cnt ACT/ACT   Iss Price 99.38700 Issuance & Trading
10) Schedules    Maturit 11/26/2018 Reoffer  99.387 Amt Issued/Outstanding
11) Coupons      BULLET                          GBP       450,000.00 (M) /
Quick Links      Issue Spread  400.00bp vs UKT 5 03/18 GBP  450,000.00 (M)
32) ALL  Pricing Calc Type (1) STREET CONVENTION Min Piece/Increment
33) QRD  Quote Reca Announcement Date    11/18/2008   50,000.00 / 1,000.00
34) TDH  Trade Hist Interest Accrual Date 11/26/2008 Par Amount     1,000.00
35) CAC  Corp Actio 1st Settle Date       11/26/2008 Book Runn   BNPPAR,HSBCL
36) CF   Prospectus 1st Coupon Date       11/26/2009 Exchang         Multiple
37) CN · Sec News   SERIES 36. TRANCHE 1.
38) HDS  Holders

66) Send Bond
Australia 61 2 9777 8600 Brazil 5511 3048 4500 Europe 44 20 7330 7500 Germany 49 69 9204 1210 Hong Kong 852 2977 6000
Japan 81 3 3201 8900    Singapore 65 6212 1000    U.S. 1 212 318 2000    Copyright 2012 Bloomberg Finance L.P.
                                          SN 860381 BST  GMT+1:00 H441-1299-1 04-Oct-2012 08:59:38
```

← This is a corporate bond issued by Vodafone, the mobile telecommunications giant. The bond is essentially a ten-year loan of £450 million ($708 million) to the company from investors. In return for their loan, which was made in November 2008 and will be repaid in November 2018, the original investors receive a fixed coupon (interest) of 8.125 percent per annum. The bond was issued at just below par (100.00) and when this snapshot was taken it was trading at a price of around 134.00, a hefty premium to its issue price (meaning that the bond's yield, which moves inversely to price, has fallen). A high-quality bond, it ranks highly in the capital structure of the company and is duly rated A3, A- and A- by the ratings agencies Moody's, Standard & Poor's and Fitch respectively.

Retail investors

Typically, bonds are only issued by large companies and are aimed at institutional investors. Because of this they have, historically, only been available in minimum lots of $50,000 or $100,000; only recently have bonds been made available to retail investors in smaller denominations – $1,000 or $2,000 – and with live, quoted prices on the Internet. Still in its infancy, the market for retail bonds looks set to grow, with major exchanges now listing bonds from blue-chip companies that can be bought and sold in small lots.

Equally, there are moves underway to allow smaller companies, known as small- and medium-sized enterprises or SMEs, to issue bonds, which would allow them to access capital without surrendering valuable equity or struggling to secure bank finance. In countries such as Germany, which has a longstanding tradition of smaller, family-owned business, known collectively as the *Mittelstand*, there are already junior bond exchanges for smaller issues.

"I USED TO THINK IF THERE WAS REINCARNATION, I WANTED TO COME BACK AS THE PRESIDENT OR THE POPE OR A .400 BASEBALL HITTER. BUT NOW I WANT TO COME BACK AS THE BOND MARKET. YOU CAN INTIMIDATE EVERYBODY."
JAMES CARVILLE, CAMPAIGN ADVISOR TO PRESIDENT BILL CLINTON, *WALL STREET JOURNAL*, FEBRUARY 1993

While the bond markets continue to intimidate both politicians and the public alike, the equities markets have historically been much more welcoming to investors. Although, when measured by volume, most shares are still bought and sold in large blocks by institutions, trading "stocks and shares" (technically stocks refers to holdings in groups of companies, shares to single company holdings, but they are essentially one and the same thing) has become something of a national hobby in many countries.

THE EQUITIES MARKETS

The equity markets are a broad church, with megacaps – companies whose share value runs into the billions of dollars – rubbing shoulders with microcaps, which may have a capitalization of less than $1 million. They represent the broadest possible range of industries and sectors.

Stock market flotation

An Initial Public Offering (IPO) is the moment when a privately held company offers some of its shares to the public via a stock market listing. These can either be shares held by the founders, who have the opportunity to cash in some of their investment, or new shares created by the company to expand its capital base by attracting new investors. An IPO is sometimes thought of as an exit for the company's founders, but in reality it is more of an entry into a tough, highly regulated public arena in which their newfound public investors will demand more of them than ever before. Nevertheless, a public offering does create liquidity – allowing people to buy and sell a company's stock – and gives them a

↓

Few IPOs create such a stir as the Facebook flotation in May 2012. The hype surrounding it led to an overestimation in the profits that would follow and the share price fell alarmingly in the first few days of trading. Despite this, around a thousand of the company's backers were made instant millionaires after shares in the social media phenomenon went on sale, while its founder Mark Zuckerberg pocketed an estimated $1.15 billion.

FACEBOOK "UNFRIENDED"

The NASDAQ flotation of Facebook, Inc, in May 2012, was the world's largest ever for a technology company (and the third largest ever, behind Visa and the power utility Enel). Its bankers valued the social media giant at $38 a share with an overall value (its market capitalization) on the first day of $104 billion. But these huge numbers required investors to believe that the company was worth some hundred times its annual earnings (not to mention two-and-a-half times the value of that other tech behemoth Google). The market swiftly decided it was not and the share price fell by over 10 percent in its first few days of trading. There followed bitter recriminations and lawsuits, as investors accused the company and its banks of not sharing all of its information equally. While the IPO made a multi-billionaire of its founder Mark Zuckerberg and many millionaires among his staff and early investors, it also exposed them to the full force of the market, forcing the company to prove every quarter-year that its value is justified by actual, as well as prospective, growth.

IPO PREPARATION

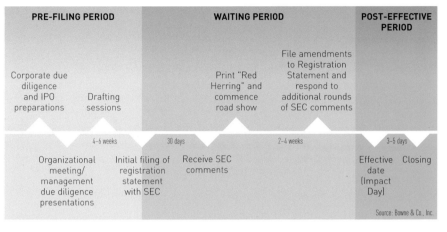

PRE-FILING PERIOD		WAITING PERIOD		POST-EFFECTIVE PERIOD
Corporate due diligence and IPO preparations	Drafting sessions	Print "Red Herring" and commence road show	File amendments to Registration Statement and respond to additional rounds of SEC comments	
	4–6 weeks	30 days	2–4 weeks	3–5 days
Organizational meeting/ management due diligence presentations	Initial filing of registration statement with SEC	Receive SEC comments		Effective date (Impact Day) Closing

Source: Bowne & Co., Inc.

← Preparations for an IPO begin when the decision to go public is taken. The final phase involves a public announcement of the flotation, the setting of the share price, the search for investors and impact day when shares are made available to trade.

↓ Since 1985 trading on the New York Stock Exchange has begun with the ringing of the Opening Bell at 9:30 a.m. More recently executives or celebrities publicizing a particular company's IPO are invited to do the honors. Here, members of the cast of TV's *Mad Men* mark the flotation of its production company Lionsgate.

currency with which to reward employees (who can receive both real shares and options – the right to buy further shares at a designated time and price in the future).

While company founders concentrate on ensuring that their business is stable and growing, IPOs themselves are largely organized by investment banks and lawyers, who will draw up a share prospectus (known in the US as a "Red Herring") and build a book of investors who wish to buy the company's stock. At the same time, there are regulatory hoops to go through, to ensure the company is compliant with stock market listing rules. A successful IPO – and many are withdrawn because of lack of investor interest or unfavorable stock market conditions – culminates in what is called impact day, when shares are made available to trade. The company will be given a ticker symbol – a market identifier that is usually an abbreviation of its name – and a welcome to its chosen stock exchange. The New York Stock Exchange famously rings its Opening Bell to greet newly listed companies, whose executives often turn up to do the honors.

FLOTATION – WHAT HAPPENS NEXT?

In the melee that accompanies impact day, the banks that have run the process for the company will carefully monitor the new shares' volatility. In many cases, they will intervene in a process called stabilization, where they will buy stock to steady the price. They can only do so much, however. Eventually, the market will form its own view of the value of the newly listed company: the banks will have to let their protégé both fend for itself and defend its declared value. In good times, companies see their shares trade up on their stock market debut, as new investors pile in; but in more sceptical times, they may see their stock savaged. For company founders, who tend to be locked in – forbidden to sell their own stock – for at least six months, taking this step into the public markets can be a salutary and brutal process.

The fluctuations in the value of one currency against another form the basis of the foreign exchange market – Forex, or FX for short – and is driven by traders' belief that one currency will appreciate or depreciate against another. So, a typical foreign exchange trade might be to buy the euro while at the same time selling the US dollar, described as going long on the EUR/USD, in the hope and expectation that the euro will appreciate against the dollar.

CURRENCIES/FX

↓

The changing values of the world's currencies provide the basis of forex trading. The object of this trading is to exchange one currency for another in the expectation that the price will change, so that the currency you bought will increase in value compared to the one you sold.

While foreign exchange trading has a huge institutional following and entire investment bank trading floors devoted to speculation on the changing value of foreign currencies, it is also a vital conduit for both corporate and individual transactions. When a company earns revenue in a foreign country, for example, it must repatriate those funds while limiting its exposure to market fluctuations.

Similarly, an individual buying a house overseas who needs to change their home currency will have to transact in the foreign exchange market. In both cases, if sums are held on deposit, investors may wish to hedge the risk of currency fluctuations for the duration.

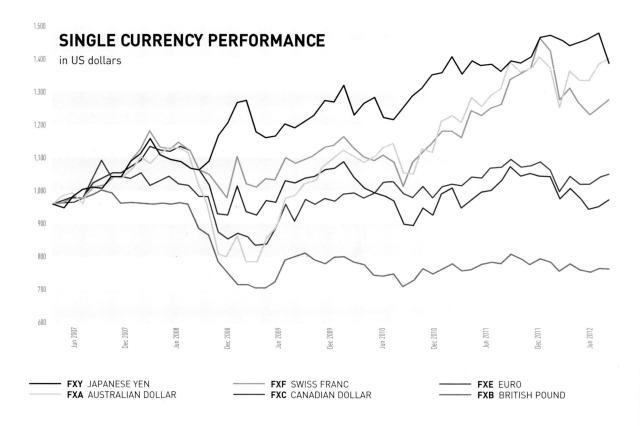

SINGLE CURRENCY PERFORMANCE
in US dollars

— **FXY** JAPANESE YEN
— **FXA** AUSTRALIAN DOLLAR
— **FXF** SWISS FRANC
— **FXC** CANADIAN DOLLAR
— **FXE** EURO
— **FXB** BRITISH POUND

CURRENCY DISTRIBUTION IN THE FX MARKET

84.9% USD

39.1% EUR

19.0% JPY

12.9% GBP

7.6% AUD

6.4% CHF

5.3% CAD

25.0% OTHERS

↑
Currencies are always quoted in pairs, such as GBP/USD or USD/JPY. This is because in every foreign exchange transaction you are simultaneously buying one currency and selling another. Here forex traders in Tokyo work below a screen showing the price of the yen (the quote currency) against the dollar (the base currency).

←
Although declining in recent years, the dollar is still the world's most traded currency by some considerable distance. It is followed by the euro, the yen and the pound while the Australian and Canadian dollars have recently shown a considerable increase in market share.

US DOLLAR CURRENCY PAIR 'MAJORS' AND THEIR MARKET NICKNAMES

Pairs		Nicknames
EUR/USD	Euro vs US Dollar	The Anti-Dollar
GBP/USD	Great Britain Pound vs US Dollar	Sterling Cable
USD/JPY	US Dollar vs Japan Yen	The Yen
USD/CHF	US Dollar vs Swiss Franc	Swissie
USD/CAD	US Dollar vs Canadian Dollar	Loonie
AUD/USD	Australian Dollar vs US Dollar	Aussie
NZD/USD	New Zealand Dollar vs US Dollar	Kiwi or Kiwi Dollar

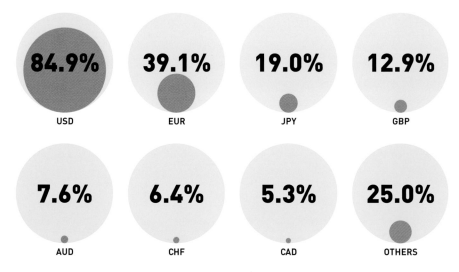

↓

The trading of copper futures, a material primarily used in the construction industry and electrical communications wiring, is seen as an accurate barometer of a country's economic growth as changes in demand suggest an expansion or contraction of the economy.

The commodities markets have their feet firmly planted in the decidedly real worlds of agriculture and mining (though some commodities, notably oil and gold, have become their own markets). So-called soft commodities include the staples of everyday diet for millions of people around the world: soya, oilseed, wheat and maize, as well as tea, coffee and even orange juice. Their cousins, hard commodities such as iron ore, steel and metals such as copper, nickel and palladium, end up in major industrial processes or as components in everything from car engines to mobile phone microchips.

COMMODITIES

All these commodities are traded on various specialist exchanges around the world and have built up their own following of producers, traders and analysts. The Minneapolis Grain Exchange, for example, is a marketplace for producers and processors of wheat, oats and corn, while the London Metal Exchange has become a global hub for traders of non-ferrous metals such as aluminum, copper, tin, nickel, zinc, lead, aluminum alloy, cobalt and molybdenum.

↓

Wheat has always been of interest to investors because it represents one of the single most important components of the world's key staple food products such as bread, biscuits, pizzas and pasta.

Controlling costs

Many commodity trades are in futures and options, which allow both actual consumers (for example, large companies that rely on a certain metal or ingredient to manufacture their own goods), as well as speculators to bet on future prices and, if necessary, secure supplies for delivery on a future date. By planning ahead on their raw materials, manufacturers are able to keep their costs under control, predict cash flow and, crucially, reassure investors that their margins can be kept intact.

Purely financial investors, which now include large hedge funds who devote enormous resources to try to predict the ups and downs of commodity markets, will normally sell or rollover (reinvest) their positions before delivery takes place.

CORNERING THE MARKET

The peculiarities of some commodity markets attract colorful and often wayward characters. In 1979, the silver market was cornered by two brothers, Nelson (below right) and William Bunker Hunt, who accumulated vast holdings, via futures contracts, of around 100 million ounces of the precious metal, amounting to several billion dollars in value. Their positions caused a squeeze that saw silver futures contracts rocket from $11 an ounce in September 1979 to $50 an ounce three months later, only to collapse back to $11 in a market debacle on so-called Silver Thursday in March 1980. It took a further nine years for the Bunker Hunt brothers to reach a settlement with the United States Commodity Futures Trading Commission, which saw Nelson fined $10 million and receive a ban from silver trading. While such antics are now few and far between, as regulators have tightened up, "squeezes" (whether orchestrated or accidental) still occur. Recently, banks wishing to launch an exchange-traded fund (ETF) in physical copper, for example, faced questions about how such contracts could effectively corner the market in certain circumstances.

JARGON BUSTER

A **futures** contract represents an agreement to buy or sell a financial product or commodity at a given price at a specified day in the future. The owner of an **option** has the choice to buy or sell a financial product or commodity at a given price at a specified date in the future if it would be advantageous for them to do so.

Liquid/illiquid: liquidity is an asset's ability to be sold quickly without any loss of value (cash is the best example); an illiquid asset is one that cannot be sold quickly without a substantial loss in value.

▶
See also Oil (pages 100–1), Gold (pages 104–5) and Carbon Trading (pages 108–9)

Oil – properly called crude oil or petroleum – is the world's most important source of energy and, as a result, the lifeblood of the global economy. A fossil fuel because it derives from prehistoric organisms, oil is essentially a mixture of hydrocarbons that can be separated from each other, processed and put to work. Its associated gases, such as butane and propane, are equally useful. Despite the expense of extracting oil and gas and the rapid rise of alternative energies, they still power the vast bulk of the world's industry, providing the fuel for its transport and heating and the raw materials for all manner of consumer goods.

OIL

↓

OPEC was founded in Baghdad in September 1960 by five oil-producing countries: the Islamic Republic of Iran, Iraq, Kuwait, Saudi Arabia and Venezuela. Today the organization is 12-strong with the addition of Algeria, Angola, Ecuador, Libya, Nigeria, Qatar and the United Arab Emirates. Able to control production and therefore the price of oil during the 1970s, its power has diminished somewhat following the discovery of large oil reserves in other parts of the world.

This billion-dollar industry is served by markets that trade a variety of crude and refined oil products and act as a barometer of industrial growth, stagnation or downturn. They are particularly sensitive to supply and demand issues and to political risk. As such, any indication of a possible interruption to supply – the threat of war or civil unrest, for example, in a major oil-producing country – causes price volatility, a scramble to secure supplies and to hedge against future price rises or falls. High oil prices mean expensive fuel costs and will likely slow down economic growth; low oil prices, on the other hand, can act as a spur.

That price is invariably the spot price per barrel, a barrel being 159 liters of oil, quoted on the major exchanges: the New York Mercantile Exchange (NYMEX) and the Intercontinental Exchange (ICE). Although there are many different flavors, or grades, of oil, the benchmarks are West Texas Intermediate (WTI), Brent crude and Dubai/Oman. The global oil price is commonly calculated as a weighted average price of all oil imported into the United States and is quoted in US dollars.

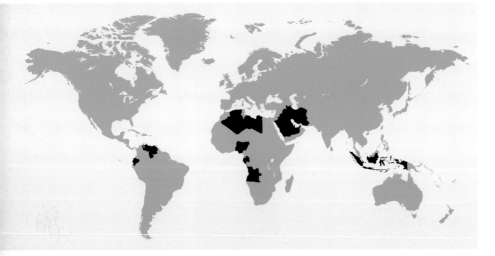

→

Given the importance of crude oil derivative products, some people may choose to invest in refineries. To be useful, crude oil must be refined into consumable products, such as gasoline, diesel and jet fuel, automotive oil, propane and kerosene. For this reason, refineries, like this one in Richmond, California, are a critical link in the crude oil supply chain.

CRUDE OIL PRICE PER BARREL
in US dollars
Source: Energy Information Administration and Bureau of Labor Statistics

TOP 30 OIL PRODUCERS/ BARRELS PER DAY

1	Saudi Arabia	10,520,000
2	Russia	10,130,000
3	United States	9,688,000
4	China	4,273,000
5	Iran	4,252,000
6	Canada	3,483,000
7	Mexico	2,983,000
8	United Arab Emirates	2,813,000
9	Brazil	2,746,000
10	Nigeria	2,458,000
11	Kuwait	2,450,000
12	Iraq	2,408,000
13	Venezuela	2,375,000
14	European Union	2,276,000
15	Norway	2,134,000
16	Algeria	2,078,000
17	Angola	1,988,000
18	Libya	1,789,000
19	Kazakhstan	1,610,000
20	Qatar	1,437,000
21	United Kingdom	1,393,000
22	Azerbaijan	1,041,000
23	Indonesia	1,030,000
24	India	954,000
25	Oman	867,900
26	Colombia	800,100
27	Argentina	763,600
28	Malaysia	664,800
29	Egypt	662,600
30	Australia	549,200

Source: CIA World Factbook 2010

Roller-coaster ride

Oil's post-Second World War history has been fraught with squabbles, market manipulation and cartels. OPEC, the Organization of the Petroleum Exporting Countries, was established in 1960 and managed to impose stability for over a decade. But the oil crisis of 1973 saw huge price fluctuations after OPEC imposed an oil embargo in response to the United States' decision to supply Israeli forces during the Yom Kippur War. A second energy crisis was triggered in 1979 when the Iranian Revolution curtailed vital supplies from the Gulf to the United States. From then on, the oil market has had a roller-coaster ride. The oil price hit a low of $17 per barrel in 1999, due to increased Middle Eastern production and slack demand from Asia, and then rocketed to $35 in 2000. After 2000, it had a bumpy but generally upward trajectory, reaching a peak of $145 in July 2008. A dramatic fall to just $30 followed, but the last few years have seen a recovery, with the price pushing past $100 in January 2011.

While the oil market retains pole position in the group of energy commodities, other energy products are also big business. Coal, mainly used to fire power stations, has historically been cheaper than oil and gas but remains difficult and expensive to transport.

ENERGY

↓

Coal is the most abundant fossil fuel on the planet and plays a vital role in electricity generation worldwide. Coal-fired power plants currently fuel 41 percent of global electricity. However, investors are wary because even though worldwide demand is set to grow, environmental concerns are making it harder to get permission to build new coal-fired facilities.

Mined in around fifty countries, a great deal of its two main types – steam and coking coal – is exported, but most stays in its home country: in 2010, overall international trade in coal reached 1,083Mt, which still only accounted for some 16 percent of the total amount consumed. Because it is such an expensive commodity to export large distances, the coal market has divided into two geographic areas – the Atlantic market, made up of importing countries in Europe including the United Kingdom, Spain and Germany, and the Pacific market, which includes heavy importers such as Japan and Korea.

THE ODD ONE OUT

Uranium – that is, yellowcake or U308 – mined out of remote regions of Australia, Canada, Russia and Africa and used in nuclear power generation is bought and sold by large power utilities, as well as by institutional and private investors. But, unlike most commodities, there is no spot price, or instant market. Instead, two longstanding industry bodies, UxC and TradeTech, report weekly prices based on recent trades in the market. The uranium market, which had been the beneficiary of an increased interest in the nuclear power renaissance, was severely disrupted by the Fukushima nuclear plant disaster in Japan in 2011, and a previous upward price trend is now in doubt as nuclear new-build projects have been put on hold. Despite this, uranium remains a vital fuel source for the world's existing nuclear industry and its price has a direct effect on end-user energy costs.

URANIUM (U308) PRICE
in US dollars
Source: UXC

140
120
100
80
60
40
20
0

1988   1994   2000   2006   2012

←

The uranium market is unusual in that its only significant commercial use is to fuel nuclear reactors and this makes it particularly vulnerable to geopolitical interference. The price spiked in 2007 due to excitement about nuclear energy's future. At the same time one of the world's biggest sources – the Cigar Lake mine in Saskatchewan, Canada – was flooded and production was stopped, creating fears about future supplies.

The gold, or bullion, market has a heritage that few others can claim. For thousands of years, the yellow metal has exercised a fascination over investors; but it is for sound commercial reasons as well as for its rather mystical character. Traditionally, gold has been an important part of countries' national reserves, acting as a bulwark against crises and the foundation that underpins paper money, a so-called value of last resort. Many investors, sometimes known as "gold bugs," have followed suit, holding gold against a rainy day, or worse.

GOLD

Why? First, gold is mostly tradable even in an emergency: although it is mainly priced in dollars, it does not defer to a particular currency, and is accepted around the world. Almost invariably, therefore, the gold price rises when war or financial catastrophe threatens. Secondly, gold has often kept its value (in terms of its real purchasing power) in inflationary times and is regarded by many as a hedge – an insurance – against rising inflation. Finally, gold carries no risk of default. Unlike, for example, a bond, there is no counterparty risk and trading it does not engender a liability.

↓

Traditionally, a nation's central bank holds much of its national reserves in the form of gold bullion or bars. This is held as a hedge: a guarantee to pay depositors, note holders and trading peers or to underpin the nation's currency. It is estimated that the total amount of gold mined during human history is about 160,000 metric tonnes – at today's prices the total value of this would exceed $10 trillion.

The sceptics' view

While these characteristics continue to give gold a following, some are sceptical about the bullion market. Gold, they say, no longer acts as the backstop to the global financial system in the way it once did and, as for its value, they point to a price that often responds to rumor and speculation. Sceptics also point out that gold does not really work for its living – it pays no interest or dividend; equally, it is expensive to store and to move around.

THE GOLD STANDARD

Confidence in gold goes back to ancient times, but is still used as a benchmark monetary unit to underpin coinage and paper money. Measuring gold against currency units is known as convertibility. This so-called gold standard monetary system has been adopted and then unadopted by many countries, as circumstances dictate. In times of war, when governments need to spend much but have limited tax revenues they will often suspend convertibility, or come off the gold standard, only to resume it at the end of the crisis (or, more commonly, stay off it for good). Although being on the gold standard encourages fiscal prudence, equally, staying on it can restrict money supply, thwarting attempts to increase the monetary base.

Its core principle was used in the post-Second World War Bretton Woods agreements, when numerous countries fixed their exchange rates to the US dollar (the new reserve currency). The US fixed its gold at a certain price – $35 – and therefore all the other currencies had a gold peg too. The debate over whether the gold standard represents long-term stability and controls inflation, or whether it encourages stasis continues. In the end, the world's supplies of gold may just be too small to act as a credible monetary base for the global economy.

THE GOLD FIX

Each weekday at 10:30 a.m. and 3:00 p.m. GMT, at the offices of investment bank NM Rothschild in the City of London, the London gold fixes are conducted – in US dollars, euros and pounds sterling – between five market-makers who are members of an organization called simply The London Gold Market Fixing Ltd. The company's primary purpose is to set a price for contracts on the London bullion market, but in reality it provides a benchmark for gold pricing around the world. The price is announced via a dedicated telephone conference facility. The Fix dates back to September 1919, when the gold price per fine ounce (troy ounce) was decided as £4/18/9d. The fix has continued ever since, albeit with a long interruption between 1939 and 1954 when wartime restrictions meant the London gold market was suspended.

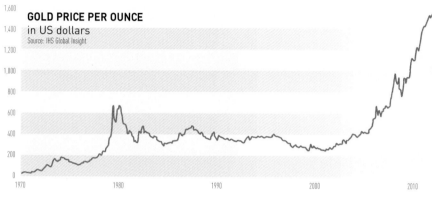

GOLD PRICE PER OUNCE
in US dollars
Source: IHS Global Insight

To counter this the gold market itself has seen considerable innovation in recent years. The plethora of small gold mining companies has lent itself to Exchange Traded Funds, which gather together a basket of gold mining stocks and offer a single price for them, allowing investors to spread their risk. Equally, the miners themselves have increasingly turned to hedging products to manage price volatility in the end-market. So gold has caught up with many other commodities in this regard.

As the market has modernized and attracted new investors, particularly retail investors from China and India, over the past two decades, the price of gold has performed strongly as the demand for gold has been sustained, in recent years, heading toward the $2,000 per ounce figure – an all-time high.

↓

A shop assistant in Nanjing, China, helps assemble a huge display of gold roses. More than 50 percent of the world's gold is used to make jewelry. Rapid growth in the economies of India and China have been accompanied by an equally rapid increase in demand for gold jewelry in these countries, helping it maintain its rising value on the world's financial markets.

The clue to derivatives is really in the name. Literally, these financial products derive from very basic ones, such as equities, bonds or indices. They were originally designed to piggyback on their grown-up relations but as the derivatives market has become ever larger, they have all too often outgrown – and outfoxed – them.

DERIVATIVES

CDOs played a pivotal role in financing the housing bubble that peaked in the US during 2006. However, within a year the number of mortgage defaults had risen alarmingly and it became clear that many CDOs included derivatives based on mortgages and, in particular, on subprime mortgages. By 2008 the subprime crisis had become the credit crunch, which was shortly followed by the collapse of Bear Stearns, one of America's major investment banks.

Many derivatives owe their parentage to the insurance market and were devised as a form of protection for investors. Take credit default swaps (CDS), for example. Unravelled, they are literally a swap, or insurance trade, against the risk of 'default', or failure to pay a promised return, by a credit, which is a bond. In other words, a credit default swap can be bought as insurance against a bond defaulting on its interest payments or on the repayment of its principal.

We may also count futures and options in the increasingly complex derivatives family. These have long been used by traders to hedge their bets against price rises – and falls – in the future. An option to buy stock at a specific price sometime in the future, a very common sort of derivative, can be traded just like an ordinary equity share. Bundled, synthesized and swapped, such innocent products can quickly become alarmingly complex to understand. When a layer of leverage boosts their buying power, they can also become highly toxic.

QUICK REFERENCE

The most common financial derivatives

Credit derivatives: relate to loans, bonds and other debt instruments.
Commodity derivatives: relate to energy (oil, natural gas and electricity), precious metals, base metals and agricultural produce.
Equity derivatives: contracts linked to the performance of equities (shares).
Index options: linked to the performance of an index of shares like the FTSE, or S&P 500FX options that relate to foreign currencies.
Weather futures: relate to the climate (a farmer might use these to hedge against extremes in climate and, hence, bad harvests).

Huge profits v. huge risks

The large investment banks stand at the center of the derivatives market. When that market functions efficiently, it generates huge fees – and profits – for them. When it does not, it can be catastrophic, as witnessed in 2007, when derivatives products such as Collateralized Debt Obligations and structures such as Special Investment Vehicles began to falter and fail. But the opacity of such derivatives and their wrappers is compounded by the fact that there has often been very little line of sight between participants.

Because derivative instruments have generally been traded between banks, the risks of failure has often been systemic. To address this problem, the industry is adopting a new methodology, whereby a clearinghouse stands between the banks. Traders must post collateral with the clearinghouse to ensure they can meet their obligations. This lends a degree of transparency to the derivatives market, although critics point out that oversight committees at the clearing houses are still peopled with banks' representatives.

↑
Chief derivatives trader of Barings Bank in Singapore, Nick Leeson's unauthorized speculative trading was exposed in January 1995. When a series of bad investments – eventually thought to total some $1.4 billion – that had been hidden through an internal company finally came to light, Leeson was arrested and sentenced to more than six years in prison. In the meantime, Barings Bank had collapsed.

←

The new clearinghouse system, which was adopted in the US in 2010, has proved so effective that several of the most-used clearinghouses are trading over a trillion dollars a year. With so much money at stake they cannot be allowed to fail when the only option would be a government bailout.

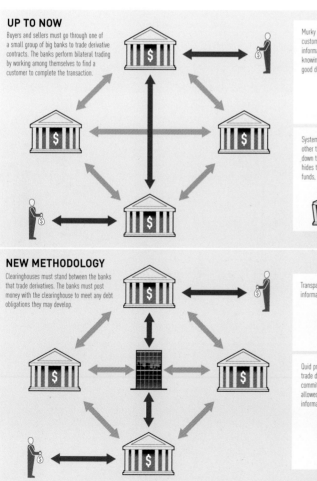

UP TO NOW
Buyers and sellers must go through one of a small group of big banks to trade derivative contracts. The banks perform bilateral trading by working among themselves to find a customer to complete the transaction.

Murky market: unlike the stock market, customers cannot see pricing or other trading information. Buyers and sellers are left not knowing whether they have overpaid or made a good deal.

Systemic risks: as banks trade directly with each other the risk of one bank failing and bringing down the others is heightened. The system also hides the risks that some big players, like hedge funds, might be taking.

NEW METHODOLOGY
Clearinghouses must stand between the banks that trade derivatives. The banks must post money with the clearinghouse to meet any debt obligations they may develop.

Transparent market: clearinghouses make some information more easily available.

Quid pro quo: representatives from the banks that trade derivatives dominate the clearinghouse committees. Other institutions have not been allowed to enter the market and trading information is still not completely transparent.

↓
Norfolk Island, has introduced the world's first personal carbon trading scheme. Residents are allocated the same number of carbon units on a credit card, which they spend whenever they buy petrol and power. If they are frugal with non-renewable energy consumption, and walk, cycle or drive an electric car, they will be able to trade in leftover carbon credits for cash at the carbon bank at the end of a set period. Each year the quota of carbon units will be reduced, and the price of a high carbon emission lifestyle will rise.

The 1997 Kyoto Agreement, in which an initial 37 countries (now nearly 200) agreed to reductions in the levels of greenhouse gases emitted into the atmosphere, opened the door to an entirely new market: carbon, or emissions, trading. This is a market with a conscience, in that it has grown out of a desire by industrialized countries to reduce their carbon emissions, and it is supported by the likes of the UN and the World Bank. Importantly, it is not carbon or CO_2 that is actually being traded, but the excess emissions or offsets of greenhouse gas polluters. In this regard, the market has been likened to a medieval exchange of sin for a pardon.

CARBON TRADING

Not that there is anything medieval about the market itself. Trading volumes have grown by over 1,000 percent since 2005 and some believe that the carbon-trading market could eventually be the world's largest commodity market. In Europe, a landmark was achieved in 2005, with the establishment of the European Union Emissions Trading System (EUETS), a compliance system for polluters.

At the crossroads

Carbon trading uses tonnes of CO_2 as its unit of currency, while the tradable certificate known as a carbon credit is the permit that allows a country

or a company to emit one tonne of carbon dioxide (or another greenhouse gas). There are a number of carbon exchanges around the world, including the European Climate Exchange, the NASDAQ OMX Commodities Exchanges and the electronic Carbon Trade Exchange. However, the recent economic downturn has seen a collapse in the price of credits, a situation that many believe will require government intervention for the system to survive.

→

The idea behind carbon trading is that from the planet's point of view where carbon dioxide comes from is far less important than total amounts. So, rather than rigidly forcing the reduction of emissions country-by-country, (or company-by-company), the market creates a choice: either spend the money to cut your own pollution; or continue polluting yourself and pay someone else to cut theirs.

THE GROWING TRADE IN CO$_2$

in metric tons
Source: Bloomberg

2003
7

2005
12

2002
11

2004
13

2006
28

2007
68

2008
130

2009
98

2010
131

←

The carbon trading market is growing fast. It's appeal is twofold: at one end of the spectrum it is intended to help mitigate global warming, at the other it can help bolster the image of companies perceived to be the world's major polluters.

TRADING YOUR OWN CARBON

Personal carbon trading brings the emissions market down to an individual level. The idea, first proposed by environmental economists, would see each of us allocated emissions credits from national carbon budgets. We would then exchange these credits for units of fuel or power; those requiring more power could buy them from those others who consume less, thus encouraging a market in individual emissions that would reward low consumers with a potential profit. So far, these credits have received a suitably warm welcome. A number of European governments are actively considering so-called Tradable Energy Quotas; elsewhere there are experiments in actual trading. On Norfolk Island, for example – a Pacific island that sits between Australia and New Zealand – the population has started the first pilot personal carbon-trading program.

The insurance market is all about risk. Whether that risk is of a life being lost, a ship sinking, a car being damaged, a house being burgled or a piece of luggage going astray, it will, ultimately, be assessed, underwritten and bought and sold on the insurance market. And the chance of these – and a myriad other – events happening, the risk being crystallized and compensation having to be paid out are the pivots on which the market turns.

INSURANCE

Insurance contracts, widely known as policies, are the key commodity in the insurance market and insurers' business derives from creating such policies, guaranteeing them in return for a premium. These premiums, collectively known as "float," can be invested, meaning that the world's insurers also constitute some of its largest investors and fund managers.

Risk assessment

↓

The estimated total losses to the world insurance market from the World Trade Center terrorist attacks are thought to be somewhere around $40 billion.

The means by which insurers assess risk – and how they then calculate insurance premiums – has long been the preserve of actuaries, whose forecasting models are now hugely sophisticated, if not entirely infallible. Faced with a request for insurance against a particular peril, actuaries will look at the frequency and severity of the risk, as well as the historical precedents. A present value of the risk will then be calculated, allowing the insurer to price a premium correctly.

The insurance market divides broadly into two: life and non-life. The former concerns itself with life insurance policies, pensions and annuities, while the latter comprises a plethora of business lines, from travel and transport to property and credit.

Cat-modeling

The risk of major catastrophes keeps the insurance industry awake at night. Whether it is natural disaster (known as "nat cat") such as hurricane, earthquake or flood damage, or acts of war and terrorism, the potential payouts to hundreds of thousands of claimants can make or break an insurance market. As a result, many millions are poured into cat-modeling wherein sophisticated computer simulations, which extend into the fields of meteorology and seismology, are run to try to calculate potential risks. Inevitably, this is an area of insurance particularly prone to dispute and litigation. Acts of terror such as the 9/11 attacks on the World Trade Center, in New York, attracted huge claims from property landlords, which took years to conclude.

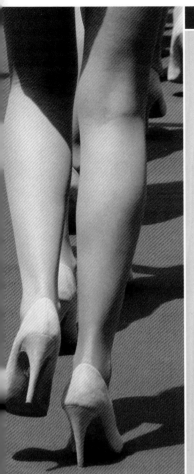

THE STORY OF LLOYD'S

Lloyd's of London (motto *uberrimae fidei* – "of the utmost good faith"), the world's oldest insurance house, remains a stalwart of the insurance industry. An insurance and reinsurance market, it brings together investors and insurance underwriters – known as Names – to aggregate and trade risk. Located in the heart of the City of London, Lloyd's traces its history back to 1688 and Edward Lloyd's coffee house, where ship-owners and merchants used to gather to swap news about arrivals and departures from London's bustling ports. In modern times it has become a symbol of the City, housed in its iconic Richard Rogers-designed inside-out building, which was completed in 1986. Its core business has been to insure all manner of risk, from shipping to film stars' legs. Historically, wealthy individuals underwrote Lloyd's insurance policies with unlimited liability (i.e. they stood to lose everything if the policy failed), but that changed in 1994 when a string of natural and industrial disasters caused huge losses and members who would bear only limited liability were admitted. These days, Lloyd's is largely a corporate world with a small minority of individual investors, although it still wields enormous power in the insurance market.

↓

Marine insurance is the oldest in the world; hardly surprising as the UN estimates that there are more than three million shipwrecks on the ocean floor. When a ship sinks, like the oil tanker *Prestige*, which sank off the coast of Spain in 2002, a raft of business activities begins: including insurance (hull, cargo and crew), salvage operations and the determination of the ecological costs of the disaster.

"WALL STREET IS THE ONLY PLACE THAT PEOPLE RIDE TO IN A ROLLS-ROYCE TO GET ADVICE FROM THOSE WHO TAKE THE SUBWAY."
WARREN BUFFETT (B. 1930),
THE TAO OF WARREN BUFFETT, 2008

6 INVESTING AND FINANCE

↑
The world's stock markets are vibrant places, full of the hustle, bustle and noise of commerce. At the center of each is a trading pit, so-called because of the apparent chaotic nature of its routine.

Left to its own devices, money tends to atrophy. In inflationary times, its purchasing power will diminish: currencies fluctuate, sometimes dramatically; and cash per se, while it certainly has its uses as an asset class, is not particularly productive. Putting it to work – investing – is both an art and a science. Even the science, which has become astonishingly sophisticated, is far from perfect: the investment strategy that can genuinely offer an absolute return (a return regardless of market conditions) has yet to be discovered.

While we wait for this breakthrough – and it may never come – there is a virtually limitless universe of single investments, collective schemes and a plethora of exotic opportunities designed to get the most out of money. Many of them depend on building value in physical assets, but many others are decidedly synthetic, responding to minute movements in prices, the probability of events occurring (or not occurring) and, indeed, the entirely unexpected. Of course, it could be argued that this uncertainty is exactly what makes it so attractive.

A delicate balance

But before dipping a toe in these shark-infested waters, it is worth bearing in mind that capital preservation – making sure that money does not lose value – is, in many ways, just as important as capital appreciation. Which brings us to the very human emotions that run through the entire world of investing and finance: greed and fear. Of course, we want money to grow but, equally, we fear losing it. Some neuroeconomic studies conclude that there is some primacy of emotion over cognition in the decison-making process. Whatever the truth, this delicate balance still drives the vast majority of investment decisions and, indeed, informs the financial markets themselves: when enough people act together – exhibiting the herd instinct – prices rise or fall. And en masse that causes market rallies and market crashes – the greatest expression of accumulation or destruction of the value of investments.

Trying to predict and exploit the drivers of those emotions is the preoccupation of a large part of the financial industry. No one, however, has ever really bettered the legendary American J. Pierpont Morgan, of banking fame, who, when asked "What will the market do?" replied, "It will fluctuate."

> **"WALL STREET NEVER CHANGES, THE POCKETS CHANGE, THE SUCKERS CHANGE, THE STOCKS CHANGE, BUT WALL STREET NEVER CHANGES, BECAUSE HUMAN NATURE NEVER CHANGES."**
> JESSE LIVERMORE (1877–1940), STOCK SPECULATOR

Financier and philanthropist John Pierpont Morgan (center) was one of the fathers of corporate finance in the United States. His company, J.P. Morgan & Co., had a great impact on enterprises such as railroads, steel, mining and other utilities that helped establish the United States as an industrial power.

No two investors are alike, but many have common characteristics that derive from basic human characteristics. The psychology of investing has spawned its own highly developed academic discipline, known as behavioral finance, which studies the cognitive and emotional factors that play a part in investment decisions.

PSYCHOLOGY

Making judgment calls

Even unconsciously, investors are often prone to reaching decisions based on heuristics – approximations rather than strictly logical steps. Equally, they will frequently employ framing, using a set of familiar scenarios, to make sense of rapidly moving events in the market. Investors, who observe their stocks and shares rise and fall, making and losing them money, run the whole gamut of emotions and even the most rational can make entirely irrational judgment calls. One of the most obvious and frequently cited is groupthink, also known

→

If investing was all about the numbers then the majority of traders would be very rich. They are not. Anything involving winning or losing money becomes emotionally charged. Though there is no perfect formula, success in investing involves a psychological commitment to the purpose and a potent mix of information, judgment, confidence, discipline and consistency ... even then success is not guaranteed.

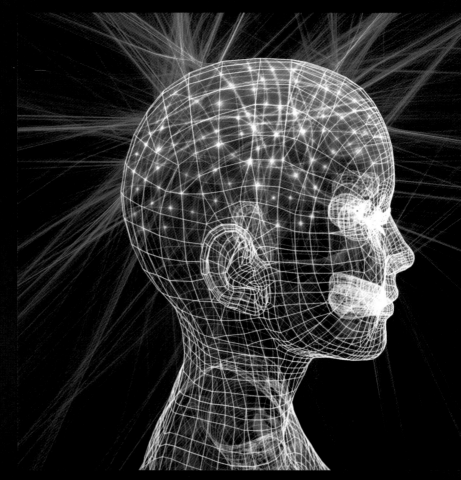

as herding, when a particular theory about the way the market is heading influences large numbers of investors.

Groupthink can sometimes lead to stock market bubbles – the 1999 dot-com bubble in technology stocks, which investors piled into without much thought, is a classic example. Behaviors vary widely, however. So-called contrarian investors take conscious decisions to unfollow the herd, often buying cheap, unwanted stocks in unloved sectors and selling those they feel are overly popular. Warren Buffett is a famous contrarian. His belief is that the best time to invest in a stock is when the shortsightedness of the market has beaten down the price.

FEAR, HOPE AND GREED

Source: Raymond James research

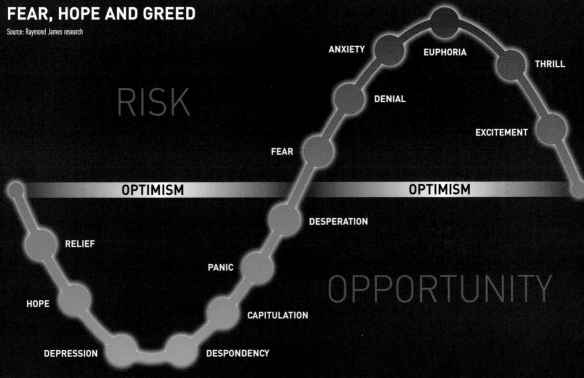

The roller coaster of emotions that drives stock market investing has been described in many ways; here's one way of looking at the cycle of fear, hope and greed that accompanies the ups and downs of the markets.

ANIMAL SPIRITS

The eminent economist John Maynard Keynes reckoned that what he termed "animal spirits" – innate human emotions – contributed greatly to financial matters. In his 1936 book *The General Theory of Employment, Interest and Money*, he wrote that it was this "spontaneous urge to action rather than inaction" that drove what he called "positive activities ... whether moral or hedonistic or economic." Alan Greenspan, the famously gloomy former head of the Federal Reserve, referred to a similar sense of "irrational exuberance" in boom times. On the other hand, animal spirits have also been credited with driving rebounds in moribund stock markets, as investors prefer to take an optimistic view of economies emerging from recession into recovery.

The Dow Jones Industrial Average's performance over the last hundred years describes three economic booms, each one larger than the previous one. First, there was an industry-led boom in the 1920s, the age of the automobile and stock market speculation; second, the period following the end of the Second World War saw a huge population increase accompanied by a surge in consumer spending.

BOOM AND BUST

The third boom occurred in the 1990s and 2000s, when technology and finance combined to spur the economy. Equally, we can see busts at the end of the 1920s, with the Wall Street Crash, the 1970s slump precipitated by the oil crisis, and a double-whammy of the dot-com crash in 2000–2002 and the wider global credit crunch from 2007–2009.

Cyclicality

The world of finance is in an almost constant state of trading as it responds to a plethora of data, information and analysis – as well as to rumor and speculation.

At a macro level, investors look for the emergence and progression of big economic cycles. At a micro level, they examine regular updates from governments and central banks, as well as company results, trading updates and news of corporate events.

All these factors play into decisions about whether to invest – or simply stay in cash – and what to invest in. Hardened investors realize that long-term patterns have emerged and that they often repeat. The investment clock, devised by the Bank of America Merrill Lynch, shows one way of looking at cyclical investing, through periods of economic boom, slowdown, recession and recovery. In each

↓

The Dow Jones Industrial Average is an index that tracks how 30 large publicly owned companies in the US have performed in a standard trading session on the stock market. A record of its value over the last hundred years reveals the cyclical nature of the global economy, punctuated by periods of boom and bust, and the reasons behind them.

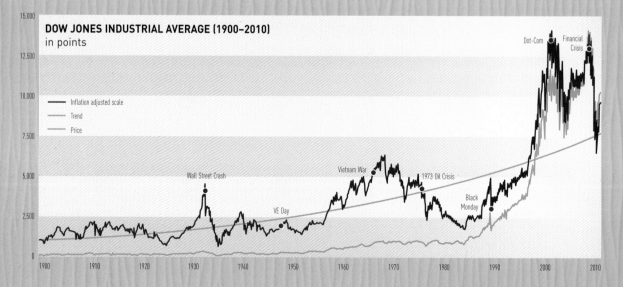

DOW JONES INDUSTRIAL AVERAGE (1900–2010)
in points

— Inflation adjusted scale
— Trend
— Price

Wall Street Crash
VE Day
Vietnam War
1973 Oil Crisis
Black Monday
Dot-Com
Financial Crisis

THE FLASH CRASH

On May 6, 2010, the Dow Jones fell by 700 points in under five minutes (right), before recovering almost as quickly, after a flood of sell orders made by "quant" computer-driven trading programs (based on a sophisticated trading model, these programs scour company data looking for stocks that meet the model's requirements and either buys the stock or sells companies that fall below its requirements). Had the losses – some $800 billion – not been reversed when the automatic programs were overridden, the Dow would have suffered one of its biggest ever one-day falls.

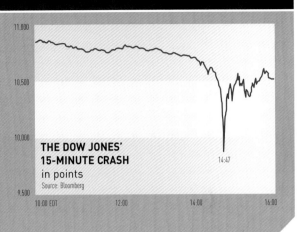

**THE DOW JONES'
15-MINUTE CRASH**
in points
Source: Bloomberg

14:47

11,000
10,500
10,000
9,500
10:00 EDT   12:00   14:00   16:00

of these episodes certain assets become more attractive and others less so, either because they are perceived to be less risky or to offer more value. It's no surprise, for example, that in an economic slowdown investors shift their money into high-quality assets such as government bonds (which are guaranteed by the issuing government); as a recession unfolds, they will seek out so-called growth stocks, which will power the recovery. Equally, when that recovery arrives and when there is more optimism in the air, investors are tempted into riskier assets such as small-cap stocks.

THE GLOBAL ECONOMIC CYCLE

VALUE STOCKS
MUNICIPALS
EARLY CYCLE SECTORS
SMALL CAP
HIGH-YIELD BONDS

RECOVERY

BOOM

COMMODITIES
OVERSEAS EQUITIES
LATE CYCLE SECTORS
TIPS*
LARGE CAP

CORPORATE BONDS
RATE SENSITIVE SECTORS
GROWTH STOCKS

RECESSION

SLOWDOWN

SHORT-TERM TREASURIES
DEFENSIVE SECTORS
HIGH-QUALITY ASSETS
LONG-TERM TREASURIES

←

The Merrill Lynch investment clock hinges on cyclical investing, believing that different asset classes will outperform one another depending on the economic condition or cycle. During recession it advises investment in bonds, as the economy recovers then stocks become more attractive, during the boom time go for commodities, but as the economy slows down then long-term investments and the money market are often suggested.

*Inflation protected bonds

A bond is often described as an IOU – a promise by a borrower to pay a lender back. The borrower is the company that issues the bond; the lender is the investor who buys it. The main characteristics of a bond are (1) the principal amount, which is repaid to the investor by the issuer at the end of the bond's term; and (2) interest payments on the principal amount, which are made to the investor by the issuer at regular intervals during the bond's term. In many cases, these interest payments are fixed – for example, at 5 percent per annum. These fixed payments have given bonds their generic names Fixed Interest or Fixed Income (which are the same thing).

BONDS

Besides (1) the principal amount; and (2) interest payments, a bond also has (3) a price. Almost all bonds are initially issued at a price of 100.00. After issue, a bond's price can – and does – move up and down. It is quite common to see a bond trading at, say, 85.00 or at 115.00. This is because it is being bought and sold in the bond market in just the same way as a share in the equity or stock markets. Although it may move up and down like this throughout its life, the bond will almost always be bought back at the end of its term at 100.00 again. The final characteristic of a bond is (4) its yield – the value of the interest – which is connected to (3), its price.

Ups and downs

Interest payments are paid by a bond's issuer to an investor. The rate of this interest depends on the creditworthiness of the issuer and the length of the term of the bond, as well as the overall economic climate.

The rate of interest a bond pays is known as its coupon and, typically, it will be paid annually or semi-annually. So, a $10,000 bond with an annual coupon of 5.625 percent will pay the bondholder $562.50 per annum, every year for the life of the bond. It will remain the same amount, no matter what the price and the yield of a bond are. In this example, a bond with a semi-annual coupon would pay $281.25 every six months.

The Scylla and Charybdis of the bond world are interest rates (that is, central bank interest rates) and inflation. Like any other investment, bonds must compete to provide better returns than an investor would receive elsewhere. So, low central bank interest rates mean that bonds often provide better returns

KEY FEATURES

There are four key characteristics of a bond: principal amount, interest payments, price and yield. The principal amount and the interest payment are fixed, while the price and yield move up and down.

than simply keeping money in the bank. But higher central bank rates are good for savers who will often leave bonds in favor of bank deposit accounts.

Equally, inflation reduces the real value – the purchasing power – of money. If inflation rises, investors demand a higher return on their money. Because the interest and repayment value of bonds are fixed, the real value of money invested in them can erode very quickly if inflation rises. If this happens, investors demand a higher yield, which in turn, means bond prices fall.

Maturity dates

Almost all bonds have a maturity date, which is the date that the principal amount will be repaid in full by the issuer. Bonds are issued with a wide range of maturity dates – it is possible to buy bonds that will run for as little as six months or as much as thirty years. As the bond gets nearer to its maturity date, its price may move closer to its 100.00 issue price, reflecting the gradually diminishing risk of the issuer not being able to pay back the principal. Conversely, a long-dated bond may be trading at a substantial discount or premium to that 100.00 issue price, which, in part, reflects the long-term uncertainty of a distant redemption date.

BOND VALUE PYRAMID

Source: OppenheimerFunds.com

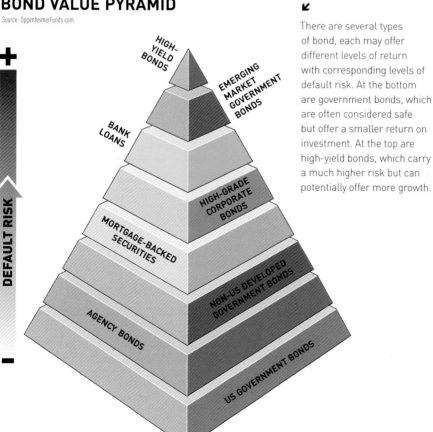

There are several types of bond, each may offer different levels of return with corresponding levels of default risk. At the bottom are government bonds, which are often considered safe but offer a smaller return on investment. At the top are high-yield bonds, which carry a much higher risk but can potentially offer more growth.

► See also The Bond Markets (pages 92–3)

JARGON BUSTER

Credit spreads: often known just as "spreads" – are used to define the differential in yields of different corporations' or countries' bonds compared to a benchmark, often a ten-year government bond. Spreads are measured in basis points, and either widen or tighten, depending on the perceived risk compared to the safe equivalent duration government bond.

Basis points: many securities, rates and credit spreads move around in very small increments commonly measured in hundredths of percentage points. These are known as basis points. One basis point equals 0.01 percent, so one hundred basis points equals 1 percent. The shorthand for basis points is bps and the abbreviation is pronounced *bips*.

Bonds and issuers are graded according to their perceived quality and this grading is an important factor in how bonds behave in the market. The concept of quality is strongly linked to the characteristics of a bond itself and to the creditworthiness of its issuer.

CREDIT RATINGS

The overriding concern of any investor, of course, is that the bond he or she has bought will do what it has promised: repay its principal amount when it says it will and, in the meantime, honor its interest payments. The grading system for calibrating the likelihood of a bond's possible default is fairly straightforward, running from AAA downwards. A bond rated AAA has been given the highest possible rating. This means it is regarded as virtually impossible that it will default on any and all of its obligations. At the other end of the scale, a bond rated D will already have defaulted and is likely to do so again.

INVESTMENT GRADE RATINGS

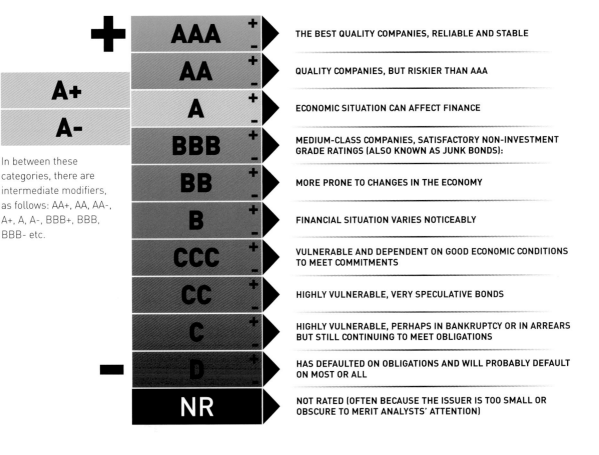

In between these categories, there are intermediate modifiers, as follows: AA+, AA, AA-, A+, A, A-, BBB+, BBB, BBB- etc.

AAA	THE BEST QUALITY COMPANIES, RELIABLE AND STABLE
AA	QUALITY COMPANIES, BUT RISKIER THAN AAA
A	ECONOMIC SITUATION CAN AFFECT FINANCE
BBB	MEDIUM-CLASS COMPANIES, SATISFACTORY NON-INVESTMENT GRADE RATINGS (ALSO KNOWN AS JUNK BONDS):
BB	MORE PRONE TO CHANGES IN THE ECONOMY
B	FINANCIAL SITUATION VARIES NOTICEABLY
CCC	VULNERABLE AND DEPENDENT ON GOOD ECONOMIC CONDITIONS TO MEET COMMITMENTS
CC	HIGHLY VULNERABLE, VERY SPECULATIVE BONDS
C	HIGHLY VULNERABLE, PERHAPS IN BANKRUPTCY OR IN ARREARS BUT STILL CONTINUING TO MEET OBLIGATIONS
D	HAS DEFAULTED ON OBLIGATIONS AND WILL PROBABLY DEFAULT ON MOST OR ALL
NR	NOT RATED (OFTEN BECAUSE THE ISSUER IS TOO SMALL OR OBSCURE TO MERIT ANALYSTS' ATTENTION)

Rating agencies

Credit ratings are marks given by independent ratings agencies (principally Moody's, Standard & Poor's and Fitch) to individual bonds, as well as to companies and sovereign governments. Their ratings are grouped into two – Investment Grade and Non-Investment Grade – which already give some indication of risk; Non-Investment Grade is clearly inferior and has acquired the nickname "junk." Agencies typically receive payment for their services either from the borrower that requests the rating or from subscribers who receive the published ratings and related credit reports.

Although credit quality is important, some investors actively seek out bonds with lower – or no – ratings because they are often priced attractively with high interest rates. This high yield group of bonds has become an entire investment class of its own.

THE KING OF JUNK

The financier Michael Milken is credited with coining the term "junk bonds," which describes high-yield debt that is considered below – and, in some cases, well below, investment grade. Milken pioneered the issuance of junk bonds by cash-strapped companies in the 1980s, which rose from a mere $1.5 billion in 1981 to $16 billion three years later and $33 billion by 1986. Often the debt raised, which attracted investors because it paid a much higher coupon, or interest rate, than normal debt, was used for a spree of mergers and acquisitions in corporate America. The party, which earned millions of dollars in fees for bankers such as Milken, continued until the end of the decade, when the global economy slowed and the junk bond market collapsed. Many bond issuers, unable to meet their repayments, defaulted and losses were put at some $20 billion. When the dust settled, it became clear that Milken and his fellow financiers such as Ivan Boeskey had overstated the investments and were either jailed or paid huge fines. Reflecting on this bond bubble, commentators note that although junk bonds heralded an age of irresponsibility (in an up until now, sedate corner of the investment world), they did provide much-needed financing for America's burgeoning computer and telecommunications industries, which used the proceeds to roll out their new technologies.

Stocks and shares remain the security of choice for many investors. Mostly straightforward, easy to buy and sell and widely issued by a multitude of companies around the world, equities are the foundation of individual investors' portfolios, long-term investment plans and pensions schemes alike.

EQUITIES

Open outcry is the name of the method of communication between professionals on a stock or futures exchange. Traders usually flash the signals quickly across a room. Signals that occur with palms facing out and hands away from the body are an indication the gesturer wishes to sell. When traders face their palms in and hold their hands up, they are gesturing to buy.

These slivers – literally shares – of a company's value or equity have proved remarkably popular with investors over the long-term, in the hope and expectation – not always realized – that, in time, a company's value will grow, that it will pay dividends from profits and that, one day, its shares may be acquired in their entirety for a premium. While this can and does happen, equally there are many instances of companies failing and their shares becoming worthless.

Types of stocks and shares

Ordinary shares – also known as common stock – not only confer a degree of ownership over a company for an investor (unless the wily founders own all the voting shares in another class of share), but also allow them to vote at annual meetings on issues of company governance and the directors' remuneration. Shareholders voting together wield considerable power and, if they feel like it, can remove a company's chief executive or, indeed, an entire board.

Not content with ordinary shares, some investors prefer preferred stock, which allows them certain defined privileges: the right to a dividend, for example, or the ability to get their money out of a company ahead of ordinary shareholders in the event that it should fail. Warming to this theme, many investors – and their lawyers – have decorated their shares with all sorts of provisions to protect their positions and enhance their putative returns.

DAY TRADING

While the professionals like Warren Buffett (right) prefer long-term investing, the advent of the Internet, providing cheap real-time equities prices and execution-only (i.e. no advice is given to investors on which stocks to buy and sell) stockbroking services, has brought a new breed of home-based investors who often trade intra-day, that is they do not hold positions overnight but liquidate them to cash before the market closes. Often utilizing spread-betting to provide leverage to their positions and to maximize tax advantages on their gains, such trading is particularly risky and short-term. Strategies are often event-driven, where traders will follow a company's announcement, invest heavily and take any profits on any uplift in prices almost immediately. Day traders may work singly or sometimes in groups, often swapping investment ideas on online bulletin boards.

So equity shares are a highly flexible investment mechanism, even if they always rank behind the taxman, debt (bonds and bondholders) and, in the case of banks and other financial institutions, depositors.

Buffettology

Many investors prefer the homespun wisdom – known as Buffettology – of their hero Warren Buffett to the fancy investment banks of Wall Street, Tokyo and the City of London. Buffett, who resides in Nebraska and is fondly known as The Sage of Omaha, has spent his entire life investing for long-term growth in an eclectic mix of companies and industries, including insurance and financial services. In recent years he has placed big bets on American behemoths such as General Electric, IBM and, saving it from a wobbly moment during the financial crisis, Goldman Sachs. Buffett invests for the long-term: he declares his preferred investment horizon is forever.

His annual letter to shareholders in his holding company Berkshire Hathaway contains his wit and wisdom, often peppered with quotations from the Bible, and those shareholders loyally make a pilgrimage to Nebraska for the company's idiosyncratic annual meeting. A modest man, in spite of the many billions of dollars to his name, Buffett continues to acknowledge his mentors Benjamin Graham and David Dodd (authors and academics whom Buffett studied at Columbia Business School in the late 1940s); his overriding philosophy remains that "the basic ideas of investing are to look at stocks as business, use the market's fluctuations to your advantage, and seek a margin of safety."

"WHETHER WE'RE TALKING ABOUT SOCKS OR STOCKS, I LIKE BUYING QUALITY MERCHANDISE WHEN IT IS MARKED DOWN."

"IF A BUSINESS DOES WELL, THE STOCK EVENTUALLY FOLLOWS."

"IT'S FAR BETTER TO BUY A WONDERFUL COMPANY AT A FAIR PRICE THAN A FAIR COMPANY AT A WONDERFUL PRICE."

"I TRY TO BUY STOCK IN BUSINESSES THAT ARE SO WONDERFUL THAT AN IDIOT CAN RUN THEM. BECAUSE SOONER OR LATER, ONE WILL."

WARREN BUFFETT (B. 1930), BUSINESSMAN, INVESTOR, PHILANTHROPIST

There is no shortage of terminology to describe financial transactions and investment classes, but private equity has always been a puzzle. The phrase grew out of the fact that this part of the investment community uses private funds, or equity, often drawn from wealthy individual investors, to buy into growing companies.

PRIVATE EQUITY

↓
Private equity traditionally has large cash flows allowing for capital expenditures. Additionally, private equity firms generally know how to run organizations successfully. With huge costs, the need for long-term investment and huge potential profits, the healthcare industry is a popular option for this type of company.

However, as the industry has matured and the transactions have become more complicated, private equity investors have relied as much upon debt as equity to finance their acquisitions. In fact, the availability or unavailability of debt, in the form of bank loans, has tended to give the private equity industry its famously cyclical nature, with years of plenty often followed by lean periods.

In recent years, too, private equity investors have strayed beyond their normal hunting ground – the arena of privately held companies – into the public markets, sometimes investing their funds in companies already quoted on the stock market in what are called PIPE deals – private investment in public equity.

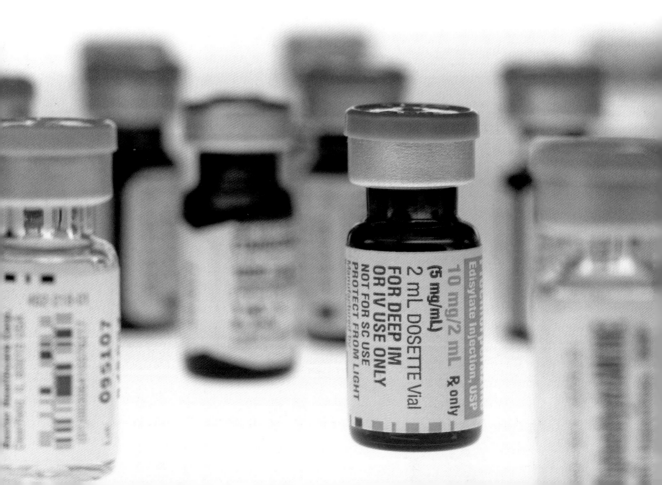

VENTURE CAPITAL

This is private equity's little brother, although it now comprises its own asset class and often makes up part of a balanced investment portfolio. Typically, venture capitalists invest relatively small sums (typically $250,000 to $1 million) in start-up or very early stage companies – the technology and biotech sectors are favorites – in return for sizeable equity stakes and often-onerous follow-on rights and other provisions. For entrepreneurs this is expensive fundraising, but often vital nevertheless to grow their company from its embryonic first stages. Venture capital is now a mature industry, with its own legends (Silicon Valley start-up investors such as Kleiner Perkins Caufield & Byers, which has invested in over 500 companies including Amazon and Google) often generating astronomical returns for its partners, but with many failures, too. A sub-set of the venture sector are so-called angel investors, who are mostly wealthy individuals who act alone or club together to make investments in small companies that catch their eye.

Private equity firms are built around their funds, which comprise long-term (typically seven-year) commitments from pension funds, wealthy families and individuals, who are known as the fund's limited partners or LPs. The private equity fund manager will put this money to work; building a portfolio of businesses that can eventually be sold on, generating returns for their investors.

Superior returns

While some of their investment parameters have blurred, private equity fund managers are still quite a recognizable breed. These firms tend to be tight-knit and entrepreneurial, with teams often drawn from investment banking or accounting backgrounds. They will tend to specialize in a particular industry sector, such as technology, healthcare, retail or services business and become expert in spotting fast-growing companies with strong management teams that need development capital.

The private equity industry has grown very considerably in recent decades, driven in large part by the superior returns that fund managers have been able to generate from their investors' equity. But this has often been achieved by loading their investments with unsustainable levels of debt. Debt is cheap (in that it does not involve giving away valuable shares in the company), but it must still be repaid. Where companies slow down and cannot generate enough cash to service their debt, the private equity model has often become overstretched.

Despite these large pitfalls, private equity has scored huge successes for some investors, particularly those fortunate enough to be in early on investments that have grown into industry leaders. As the industry has grown

↑
Institutional investors and wealthy individuals are often attracted to private-equity investments. Their money represents a source of funding for early-stage, high-risk ventures. Often, the money will go into new companies believed to have significant growth possibilities such as computer hardware and software developers.

it has divided into, broadly, three layers: at the top are large buyout funds, which may deploy several hundred million dollars of equity in a single transaction; these are followed by mid-market funds, which tend to target medium-sized companies and deals of between $50 million and $250 million and by venture capital funds (now an entire industry of its own), which spot much smaller deals in early stage companies and start-ups.

↓

Seen regularly on the red carpet at the Oscars, immortalized by TVs *Sex and the City* and the go-to shoes of the world's glitterati, Jimmy Choo shoes are one of private equity's greatest success stories. Tamara Mellon, one of a number of "seed corn" investors, put in $200,000 when she co-founded the company in 1996. In 2011, she sold her stake for $130 million as part of a $800 million deal.

THE PRIVATE EQUITY MACHINE

Private equity can seem like a game of pass-the-parcel. Companies invested in by one private equity fund are often sold to another, larger fund with deeper pockets to help it grow, before being sold on to another fund and so on. Take a fashion brand like Jimmy Choo. No Hollywood starlet would be seen without her Jimmy Choo shoes but, despite the money-can't-buy celebrity endorsement, the business also owes its iconic brand status to the private equity machine. The original Jimmy Choo, a Malaysian shoemaker who set up shop in London in 1996, raised seed capital from investors including Tamara Mellon (below), its longstanding creative director. In 2001 the business received further investment from Equinox Luxury Holdings. It was sold to Lion Capital for around $187 million in 2004. In 2007 Lion Capital sold it to TowerBrook Capital for $364 million and in 2011 TowerBrook sold it on to Labelux for $800 million. For Mellon, riding the private equity train for a decade had its compensations (her stake became worth around $130 million), but also its drawbacks: "I wouldn't necessarily recommend bringing private equity into your business," she told a conference after her exit, "because they don't put capital in for growth, they have short time frames. Their main goal is to show a return for their investors, not the long-term growth of your business."

Hedge funds have a not-wholly-deserved reputation as being the investment community's Wild West. The very first hedge fund was developed in the United States in 1949 by Alfred Winslow Jones, who pioneered the idea of hedging risk by guarding against a potential loss if the market moved away from an investor. Using borrowed money (leverage) and placing bets that both maximized upside and protected downside, Jones laid the foundations of the modern hedge fund industry.

HEDGE FUNDS

Jones' investment methods found their way into investment banks and, for the next forty-odd years, were the preserve of trading desks using both client and proprietary (i.e. home) funds to generate returns.

Coming in from the warmth

By the early 1990s, some of these traders were becoming restless. Talented equity, bond and derivatives traders (soon joined by all manner of other disciplines) began setting up shop on their own. These traders – now hedge fund managers – offered investors big-bank expertise and boutique-style service. They also offered risk, but – crucially – hedged or constrained risk.

↓

Most often set up as private investment partnerships, hedge funds are only open to a limited number of investors and require a very large minimum investment. Hedge funds aggressively manage a portfolio of investments and use advanced financial strategies with the goal of generating high returns. Here is a simple diagram that shows the entities typically involved in a hedge fund and what each contributes.

HEDGE FUND STRUCTURE

MANAGEMENT COMPANY (LLP)

HEDGE FUND (LP)

Cash

Cash

Trades

INVESTMENT PORTFOLIO

GENERAL PARTNER (LLP)
The General Partner has ultimate responsibility for the hedge fund; it will often be domiciled in an offshore jurisdiction such as the Cayman Islands, for tax purposes

Strategic direction

OUTSIDE INVESTORS (LIMITED PARTNERS)
Limited Partners are often high-net-worth individuals, family offices or institutional investors such as pension funds

QUICK REFERENCE

Volatility

Low volatility: low risk and steady returns.
Medium volatility: some risk in order to improve returns.
High volatility: higher risk in order to maximize returns.

For the adventurous investor, they represented a way to play the markets with potentially very large returns. As a result, from the 1990s until the early 2000s, the industry boomed, with some funds ballooning to manage billions of dollars apiece, often funded by wealthy families as well as by institutions seeking better-than-average returns, often from investments of high volatility.

This heady mix was not always to the taste of financial regulators and the hedge fund industry has often preferred to be off-grid and offshore, at the very least to protect its investors' returns. With maturity, it has, however, gradually come in from the warmth (most funds gravitated to the Caribbean tax havens such as the Cayman Islands for their administrative headquarters) and submitted itself to increased regulatory oversight.

Beating the market average

But what does a hedge fund do, exactly? The mystique that surrounds them is largely undeserved. In reality, most continue to trade bonds, equities and derivatives using a variety of industry-standard strategies. The best known of these are long-only, where a fund manager will buy securities in the hope they will rise in value; long-short, where a manager will also short some securities in the expectation they will fall; absolute return, where techniques are employed to ensure a positive return whatever the fluctuations of the market (in fact, very few absolute return funds always deliver positive returns); and, finally, multi-strategy – known as "multi-strat" – which combines all of a fund's best ideas.

What gives hedge funds their edge? Ultimately, it is their star managers' ability to generate so-called "alpha," winning strategies that beat the market average. Such star managers – an eclectic crowd of larger-than-life traders and reclusive mathematical geniuses – have become the stuff of legend. Particularly sought-after funds, which often charge fees of 2 percent of funds under management and hefty performance fees – rarely accept new investors, never advertise and prefer to keep out of the media spotlight.

BLACK BOXES AND HIGH FREQUENCIES

Sometimes, hedge fund trading really is rocket science. Specialist firms such as Winton Capital and Man Group have earned their reputations for successful investment strategies with the help of computer-driven trading algorithms. Often, those algorithms, which rely on huge datasets and armies of highly skilled mathematicians and physicists, have proved so effective that the fund managers simply let the computers get on with it: hence algorithmic – or Algo- trading, which finds and studies short, medium and long-term trends and places bets with mathematical precision. Similarly, other managers have developed high-frequency trading (HFT) strategies, which exploit miniscule and momentary differences in asset prices to generate profits. The billion-dollar question of whether such technology can beat the market is best answered by the words "it depends." Flash crashes tend to throw the algorithms off course, but over the long term they have proved remarkably successful.

GOING SHORT

This is a technique used by investors who think the price of an asset, such as shares or oil contracts, will fall. They borrow the asset from another investor and then sell it – known as shorting – in the relevant market. The aim is to buy back the asset at a lower price and return it to its owner, pocketing the difference. Naked short-selling is a version of short-selling, illegal or restricted in some jurisdictions, where the trader does not first establish that he is able to borrow the relevant asset before selling it on. Where hedge funds place unusually large short bets, the sheer weight of downward pressure on a stock or an index can make it fall; in times of stock market crisis – in the autumn of 2008, for example – some stock exchanges introduced temporary bans on short-selling to prevent the shares of banks and other financial institutions, which investors deemed precarious, from collapsing. These moves caused fierce debate, with some arguing that the market should be allowed to operate freely; others maintained that short-sellers are invariably also short-term players who should be discouraged.

←

A hedge fund's success depends on the ability of its managers to deliver high returns. Although there are limits to what they can do, hedge funds are not regulated. The implications of this are that an investor should be properly informed about a hedge fund, its strategy and the character of its management team before investing.

While there have been wild successes, there have also been spectacular failures when managers have miscalled the market. A prime (or more accurately sub-prime) example of the former came in 2007, when Paulson & Co, a New York-based hedge fund famously anticipated the credit crunch and made millions for its investors by betting against overvalued but low-grade mortgage securities. Others were less prescient. The ensuing credit crisis caused a huge shakeout in the hedge fund industry as returns plummeted, investors rushed to redeem their money (many found them frozen and had to pursue the fund managers through the courts) and funds folded. A gradual recovery in the market has been accompanied by a more cautious approach, demands for greater transparency and better regulation. But the risk – hedge funds' stock-in-trade – remains.

In every asset management pie chart, which contains segments labelled equities, bonds, cash and so on, there is invariably a chunk called alternatives, which covers a multitude of other assets, from property and land to art and vintage wines, racehorses, classic cars, jewelry and coins and stamps.

ALTERNATIVES

Historically, investors turn to these assets when the equity and bond markets are suffering from prolonged periods of uncertainty or volatility, and they are seeking tangible items that may hold and also appreciate in value. Although many such assets are uncorrelated to financial markets, they can still suffer dramatic swings in value and are by no means immune to their own shocks.

Rocking the foundations

Property remains the alternative asset of choice, particularly in Western economies although increasingly so in rapidly developing countries such as China and India. Property's long-term value trend is undeniably upward, notwithstanding some fairly severe corrections along the way. Ultimately, as with many alternative assets, property values depend on supply and demand although, unlike many, also on the availability of leverage – that is, mortgages or simply debt. Property investors have long been indulged by banks willing to lend against (essentially, take a charge over) bricks and mortar. But since the financial crisis of 2007–2009, during which many mortgagees defaulted, such debt has been harder to come by. The trickle-down effect of this will be felt for many years, as younger

→

Art sits at the top end of the investment spectrum. Unlike other investments, art has an advantage over other hard assets because it can be enjoyed and confers status – so called wall power – on its owner. Art is also increasingly viewed as a good way to diversify a portfolio, because although prices appear to move independently of stocks, they perform at least as well in the long term.

buyers at the bottom of the property ladder, who are essential to
stabilize the higher echelons of the market, are denied access.
As an asset class, property has moved from being a fairly sure-fire
long-term bet to being prone to boom and bust.

The attraction of collectables

Art has become an increasingly popular investment, at the very
least because it can be bought in one currency and, if the market
moves, sold on in another. So a Picasso, a Monet or a Warhol
acquired in New York in US dollars may be disposed of at auction
in London or Hong Kong in sterling or yen, making the most
of the relative strength or weakness of the latter currencies against
the dollar. Even for investors who do not play the currency game,
art has proven to be a good investment, with some indices that
track sales at auction showing double-digit annual returns in
recent years.

While the art world, particularly the rarefied world of
Impressionist, Modern and Contemporary art, has seen spectacular
gains, fine wine has also benefited from the surge of interest from
China, Japan and Russia. The most sought-after first growth
Bordeaux vintages have seen their values rocket year-by-year as
inherently limited supply meets more or less unlimited demand.
While some investors choose to build their own cellar collections,
others have flocked to specialist wine funds, set up to provide
returns from a broad spread of wines, which are traded by portfolio
managers just as they might otherwise do with equities or bonds.

↑
Property investments are
popular because some
investors believe they offer
stability, simplicity and a
good rate of return. No other
investment allows you to
purchase with other people's
money (the bank's). At the
top end, however, property is
incredibly expensive, like this
townhouse on Fifth Avenue
in New York, bought by
Carlos Slim (see page 34)
for $44 million in 2010.

7 MONEY AND BUSINESS

↑
Nearly 400 years ago, Avedis Zildjian founded a cymbal-manufacturing company in Istanbul. Around 1928, Avedis III decided to relocate to the USA to develop the business. Today the company – now the oldest in the world – is based in Norwell, Massachusetts. It controls 65 percent of the world's cymbal market and took in more than $50 million in revenues in 2011.

Though a fact easy to forget, money is not an end in itself, but rather a medium for the exchange of goods and services. This system of exchange, in which each product or service is given a perceived value agreed by both buyer and seller, is what we commonly call *business*. A complex dance is played out between buyers in search of good value and sellers seeking the maximum profit, and it is fair to say that this merry jig helps the world go round.

Business sectors

A business is any enterprise engaged in industrial, professional or commercial activity, either for-profit or not-for-profit. The organization itself may be in private hands or state-owned. However, in recent times the traditional public/private divide has blurred with the emergence of Public-Private Partnerships. Typically, in such an alliance a private enterprise works with a government body to complete a public project in return for future operating profits.

In our interconnected world, everyone from the individual selling sandwiches from a van to the CEO of the biggest supranational firm can claim a vital role in the global dance of business. Traditionally, the business world is considered to have three distinct sectors:

- **The primary sector:** dealing in natural resources and raw materials.
- **The secondary sector:** in which raw materials are manufactured into finished products.
- **The tertiary sector:** comprising all those businesses offering services, comprising everything from banking and insurance to cleaning.

Broadly, the primary sector remains most important in developing economies, while the tertiary sector has come to dominate the economies of developed nations. For instance, some three-quarters of employees in the USA now work in services.

↓

In the richest country (USA), most people work in the tertiary sector. In the poorest country (Nepal), most people work in the primary sector. In Brazil, the labor force is more evenly distributed between the three sectors.

COMPARISON OF EMPLOYMENT STRUCTURES

Source: BBC

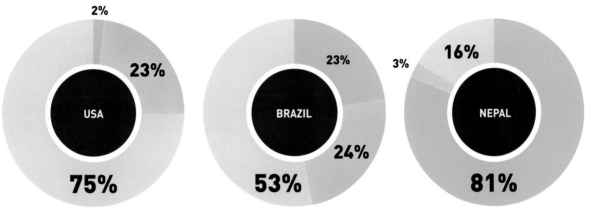

● PRIMARY
◍ SECONDARY
○ TERTIARY

Commerce can be conducted by individuals (sole traders) who are legally indistinct from their business, but many businesses choose to structure themselves as companies. While a sole trader can make a good living, the company has proved to be a far more efficient way of doing profitable, commercial business.

THE COMPANY

The word "company" derives from the French word *compagnie*, meaning "a group of soldiers." A company is a legally constituted body, distinct from the individuals within it. In the eyes of the law it is a legal personality, allowing more than one individual to act together under the banner of a single entity.

Thus a company can own property, enter into contracts and employ people. It can also sue other legal entities (though, of course, the company may be sued itself) and is subject to taxation. The owners, the management and the employees may change, but the company will live on unless it is formally wound up (undergoing insolvency). As such, companies offer a degree of security to those within it and those dealing with it.

Ownership and structure

Companies are typically owned by their members who, in the case of joint-stock companies, are the shareholders. This illustrates another great advantage of the company – the ability to pool together funds from multiple sources. In return for their investment, shareholders can expect to receive a dividend (a share of the company's profits divided in proportion to the number of shares owned). A company's members appoint a board of directors to run it. Sometimes members

Companies offer their employees and their suppliers and customers a degree of security. A company will continue to exist unless it is wound up. Employees will have a legal contract of employment, are likely to receive training, work experience and a regular wage; while suppliers and customers will be able to do business with the company for as long as they want.

JARGON BUSTER

Limited liability: if a company has limited liability, its shareholders are not responsible for any debts beyond the nominal value of their shareholding.

Unlimited liability: in a company with unlimited liability, shareholders lack the security of a limit to the level of company debt for which they are liable. This added risk can make it difficult to attract investors and generate new funds.

IN GOOD COMPANY

Businesses can be organized in all sorts of shapes and sizes, dependent on the nature of the sector they are in and in which markets they operate. Here are a few of the most familiar models:

Sole trader – an unincorporated business owned and run by an individual.

Partnership – a business with more than one owner, but is unincorporated, so that the partners are fully responsible for any debts incurred.

Family enterprise – where two or more members of the same family have a significant role in the management of the company. Family enterprises may be small-

scale (e.g. Gloomy & Sons, your friendly neighborhood undertakers), but not always. Several global giants, such as the Tata Group and Walmart, are to some degree family enterprises.

Multinational – a company that operates in more than one country, either through branches or subsidiary firms.

Social enterprise – an organization that employs commercial strategies, but that is less concerned with bottom-line profit than achieving a social objective.

Co-operative society – in which the business is owned by its employees or creditors.

will themselves sit on the board, but it is quite possible to have a company with thousands of shareholders, none of whom serve as directors.

Shareholders retain the right to sell their shares to other shareholders or to new buyers. If the company is doing well, the seller can expect to make a healthy profit, however, if not, they may want to rid themselves of stock of declining value.

↓

Most companies follow a broadly pyramidal structure, with very few people at the top but more the further down the organization you go. This graphic, for the imaginary Hungry Bunny Catering Services, gives an idea of how the classic top-down model works.

ORGANIZATION CHART

CEO

Director of Finance | Director of HR | Director of Marketing | Director of Operations

Accountancy Team | Payroll Team | HR Department | Marketing Manager (North) | Marketing Manager (South) | Catering Division | Transport Division | Logistics Division

Field Sales Teams | Field Sales Teams | Field Sales Teams | Field Sales Teams

A public company is one that has offered its securities (e.g. stocks, shares and bonds) for sale to the general public. These may then be traded on at least one stock exchange or in the "over-the-counter market" (a decentralized securities market not listed on an exchange). The daily trading of a public company's shares determines its value on a day-to-day basis. Public companies are not to be confused with publicly owned companies, which are corporations owned by a government.

PUBLIC COMPANIES

Usually, a new, small business remains privately held until it reaches a relatively advanced stage of profitability. At that stage it might consider floating to the public in order to secure large-scale capital investment and to get increased access to the debt markets. However, some companies choose never to do so – Goldman Sachs is a prime example of a global giant that has remained in private hands ever since its creation in 1869.

Getting there

Going public has profound consequences for a company's structures and operations. A public corporation is subject to greater regulatory scrutiny and is required to publish its financial statements for public inspection. Furthermore, its original owners and its management have their power diluted by the arrival of an army of new shareholders, each owning a part of the company and with voting rights for major decisions, such as the appointment of directors or the acceptance or rejection of a takeover.

↓
While we might think of America and Europe as the chief domains of the high rollers, the very biggest public companies of recent years have been developing in the Far East, reflecting the massive economic expansion of China – seen here in the rapidly evolving skyline of the Lujiazui financial district of Pudong, Shanghai.

THE DUTCH TULIP BUBBLE

The Dutch East India Company, formed in 1602, is generally regarded as the first company to issues shares to the public, enticing investors to provide capital for its international trading operations with the promise of huge returns. True to its word, the company delivered dividends over the following century at rates as high as 63 percent per year. However, the company was also at the center of the first great stock market crash in 1637. This was the year that the Dutch Tulip Bubble, driven by a pan-European craze for that particular flower, burst. The Dutch East India Company's ships had carried the bulbs between nations, helping to grow the bubble, but saw its share price slashed in the crash.

However, most shareholders are minority shareholders (holding less than 50 percent of a company's voting shares) and need to vote en masse to impose their will. In contrast, majority shareholders (owning over 50 percent of voting shares) can potentially dictate appointments and company strategy as they see fit.

A public flotation begins with an Initial Public Offering (IPO), with securities becoming available for sale at a set time and price. They can then immediately be traded, making IPOs an opportunity for investors to make quick profits and, just as quick losses. A public company may also look to secure an injection of fresh capital by making additional public offerings over time.

Though going public is a risk for both the company and for its investors, the rewards on offer when a flotation goes right are too good to resist for many businesses and speculators.

QUICK REFERENCE

Top five biggest IPOs of all time
As of 1 January 2013

1. AGRICULTURAL BANK OF CHINA
Sector: Finance
Date of IPO: July 7, 2010
Exchange: Hong Kong Stock Exchange/ Shanghai Stock Exchange
Value: US$19.23 billion

2. INDUSTRIAL AND COMMERCIAL BANK OF CHINA
Sector: Finance
Date of IPO: October 20, 2006
Exchange: Hong Kong Stock Exchange/ Shanghai Stock Exchange
Value: US$19.09 billion

3. NTT MOBILE
Sector: Communications
Date of IPO: October 22, 1998
Exchange: Tokyo Stock Exchange
Value: US$18.1 billion

4. VISA
Sector: Finance
Date of IPO: March 18, 2008
Exchange: New York Stock Exchange
Value: US$17.86 billion

5. AIA
Sector: Finance
Date of IPO: October 21, 2010
Exchange: Hong Kong Stock Exchange
Value: US$17.82 billion

▶ See also The Equities Markets (pages 94–5)

Mergers and Acquisitions (M&A) is the term used to describe the consolidation of two or more companies into a single entity. A merger sees two companies combining to form an entirely new company, while in an acquisition one company buys another and subsumes it into an existing structure. As a vital component of corporate life, many financial institutions have specially dedicated M&A departments.

MERGERS AND ACQUISITIONS

In reality, mergers are rarer than acquisitions, since usually a bigger company takes over a smaller one. Nonetheless, it can often be politically useful to describe an acquisition as a merger, which implies mutual cooperation and avoids damaging talk of buy-outs.

The driving principal behind all M&As is that two is better than one. In practical terms, a consolidation of two companies should do either or both of the following: improve efficiency and secure a greater market share. Improved efficiency (often described in quasi-mystical terms of synergies) can manifest itself in a number of ways:

- **Economies of scale** – the ability of a larger organization to produce goods and services more cheaply than a smaller one.
- **Job cuts** – saving money by losing excess staff.
- **Technology sharing** – combining specialist knowledge held within each of the original companies.
- **Increased market presence** – through the creation of a new super brand or by exploiting existing brands.

TYPES OF M&A

- **A horizontal merger** sees the coming together of two companies in direct competition, offering similar products and/or services in the same markets.
- **A vertical merger** is the joining of two companies where one is the supplier of the other (e.g. a toy manufacturer and a toy shop).
- **A market-extension merger** consolidates two companies selling similar lines but in different markets.
- **A product-extension merger** is between firms selling different but related products (e.g. pens and inks).
- **A conglomeration** occurs between businesses with no overlap in terms of product or market.

Another attraction is that a bigger company often has an inherent advantage in acquiring investment. And, of course, a consolidation of two companies previously active in the same commercial sector inevitably eliminates competition between them. For this reason, all mergers are subject to scrutiny from regulatory bodies to ensure that competition is not unfairly stifled or a monopoly created.

The M&A process begins with one company making a tender offer to the other's shareholders, often after having already bought shares of the target company in order to build position. In partnership with investment bankers, the acquiring organization will decide on an offer price and a deadline at which time shareholders must agree to or reject the sale.

At this stage, it will be clear whether or not an acquisition is hostile (i.e. whether it has the approval of the target company's management). The target company can either choose to accept the terms of a deal, negotiate for better terms, search out an alternative, preferred acquiring company ('a white knight') or attempt a defensive maneuver. For instance, the target company might activate a poison pill, allowing existing shareholders to buy new stock at rock-bottom prices to dilute the shareholding of the hostile bidder.

If a deal is accepted by the target business, the merger goes ahead either through a cash-for-stock transaction (with target shareholders paying tax on their windfall) or a stock-for-stock transaction (where share certificates are exchanged and no tax is payable).

Proceed with caution

Despite plentiful success stories, history suggests a large proportion – as many as two-thirds – of M&As are doomed to fail. This can be because expected synergies fail to materialize or an organization becomes so big that management loses control of it. There is also often an element of ego in M&As, with CEOs keen to flex their muscles before fully analyzing the implications of a deal. This is never more so than in times of apparent plenty.

Take the case of the Royal Bank of Scotland Group, which was briefly the largest company in the world in terms of assets and liabilities. In 2007 it paid €71.1 billion to acquire Dutch bank, ABN AMRO. Less than a year later, RBS had to accept a rescue package from the UK government. The FSA reported that losses and capital strain suffered as a result of the acquisition were a substantial contributing factor to RBS' vulnerability to failure.

QUICK REFERENCE

Top five biggest M&As of all time

As of 1 January 2013

1. VODAFONE AIRTOUCH (NOW VODAFONE GROUP) ACQUIRED MANNESMANN AG
Sector: Telecommunications
Date: 1999
Value: $202.8 billion

2. AMERICA ONLINE (AOL) ACQUIRED TIME WARNER TO FORM AOL TIME WARNER
Sector: Media
Date: 2000
Value: $164.7 billion

3. SHAREHOLDERS' ACQUISITION OF PHILIP MORRIS INTERNATIONAL
Sector: Tobacco
Date: 2008
Value: $107.6 billion

4. RBS ACQUIRED ABN-AMRO
Sector: Finance
Date: 2007
Value: $98.5 billion

5. PFIZER ACQUIRED PHARMACIA CORPORATION
Sector: Pharmaceuticals
Date: 2003
Value: $89.2 billion

Most successful businesses start small and grow, and a select few just keep on growing until they become global giants. Once a company has established itself in its local, regional and national markets, it must look beyond its borders to continue expanding. At the point when a business either bases its operations or offers its goods and services in more than one country, it becomes a multinational corporation.

GLOBAL COMPANIES

A quick look at *Forbes* magazine's annual list of the world's biggest companies provides ample evidence of the power of the multinational corporation. Of the ten biggest firms in 2012, only one was not a multinational – that was Fannie Mae, the US-based Federal National Mortgage Association. The biggest of the lot was the oil and gas conglomerate ExxonMobil, with annual revenues not far short of half a trillion dollars. If the company was a sovereign country, it would rank somewhere between the 20th and 30th largest economies on the planet, rubbing shoulders with the likes of Sweden and Norway.

Lower costs, higher profits

The potential financial benefits of going global are clear. Principally, it can open up vast new markets. A company operating in the US has a potential market of a little over 300 million customers. An EU firm can target about half a billion people.

There can also be the opportunity to take advantage of lower worker and production costs by moving operations into new territories. A clothing

↓

Multinational corporations, many of whom are involved in oil and gas production, represent one of the most significant forms of non-state activity on a global scale. The sheer size of many of these organizations means that they exert a significant economic and political influence around the world. It is estimated that there are more than 80,000 multinational corporations in existence and that they control 30 percent of the world's exports.

company that makes its products in Shanghai or Delhi will have significantly lower costs than if it manufactures in Sacramento or Dortmund. National governments keen to invite big business into their economies may also offer enticing tax breaks, promise to

BY EXPANDING INTO, SAY, INDIA AND CHINA, THE SAME FIRMS CAN ADD A FURTHER 2.5 BILLION TO THEIR THEORETICAL CUSTOMER BASES

ease their regulatory frameworks or provide other assistance to multinational companies. In return, the multinational offers the prospect of increased local employment (and thus local wealth), inward investment and inflows of foreign currency. Of course, the arrival of a global giant is not generally conducive to the success of small, local businesses, but that is a price that many governments are happy to pay.

There are challenges to overcome for a business operating in a new territory. They must adapt to the labor and business laws specific to that area, as well as recognize cultural differences. They may also be subject to higher transportation costs and rates of tax. However, a well-planned expansion offers potential for increased profits, which can be reinvested into research and development programs and further growth. In addition, by being able to take advantage of economies of scale, multinationals can ensure lower prices for the end consumer.

THE TASTE OF AMERICA, EVERYWHERE

Coca-Cola famously began life in the workshop of a chemist, Dr John Pemberton, in Atlanta, Georgia. First year sales came in at just nine bottles, but from these humble beginnings in the latter part of the 19th century, the brand has gone on to become the most famous and recognizable in the world.

Today the company operates in over 200 states and territories (except Cuba and North Korea), employs over 90,000 people and sells some 1.8 billion servings daily (equating to just over one serving for every five people on the planet). All of that translated into revenues of US$46.5 billion in 2011. That can get you an awful lot of soda.

Yet the Coca-Cola story throws up plenty of admonitions to other prospective multinationals.

While much of the world cannot get enough of Dr Pemberton's brew, for many others the company epitomizes the march of globalization. Indeed, modern anti-globalization protesters have adopted the phrase "Cocacolonization" as shorthand for a form of social colonization, a portmanteau apparently coined by French communists in the late 1940s.

In practical terms, the sheer size of the Coca-Cola Company ensures that it is intensely scrutinized by its critics. The product's identification with the spirit of America has brought its own set of problems too. In 2003 protestors in Thailand even emptied bottles of Coke into the streets in protest at the US-led invasion of Iraq.

The social enterprise is a relatively modern phenomenon, the phrase only significantly entering the academic lexicon in the 1970s. A social enterprise can broadly be described as an organization that follows a traditional market-based business strategy with the aim of meeting a social need. That is to say, it uses its profits for good.

SOCIAL ENTERPRISES

Unlike a traditional charity that relies on donations or grants, a social enterprise secures its funding in the competitive market but its profits, instead of going into the pockets of the organization's owners, are invested into social improvement by fulfilling a stated objective.

The model has revolutionized our understanding of the charitable sector in recent years and encompasses an enormous range of business types. A bakery set up to give employment opportunities to the socially disadvantaged (for instance, the disabled), a chocolate company established to ensure a fair deal for African cocoa-growers and a microfinance company providing funding to female Indian entrepreneurs may seem to have little in common, but all operate under the social enterprise banner.

Profit with a conscience

Social enterprises have some advantages over traditional for-profit businesses. They may be able to raise capital at lower than normal rates, owing to a willingness by backers to accept a lower monetary return. Some investors, for instance, take at least part of their reward in the form of satisfaction at the social good being done. A social enterprise may also be able to generate publicity more easily through the personal-interest angle of the work they do. Furthermore, there is evidence that a proportion of workers in the sector are prepared to work for below-market rates of pay. However, a social enterprise will ultimately fail if its underlying business model is not sound, as its ability to generate finance relies not on the generosity of donors, but on customers who want a fair exchange of goods or services for their money.

Nor is the model immune to criticism. Because of the lack of clarity as to precisely what constitutes a social enterprise, it is difficult for governments to regulate. For instance, what is a misuse of competitively earned profits in a social enterprise context? Similarly, how does one measure whether a social enterprise qualifies for tax incentives?

↓

Based in San Francisco, Sam Goldman (left) and Ned Tozun are among the world's leading social entrepreneurs. Their vision to provide clean, safe, bright light to some of the 1.6 billion people who do not have a reliable electricity supply has been a huge success. Their solar-powered d.light lanterns sell for as little as $7 and provide many hours of bright light from a single day's charge.

ONE STEP AT A TIME

Rated one of America's most inspiring companies by *Forbes* magazine, TOMS Shoes was set up in 2006 by Blake Mycoskie, a Texan entrepreneur. He had just returned from a trip to Argentina, where he had seen children suffering with a foot infection caused by walking barefoot. He decided to start selling to American consumers a traditional Argentinian farming shoe called the alpargata. The social enterprise twist was that for every pair of shoes he sold, he would donate another pair to an Argentinian child. His original idea for the business' name was the Shoes for Tomorrow Project, which evolved into TOMS Shoes. Within six years, the company had given a million pairs of shoes to children in 25 countries around the world, as well as starting a sister one-for-one operation dealing in eyeglasses.

Professor Aneel Karnani of the Stephen M. Ross School of Business at the University of Michigan has argued: "Companies should do well, citizens should do good. I think it's good to separate profit and not-for-profit organizations. Having the middle ground isn't useful. It opens up questions of governance: who is going to have the final say, the investor, the manager or the donor?"

But if proof were needed that the social enterprise is here to say, one need look no further than *Forbes* magazine, bible of the corporate world. In 2011, it produced its first annual list of the world's leading social entrepreneurs.

The recent downturn in the global economy and the blame many people have attached to finance and business has prompted increased interest in the social enterprise model. Outdated business practices are becoming a burden to many companies who are coming under pressure to adapt to new business models. This graphic indicates some of the difficulties that companies will have to overcome if they are to continue to appeal to their customers in what seems likely to be a completely new operating environment.

NEW BUSINESS MODELS

20TH-CENTURY OPERATING MODEL

- traditional business model
- hierarchy
- control
- profit at all costs
- economic downturn

21ST-CENTURY OPERATING MODEL

- collaboration and shared values
- use of technology
- environmental awareness
- accountability
- corporate social responsibilty

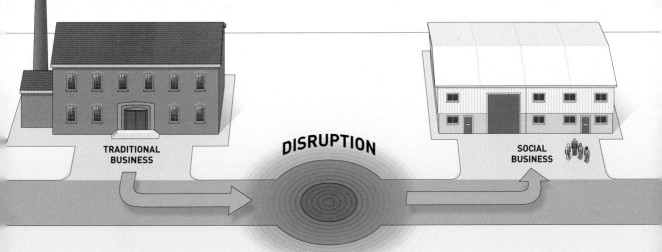

TRADITIONAL BUSINESS

DISRUPTION

SOCIAL BUSINESS

The secret to any business' success is really very basic: make sure your income is larger than your outgoings. The job of keeping a close eye on a business' finances falls to a band of much maligned professional number crunchers that we know as accountants. Their job, according to the American Institute of Certified Public Accountants, is "recording, classifying, and summarizing in a significant manner and in terms of money, transactions and events which are, in part at least, of financial character, and interpreting the results thereof."

ACCOUNTING

Mankind has spent at least 7,000 years developing the art of accountancy. Today, it encompasses two major arms:

■ **Management accounting:** providing relevant information to people within a business, such as owners and managers, in order to provide them with a broad overview of the business and guide their decision-making.

■ **Financial accounting:** for parties outside of the business itself, ranging from banks and the taxman to financial analysts and potential investors. Financial accounting is governed by Generally Accepted Accounting Principles (GAAP), a set of standardized rules and protocols in a particular jurisdiction.

"NEVER CALL AN ACCOUNTANT
A CREDIT TO HIS PROFESSION;
A GOOD ACCOUNTANT IS A DEBIT
TO HIS PROFESSION."
CHARLES LYELL (1797–1875), LAWYER

Crunching the numbers

At the heart of accountancy is the balance sheet, which is a record of the monetary values of a company's assets and liabilities at a given moment in time. A balance sheet is based on the equation:

assets = liabilities + equity

Assets are any economic resources owned by the company and might include cash, securities, land, property, capital equipment and monies due. A liability is any debt, whether secured or unsecured. Equity amounts to any claims the company's owners have on the company assets, based on their portion of ownership.

If the value of assets is greater than the value of liabilities, the excess is the net worth of the firm. This excess is treated as a liability to the owners/shareholders so that, by definition, the balance sheet always balances. However, should liabilities exceed assets, the company is technically insolvent.

While the balance sheet reflects a company's finances at a particular moment, the profit-and-loss account (or income statement) provides a record of a business' spending and its receipts over a defined period of time (typically over a month, a quarter or an entire financial year).

This statement lays out revenues over the period in question minus running costs (encompassing cost of goods sold, taxes, interest on loans and any other operating costs). The figure left after this subtraction (the bottom line of the statement) is the net profit for the period.

The third vital accounting tool is the cash flow statement. A company is solvent if it can meet its debts (including staff salaries) when they are due for payment. To do this, a firm needs working capital (capital not tied up in property and land or fixed assets). A cash flow statement calculates working capital by subtracting current liabilities from current assets.

To maintain a firm grasp of a company's finances, its management must regularly analyze each of these three major statement types.

GREEN STRIPE CLOTHING COMPANY
STATEMENT OF FINANCIAL CONDITIONS/BALANCE SHEET
At 31 December, 2012 and 2013

Assets	2012	2013
Cash	$4,550	$4,330
Accounts receivable	$4,300	$5,200
Inventory	$5,450	$6,900
Prepaid expenses	$1,050	$1,200
Current assets	$15,350	$17,630
Property, plant and equipment	$22,350	$24,900
Accumulated depreciation	($11,280)	($12,830)
Net of depreciation	$11,070	$12,070
Total assets	$26,420	$29,700

Liabilities	2012	2013
Accounts payable	$1,280	$1,530
Accrued expenses payable	$1,500	$1,800
Income tax payable	$180	$230
Short-term notes payable	$4,300	$4,500
Current liabilities	$7,260	$8,060
Long-term notes payable	$7,700	$8,000
Owners' equity		
Invested capital	$6,200	$6,500
Retained earnings	$5,260	$7,140
Total owners' equity	$11,460	$13,640
Total liabilities and owners' equity	$26,420	$29,700

↑

A balance sheet is a snapshot of a company's assets, liabilities and owners' equity at a specific point in time. It's called a balance sheet because the two sides balance out, as a company has to pay for all the things it has either by borrowing money from investors or getting it from the owners.

Bankruptcy is a legal status for businesses (and individuals) that are unable to pay their creditors. Bankruptcy laws differ significantly across the world. For instance, in the UK and Australia, only an individual may technically be declared bankrupt, while businesses are liquidated or go into administration. In the USA, however, the term is used to cover both individuals and businesses.

BANKRUPTCY

While going bankrupt is never welcome, it does offer an element of protection to the insolvent party that has not always existed. In ancient Greece, for instance, an insolvent person could find himself a debt slave of his creditor, forced (sometimes along with his family and any slaves of his own) to labor for up to five years to pay off his debt.

Not pain-free

There are two fundamental reasons for a modern business becoming insolvent, although it may come about as the result of a myriad of causes ranging from professional negligence to a market collapse or plain old bad luck. Firstly, a company may have insufficient assets to carry on trading; secondly, it may be suffering from illiquidity (insufficient cash flow).

The process involves the debtor or a creditor filing a legal petition. The debtor's total assets are then evaluated and used to repay a proportion of the debtor's obligations. Under some legal systems, certain "preferential creditors" are prioritized over others. Typically, these will include a company's employees and the tax authorities. Once the process is complete, the debtor is relieved of any further obligation for the debts incurred prior to going bankrupt.

However, going bankrupt is by no means a pain-free way to wipe the slate clean. Securing credit in the future becomes much harder, while in many

↓

American Airlines filed for Chapter 11 bankruptcy in November 2011, but on 30 September 2012 set an all-time record for company revenues – how can this be? In the US the Chapter 11 bankruptcy process enables insolvent companies to continue conducting normal business operations over a designated time period while they restructure their debt, costs and other obligations.

HENRY FORD – DRIVEN TO BANKRUPTCY

Though bankruptcy still comes with a stigma, some of the greatest business brains in history have been ensnared by insolvency at one time or another. Among them is Henry Ford. By 1899, he had secured backing to set up the Detroit Automobile Company, but had yet to get on top of his designs or to implement the production processes that would make his fortune. Having seen just 20 vehicles roll out of the factory, the business was declared bankrupt in 1901. It wasn't until 1903, when he established the Henry Ford Company, that his luck began to change. His net worth at death in 1947 has been estimated at $188 billion at today's values.

↓

Not much is certain on this planet (only death and taxes, according to Benjamin Franklin), but the commercial world is at least predictable in its unpredictability, and the truth is that plenty of companies eventually slide down the greasy pole of commerce and are declared bankrupt. This graphic shows that in the US there have been somewhere between 30,000 and 50,000 bankruptcies each year since the mid-1990s.

countries a director of a bankrupt business is disqualified from holding another directorship for a period of time.

Historically, bankruptcy legislation focused on liquidation – winding up an insolvent business and disposing of its remaining assets in order to pay off creditors. But in more recent times, the emphasis has increasingly been on restructuring a business' finances so that its debt obligations may be met, but the business can continue to operate with a view to getting back on its feet. This path – most readily taken where insolvency is down to cash-flow problems rather than a lack of assets – is often known as "going into administration."

The US bankruptcy model clearly reflects the adoption of new approaches, offering provision for two major corporate bankruptcy types – Chapter 7, a straightforward liquidation; and Chapter 11, a business rehabilitation.

US CORPORATE BANKRUPTCIES 1994–2012

Source: Amercian Bankruptcy Institute

Year	First quarter	Second quarter	Third quarter	Fourth quarter	Total
1994	13,858	13,617	12,878	12,021	52,374
1995	13,123	12,216	12,648	12,891	51,878
1996	13,388	13,992	13,198	12,887	53,465
1997	13,831	13,991	13,456	12,653	53,931
1998	12,410	11,552	10,346	9,888	44,196
1999	9,180	10,378	8,986	9,020	37,564
2000	9,456	9,243	8,211	8,413	35,472
2001	10,005	10,330	9,537	10,013	40,099
2002	9,775	9,695	9,433	9,500	38,540
2003	8,814	9,331	8,446	8,294	35,037
2004	10,566	8,249	7,574	7,778	34,317
2005	8,063	8,736	9,476	12,798	39,201
2006*	4,086	4,858	5,284	5,586	19,695
2007	6,280	6,705	7,167	7,985	28,322
2008	8,713	9,743	11,504	12,901	43,546
2009	14,319	16,014	15,177	15,020	60,837
2010	14,607	14,452	13,957	13,030	56,282
2011	12,376	12,304	11,705	11,149	47,806
2012	10,998	10,374	9,248	11,388	42,008

Quarterly business filings by year (1994–2012)
(* Change in law responsible for drop in 2006)

The growth of the Internet has brought about a genuine revolution in business, opening up previously unimaginable avenues for making money. Few serious businesses, from banks to booksellers, do without an Internet presence today and virtually anything you care to think of can be bought or sold online. The Internet has not only made it easier to carry out traditional business, but has created brand new businesses of its own. High-tech companies developing software to power the Internet are themselves among the biggest businesses in the world, while others – like social networking sites – simply couldn't exist without the Web.

THE INTERNET

Since the appearance of the first web browser in 1990 (Tim Berners-Lee's World Wide Web), the Internet's growth has been exponential. By 1995 it had just under 40 million users who were able to view some 23,500 websites. Today there are over 2 billion users and almost 300 million websites, with numbers rising all the time. Naturally enough, where people mass together, commerce soon follows and so it has proved in cyberspace.

Lessons learned

The first sign of the impending Internet boom that would redefine the commercial world came in 1995 with the IPO of Netscape, a youthful technology company that had created what was then one of the dominant Internet browsers. On the first day of trading, its share price increased from $28 to $75, giving the company a market value of nearly $3 billion. For the rest of the 1990s Internet businesses of varying pedigree and quality were traded for ever-more inflated figures in what became known as the dot-com bubble. Then the dawn of the new century saw the bubble burst. Companies previously valued in terms of hundreds of millions of dollars (even though many of them had never turned an annual profit) folded or saw their values slashed virtually overnight. Belatedly, the lesson was learned that in cyberspace, just as in the real world, a business needs a solid base and a sensible plan for growth. Nonetheless, the phenomenon of the Internet remains in its infancy and it can often be difficult to

↓
This is a visual representation of Internet traffic around the world in one day. It traces the millions of routes along which data can travel and pinpoints the hubs receiving the most traffic. Internet giants such as AT&T and Google manage the most heavily used networks, which appear here as glowing yellow orbs. The different color routes indicate traffic from different continents.

E-COMMERCE

E-commerce is the phrase used for the buying and selling of products via the Internet. It is the sort of old-fashioned business that once would have taken place in a shop or market but now happens in cyberspace. Of all the many opportunities for moneymaking that the Internet offers, it is a distinctly traditional model. Yet it underpins two of the three largest Internet businesses in the world, Amazon (the largest) and eBay (Google completes the top three).

Amazon, which made its name as a retailer of books, but now markets everything from clothing to DIY products, began operating in 1995. In 2011 the company reported profits of more than $650 million. eBay, meanwhile, represents for some the ultimate e-commerce experience: if you have something to sell, eBay's auction facility will find you a buyer if there is one out there and will establish the true market price of your goods. In 2008, it was reported that two Virginian sisters sold a cornflake the shape of Illinois (in a certain light, at least) for a cool, $1,350.

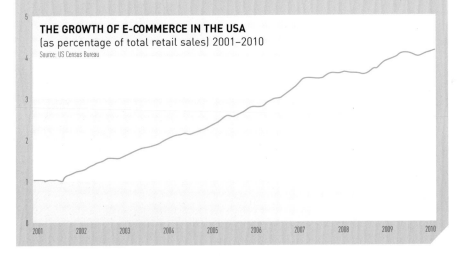

THE GROWTH OF E-COMMERCE IN THE USA
(as percentage of total retail sales) 2001–2010
Source: US Census Bureau

predict the long-term future and viability of emerging Internet business models. The troubled IPO of Facebook (see page 94) provided a timely reminder that in this nascent commercial environment, no one really knows what tomorrow holds, let alone next year or the next decade.

But for many traditional businesses, the Internet offers clear advantages. Principally, it allows companies to connect with vast numbers of new customers, regardless of the physical distance or time difference between them. It can also negate the need for expensive overheads such as real-world premises, while online payment technology allows for safe and secure financial transactions to happen with just a few clicks of a mouse.

And while the Internet has already brought about fundamental changes to the way the world does business, it may yet usher in other changes not yet foreseen or dreamt.

←
The growth in the volume of e-commerce since the turn of the 21st century has been nothing short of astonishing. For example, in the USA Internet sales represent at least 5 percent of the total of retail sales and are worth almost $160 billion a year. Although the annual percentage increase has been slowing down in the last few years, this steady rate of growth is predicted to continue for the foreseeable future. However, m-commerce, with customers using mobile devices to purchase goods, is expected to be the next challenge for traditional retailers.

"LABOUR WAS THE FIRST PRICE, THE ORIGINAL PURCHASE – MONEY THAT WAS PAID FOR ALL THINGS. IT WAS NOT BY GOLD OR BY SILVER, BUT BY LABOUR, THAT ALL WEALTH OF THE WORLD WAS ORIGINALLY PURCHASED."
ADAM SMITH (1723–90), POLITICAL ECONOMIST

8 THE SCIENCE OF MONEY

↑

The objective of economics is to use mathematical observations, calculations and reasoning to improve the welfare and well-being of society. In order to do so, an economist also has to study the social environment and human behavior.

For numismatists, the study of money is all about collecting notes and coins. As a discipline it gives us undoubted insights into how past cultures operated and how currency itself has developed, yet it barely scratches the surface of how money and society interrelate at a fundamental level. For that, we need to turn to that much broader subject: economics.

But what is it that economists actually do? The brief answer is that they study the production and distribution of wealth. Mankind has unlimited desires and needs but limited resources to try and meet them. Economics seeks to understand how humans go about making rational decisions to fulfil their wants given this scarcity. Economics is thus a social science, since it examines how human society functions and how individuals operate within it. On a practical level economics involves the generation, collection, study and analysis of both quantitative and qualitative data about the social environment to recognize trends, make predictions and arrive at conclusions that will benefit society.

THE SCARCITY SCALES

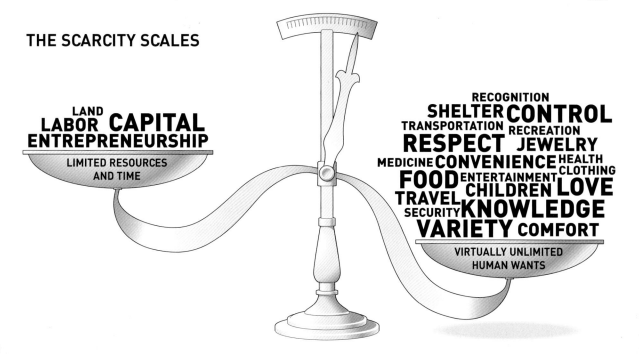

LAND
LABOR CAPITAL
ENTREPRENEURSHIP
LIMITED RESOURCES
AND TIME

RECOGNITION
SHELTER CONTROL
TRANSPORTATION RECREATION
RESPECT JEWELRY
MEDICINE **CONVENIENCE** HEALTH
CLOTHING
FOOD ENTERTAINMENT
TRAVEL CHILDREN LOVE
SECURITY **KNOWLEDGE**
VARIETY COMFORT
VIRTUALLY UNLIMITED
HUMAN WANTS

The dismal science

For as long as society has functioned, it has been challenged by limited resources and some of the greatest minds of the ancient world expounded their thoughts on how best to employ and share out what is available to us. But economics as a modern academic discipline traces its roots to a pivotal work by Adam Smith published in 1776 – *An Enquiry into the Nature and Causes of the Wealth of Nations*.

Today, economics is often subdivided into two broad streams: micro- and macro-economics. Microeconomics looks at the decision-making of small units within the economy (e.g. individuals and specific businesses), while macroeconomics looks at how all these micro-units act collectively (e.g. as a country or at the supranational level).

The modern economist must be master of an array of academic disciplines – from mathematics and computing to history, politics and psychology – as they seek to understand why economies work as they do and attempt to forecast how they will operate in the future. If proof were needed of the difficulty of this job, the economic crisis that overcame the planet in 2008 neatly illustrates how our understanding of economics is incomplete and constantly evolving, with real life often throwing up more questions than answers. Indeed, as long ago as the mid-19th century, the historian, Thomas Carlyle, described economics as the "dismal science."

↑
Scarcity is a basic economic problem that arises because people have unlimited wants, but limited resources. It occurs when people want more of something than is readily available. In economics, scarcity forces people to make choices, as everyone cannot have everything. Without scarcity, an economy cannot exist.

"THE STUDY OF MONEY, ABOVE ALL OTHER FIELDS ... IS ONE IN WHICH COMPLEXITY IS USED TO DISGUISE TRUTH OR TO EVADE TRUTH, NOT TO REVEAL IT."
JOHN KENNETH GALBRAITH (1908–2006), CANADIAN ECONOMIST

As we have seen, underpinning economics is the concept of scarcity – the limits on our resources set against our unlimited wants. But what are these resources of which we have a finite amount?

■ **Labor** (human time and work).
■ **Natural resources** (raw materials).
■ **Capital** (man-made materials needed for the production of other goods, such as buildings and machinery).

ECONOMICS –
SOME BASICS

So the economist is left to ponder these three fundamental questions, as illustrated below:

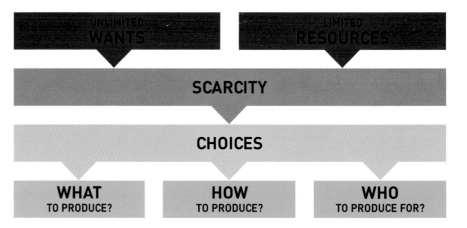

Different responses to these questions leave us with two diametrically opposed economic models for society. The first of these is the market economy, in which the market is left to determine the allocation and pricing of goods and resources. This is essentially a self-regulating model in which, according to its advocates, the amalgamation of decisions made by individual consumers and suppliers keeps the economy in long-term balance.

The alternative model is the command (or planned) economy, in which the government determines the allocation and distribution of resources. This was the model, now discredited, used by the Soviet Union. Command economies are prone to regular surpluses and shortages because of the inability of governments to accurately track how much of a product or service is required at any one time.

In reality, most of the world's economies inhabit a position somewhere between the extremes of these models, with much of the developed world inclined toward free markets.

How the market works

All market economies are based on the concept of supply and demand. Demand is the amount of a product or service that buyers want at a certain price, while supply is the amount that producers will make available at a given price.

Every economic decision that a consumer makes takes account of utility (the amount of benefit to the consumer) and comes with an opportunity cost. Opportunity cost is the value of what the buyer must give up in order to have something else – buy a pair of shoes and the opportunity cost might be the coat you could have had instead.

As a rule, when the price is high, fewer people will demand a product, since the higher the price, the greater the opportunity cost for the consumer. If the price of shoes goes up so that the opportunity cost to the consumer is now a coat and a pair of gloves, they will be less inclined to buy.

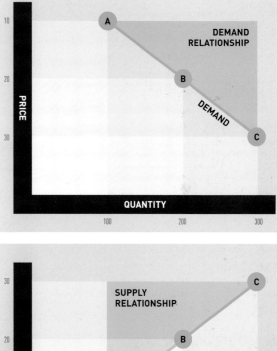

Source: Investopedia.com

SADLY, MARKET EQUILIBRIUM RARELY EXISTS OUTSIDE OF THE THEORETICAL

Conversely, the higher the price, the more will be supplied, as there is greater profit to be made for the supplier by selling more at a higher price. As these graphics (right) illustrate, supply and demand curves are inversely proportional to each other. In the Demand graph, there is a downward slope where the quantity of demand declines as price increases. In the Supply graph, the curve is upward as supply increases in proportion to the rise in price.

The point at which the supply and demand curves cross – the equilibrium – is when the volume of a product or service being supplied is exactly the same as that being demanded (see graphic on page 158, top). The extent to which demand or supply moves as a direct result of price change is known as elasticity. In general, a product deemed essential (such as a food staple) will be less elastic than a luxury, since consumers have no choice but to buy an essential regardless of price.

If real life worked like this, economics would be simple. Alas, markets are much more nuanced. For example, there may be a spike in demand for heavy coats in a cold snap, allowing for a rise in price. But it would be a foolish supplier who puts all his investment into his coats if the cold snap is due to end in a week.

↑
The relationship between supply and demand is the backbone of a market economy. The law of demand (top) – a downward slope – says that the higher the price of a good, the lower the quantity demanded. The law of supply (above) – with an upward slope in inverse proportion – says that the higher the price the greater the quantity supplied.

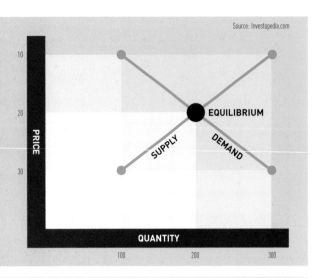

Source: Investopedia.com

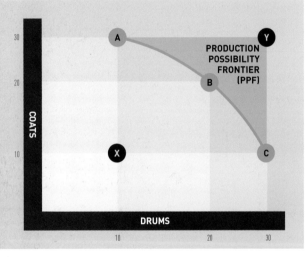

The Production Possibility Frontier

This tool is used to show the point at which an economy is producing goods and services at the optimum level. This is because all economies must decide how best to utilize their scarce resources.

The instrument is best explained by imagining an economy that produces only two goods. In this case, coats and drums. On the diagram (below left), points A, B and C show how in order to produce more of one of these items, resources must be diverted away from production of the other.

The more coats that are produced, the less drums will come off the production line, and vice versa. The curve that goes through points A, B and C is the Production Possibility Frontier. Along this arc is where an economy aims to be, but very few manage it. Point X shows a point at which an economy's resources are not being used to their full potential (the normal state of affairs), while point Y shows a level of output unachievable under current circumstances but that may be possible if more resources or improved means of production become available.

It is up to the leaders of an economy to decide where exactly upon the PPF arc they should be – that is to say, which combination of production is most suitable to the society's needs. Should the country in this example have a particularly harsh climate, its leaders may well decide that resources are best directed toward producing coats. However, if it is an island paradise with a penchant for carnivals, drums may be a more worthwhile use of scarce resources.

Specialization

While most nations can produce more than drums and coats, none are able to produce everything they need, nor would it be efficient to do so. Most economies practice specialization. Imagine that two countries (which we shall call Cowland and Sheepland) both want coats and drums. Sheepland has plentiful herds of sheep, providing wool for coats, so specializes in coat production. Cowland has lots of cows, providing hides perfect for drums, so focuses on that. Sheepland is said to have a comparative advantage over Cowland in the production of coats, while Cowland has a comparative advantage in drum-making. So each country concentrates on what it can do best and imports whatever else it needs from the other. In this way, the theory of comparative advantage underpins trading.

↑
If the market is working perfectly, the economy is in equilibrium, marked by the intersection of the supply and demand curves (top). However, this is rarely achieved. The PPF, meanwhile, is used to establish the best allocation of production resources. In this example, Cowland will strive to be on the arc close to the drums axis while Sheepland will be located much closer to the coats axis.

Ask three different economists a question, and you'll get five different answers. So goes the old adage. A number of economists have presented theories and created models to explain the functioning of the economy as a whole, as a result of which they have changed the world for all of us – whether we know it or not.

GIANTS OF ECONOMICS

Here we take a look at some of the leading figures who have developed streams of economic thought, starting with the godfather of the discipline, Adam Smith.

Adam Smith (1723–90)

A professor of moral philosophy and a leading figure of the Scottish Enlightenment, Smith's magnum opus, *The Wealth of Nations*, is widely regarded as the founding document of modern economics. In it, Smith espoused a view that competition and the self-interested pursuit of profit brings about general prosperity. He described how constraints placed on firms and individuals by competition actually cause them to behave in ways that are ultimately socially beneficial. Smith nonetheless acknowledged that governments have a vital role to play too, providing certain essential goods and services and fostering genuine competition in the market. He remains a highly influential figure, particularly in organizations such as the London-based policy institute supporting the free market, The Adam Smith Institute.

Essential Work: *An Inquiry into the Nature and Causes of the Wealth of Nations* (1776).

Adam Smith

David Ricardo (1772–1823)

A British businessman, Ricardo made a fortune from dealing government securities, but he was also one of the great economic thinkers of his age. He developed various important ideas, among them the suggestion that the value of a commodity is linked to the labor required to produce it (an idea later taken up by Marx). He also set out theories of diminishing returns and noted the impact of money supply on inflation.

However, his most famous contribution was the discovery of comparative advantage (where one person/business/country can produce a good more cheaply than another – see opposite). Arguing that international trade was a boon to all nations, he did much to undermine mercantilism, which extolled the advantages of exports over imports in order to increase national wealth. Despite the unsustainability of a system in which everyone only wants to export, mercantilism also fed into theories of colonialism where trade is to the advantage of the colonizer at the expense of the colonized. Ricardo's work helped pave the way for the laissez-faire trade models that dominated the 19th century.

Essential Work: *On the Principles of Political Economy and Taxation* (1817).

David Ricardo

Thomas Malthus

Thomas Malthus (1786–1834)

A professor of history and political economy at the East India Company College, (now known as Haileybury) in Hertfordshire, Malthus lived in an era when the dominant orthodoxy was that mankind could grow and improve almost endlessly. Malthus came to somewhat less optimistic conclusions. He argued that populations continue to grow until restrained by, for instance, war, famine, natural disaster or illness and preventative checks such as birth control. The "Malthusian problem" is that as population grows faster, land becomes increasingly unable to support this expansion so that per capita wealth decreases until it hits the subsistence level. He attempted to show through historical precedent that a part of the population is always poor and unhappy. As he put it: "The power of population is indefinitely greater than the power in the earth to produce subsistence for man."

Malthus has remained a controversial figure, his influence evident in the works of, for instance, Keynes and even Charles Darwin, who saw echoes of his theories of natural selection in Malthus' writings.

Essential Work: *An Essay on the Principle of Population* (1798).

Karl Marx (1818–83)

Karl Marx

German-born, Marx's theories were so influential that Marxist doctrine was adopted by vast swathes of the world during the 20th century, often with devastating consequences. Without Marx, for instance, there could have been no Soviet Union, though it is to be argued just how Marxist the USSR was in practice.

There is a distinction between Marxism as a political position and Marxian theories of economics. Marxism sees human history through the lens of struggle between the labor force (the proletariat) and capitalists (the owners of capital, known as the bourgeoisie). He believed that the bourgeoisie were intent on taking control of the factors of production at the expense of the proletariat, and espoused that long-term economic growth could only be secured by ending private ownership of the economy. Marxian economics, meanwhile, focuses on how labor and economic development are interconnected. In *Das Kapital*, he posits that labor is exploited in pursuit of profit since the new value created by workers beyond their own labor-cost is taken by the capitalist. This, in broad terms, locks workers into a cycle of poverty while market competition ultimately fosters monopolies. In the end, Marx argued, the capitalist society will be undermined by under-consumption and the proletariat will rise up.

Marx's philosophy foresaw the arrival of the socialist state (essentially a workers' democracy) to be replaced ultimately by communism (a classless and stateless social order). His views are in many aspects largely discredited, with the major communist experiments of the last century having either failed (the USSR) or at least succumbed to heavy market influence (China).

Essential Works: *The Communist Manifesto* (1848; written with Friedrich Engels) and *Das Kapital* (1867–94).

John Maynard Keynes (1883–1946)

A British economist widely credited as the founding father of modern macroeconomics. He argued that governments should use fiscal and monetary policy to smooth the impact of inevitable contractions and expansions in the business cycle. For instance, governments should employ economic stimuli in times of recession.

Much of his most important work was carried out in the shadow of the Great Depression in the 1930s. He argued that the crisis was the result of reduced spending on goods and services, a problem that monetary policy (i.e. government attempts to control the money supply) had failed to address. He proposed that growth needed to be prompted by fiscal policy – the government should undertake projects for which they buy up goods and services, kickstarting the entire economy.

His arguments not only won favor with governments around the world during the 1930s, but underpinned the rise of the post-Second World War welfare-state model. After a period spent in the relative wilderness, Keynesian economics re-emerged in a pivotal role in discussions as to how to overcome the global financial crisis of the 21st century.

Essential Work: *The General Theory of Employment, Interest and Money* (1936).

John Maynard Keynes

Milton Friedman (1912–2006)

A US economist and statistician, Friedman was a professor at the University of Chicago (where he became the leading figure of the Chicago school of economics) and won the 1976 Nobel Prize for Economics. He believed in the power of free-market capitalism, arguing that markets maintain stability as long as the supply of money remains fairly constant. He described how price inflation was intrinsically linked to the money supply and laid the blame for the prolonged Great Depression with monetary tinkering by government.

His teachings were widely perceived as the antithesis of those of John Maynard Keynes. His work gave rise to the monetarist movement, which argued that governments should focus on keeping prices stable, managing monetary policy principally to achieve this goal. By the 1980s, he seemed to have won the ideological battle with Keynes, his theories finding favor, for instance, with the governments of Ronald Reagan in the USA and Margaret Thatcher in the UK. Indeed, Friedman came out of retirement to serve as an economic advisor to Reagan. One magazine described him as "the most influential economist of the second half of the 20th century ... possibly of all of it."

Essential Works: *A Theory of the Consumption Function* (1957); *Capitalism and Freedom* (1962); *A Monetary History of the United States* (1963).

Milton Friedman

Money supply (sometimes called money stock) is all the monetary assets within the economy at a given moment – this normally means all cash (notes and coins) plus bank deposits repayable on demand. For a more detailed breakdown, see M is for Money on page 71.

MONEY SUPPLY

Since commerce is reliant on money, the amount of money in the system has an enormous influence on economic health. Should there be an influx of new money, interest rates go down, as there is more money in the hands of consumers and investors. This, in turn, spurs economic activity, with consumers buying more goods and services and suppliers using their wealth to buy raw materials to meet increased demand. Increased economic activity means higher employment, creating more workers with wages to spend on still more goods and services.

If that all sounds too good to be true, it is. Such economic growth in turn ushers in rising prices as demand grows. That, by another name, is inflation, to which lenders respond by increasing interest rates, prompting consumers to slow their spending. And so the cycle begins again. On the other hand, a reduction in

MONEY BREEDING MONEY

There is a proverb that says money breeds money, a sentiment to which central banks cling when they pump new money into the economy. Should a central bank release, say, $100 into the system, the expectation is that an amount much greater than this is eventually added to the money supply as a result of something called the Multiplier Effect.

The Multiplier Effect occurs as a result of bank lending. Its extent is dependent on the percentage of any deposit that banks are legally required to keep in reserve in order to be able to pay depositors on demand. If the reserve requirement is 10 percent, this means that for every $100 deposit a bank receives, it must keep $10 in reserve, but may loan out the other $90. The customer who receives a $90 loan from Bank A then deposits it in Bank B. Bank B keeps $9 (10 percent) in reserve, but loans the remaining $81 to a new customer. That customer then deposits the $81 in Bank C. Bank C keeps $8.10 (10 percent) in reserve but has $72.90 available to loan. And so the cycle goes on, until the initial $100 injection from the central bank creates up to $1,000 in new deposits.

To calculate the maximum value of new money supply (discounting the fact that some money will not be re-deposited along this path), we simply divide the amount of the initial injection by the reserve rate. The lower the reserve rate, the greater the Multiplier Effect. So in the example we are using, the central bank's $100 is divided by 0.1 (the 10 percent reserve rate), giving a potential increase in the money supply of $1,000. If the reserve rate is reduced to 5 percent, the increase in money supply is potentially $100/0.05 = $2,000. Up the rate to 20 percent (100/0.2) and the figure decreases to $500.

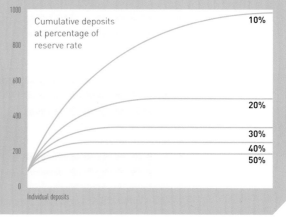

FRACTIONAL RESERVE LENDING AT VARYING RATES
$100 US dollars

Cumulative deposits at percentage of reserve rate

10%
20%
30%
40%
50%

Individual deposits

the money supply (or a decline in its growth) causes economic activity to reduce, with resultant disinflation (reduced inflation) or even deflation (falling prices).

Money supply also influences trade. Increasing the money supply may be seen as reducing the value of money. If there is $100 of a currency in the economy, each unit has a hundredth of the buying power. Double the money available to $200 and the buying power of each unit is halved. This is bad news for importers, as their money buys less, but good news for exporters, since their exports become cheaper and thus more attractive to potential buyers.

↑
This graph shows the potential expansion of an initial injection of $100, depending on the size of the reserve rate.

Who controls the supply?

Money supply is usually governed by a country's central bank: by printing more money (generally considered a bad idea as it rarely addresses underlying economic problems and can cause hyperinflation), by buying or selling government bonds (see Printing Money on page 45 and Central Banks on page 69), by adjusting the reserve requirement of banks (the money banks must keep in reserve) or by changing interest rates (raising it is likely to discourage spending, while a decrease will spur it).

Inflation – a sustained rise in the general level of prices – is a largely unloved phenomenon, but when maintained at a moderate level is a sign of a healthily functioning economy. As long as your wages or pensions are going up at a comparable rate, you have little to worry about. The problems really start if inflation gets out of control or, potentially equally damaging, if the economy falls into a deflationary cycle.

INFLATION AND DEFLATION

Inflation is most commonly measured on an annual basis and provides us with a snapshot of the purchasing power of the money in our pocket. Say you have a $10 bill. In Year 1 it can buy you a pizza from your favorite Italian restaurant. If inflation is at 3 percent, by the following year the pizza will cost $10.30. Your $10 bill can no longer buy you a whole pizza – its purchasing power has decreased. This is why there is no future in hiding your cash under the bed. Instead, wily economists will try to invest their spare money at an interest rate that outstrips inflation. That way, their cash keeps (or actually increases) its purchasing power.

The interest rate connection

The dangers of uncontrolled inflation are manifold. High inflation makes people nervous, causing them to rein back economic activity. This problem is especially acute for those who have fixed incomes (such as certain types of pension), who see the value of their money fall and do not have the opportunity to increase their income to compensate. In addition, inflation out of kilter with international norms renders a country's exports more expensive.

Disinflation – a decline in the inflation rate – can, meanwhile, be a warning sign that an economy is flatlining. As consumers, we might like the idea of lower prices, but the reality is that if sustained they result in reduced profits for businesses, declining industry, wage reductions, unemployment and loan defaults.

Many governments strive to keep control of inflation by tweaking interest rates. The mechanism by which this works is in theory quite simple. If interest rates

↓
This chart shows you how the pizza price will increase over time assuming the inflation rate remains at a constant 3 percent (something that does not happen in real life).

$10 DOLLARS WORTH OF PIZZA

VALUE TODAY	AFTER 1 YEAR	AFTER 5 YEARS	AFTER 10 YEARS	AFTER 20 YEARS
$10.00	$10.30	$11.59	$13.44	$18.06

are high, borrowing is more expensive and so consumers are more careful about spending their money. With demand low, prices stay low and inflation is kept in check. On the other hand, lower interest rates promote consumer spending, with prices rising in response to greater demand. The trick is to keep interest rates at a level where consumer spending is sufficient to keep both the economy buoyant and inflation within acceptable boundaries.

JARGON BUSTER

Basket of goods: a set of goods and services used to track annual inflation changes.

Demand-pull inflation: where demand outstrips supply, pushing up prices.

Cost-push inflation: where prices go up to compensate suppliers for increased costs.

Consumer price index: the average change in price of consumer goods and services.

Producer price index: the average price change in goods and services sold in the wholesale market.

HYPERINFLATION

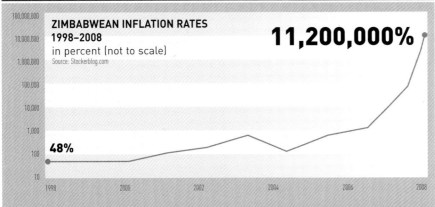

ZIMBABWEAN INFLATION RATES
1998–2008
in percent (not to scale)
Source: Stockerblog.com

11,200,000%

48%

When inflation is on a rapid rise, it is sometimes referred to as hyperinflation. What degree of inflation qualifies as hyperinflation is a moot point, though a generally accepted measure is a 50 percent monthly increase.

Among the most infamous episodes of hyperinflation was that which afflicted Germany in 1923. With the economy wracked by the demands of the Treaty of Versailles, the average monthly inflation rate reached an eye-watering 322 percent. However, that pales when compared with the hyperinflation that struck Hungary from 1945 to 1946, where the rate was some 19,000 percent per month.

More recently, Zimbabwe fell victim when its government attempted to address its economic mismanagement by simply printing more money. The result was an annual inflation figure of over 230 million percent before the government gave up counting. By October 2008 one US dollar was worth more than 2 billion Zimbabwean dollars.

Humans have always hungered to know the future and to prepare themselves accordingly, and economists are no different. While in ancient times people consulted an oracle or studied the entrails of sacrificial animals, our modern prophets of money are more inclined to process vast swathes of data with complex computer modeling programs. But that didn't stop the global economic crisis sneaking up on us unannounced.

FORECASTING

In the summer of 2006, just about the time that Peter Schiff was predicting his "real financial crisis," a wave of repossessions had a dramatic effect on house prices in the US, reversing the housing boom of the previous years and causing the first national decline in house prices since the 1930s. Four million homes remained unsold. The effect on the wider economy was swift, causing an immediate slowdown of the national economy.

Governments, bankers, investors, businesses and economists all have obvious reasons for wanting accurate predictions. But we all have an interest in predicting the economic future. Every financial decision we take forces us to consider what is around the corner. Will I have enough money tomorrow if I spend it today? Will the price be less tomorrow? Am I better off saving my money for a rainy day or investing it? There are a number of approaches open to the forecaster:

■ **Extrapolation** – calculating the future on the basis of known facts and existing trends, often likened to extending a curve on a graph.
■ **Studying leading indicators** – looking at economic factors that traditionally change ahead of the wider economy. Bond yields, for instance, classically anticipate general economic trends.
■ **Surveying** – taking a snapshot of consumers' and businesses' plans.
■ **Time series models** – looking at historical data.
■ **Econometrics** – developing mathematical and statistical models that can test hypotheses by analyzing existing data and then make predictions for the future.

While all these methods have a role to play in the forecasting game, the latter two have become prevalent. Alas, no system is infallible and many experts have summed up the problem thus: the problem is the things that we don't know we don't know.

JUST REDUCED

FOR SALE
BANK OWNED
(000) 123 4567

The global meltdown

The global economic crisis that began in the USA in 2007 and took over the planet within a year was notable at the very least in the way that it crept up unnoticed. Perhaps part of the problem was that economists thought they were better at the forecasting game than they actually were. Of course, there were economists who saw dark clouds on the horizon. Among the most vocal was Peter Schliff, who in August 2006 said: "The United States is like the *Titanic* and I am here with the lifeboat ... I see a real financial crisis coming ..."

So if he could see it, why couldn't the vast majority of analysts and commentators? The reasons are myriad and complex. Some argue that long-term low interest rates ushered in an era of consumer spending that came with a feel-good factor that no one wanted to spoil. Others point to the development of increasingly complex financial products designed to spread risk, but which too often were beyond the comprehension of even the most sophisticated banking minds. Allied to this was a financial sector culture in which workers received sizable bonuses for seemingly carrying on and not upsetting the apple cart. One eminent collection of economists retrospectively put it down to "a failure of the collective imagination."

Whatever the reason economic forecasters find themselves with a lot of ground to make up.

> "ONE OF THE SOUNDEST RULES I TRY TO REMEMBER WHEN MAKING FORECASTS IN THE FIELD OF ECONOMICS IS THAT WHATEVER IS TO HAPPEN IS HAPPENING ALREADY."
> SYLVIA PORTER (1913–91), AMERICAN ECONOMIST AND JOURNALIST

THE DISASTER THAT NO ONE FORESAW

Percentage share of subprime mortgage originations

Source: US Census Bureau

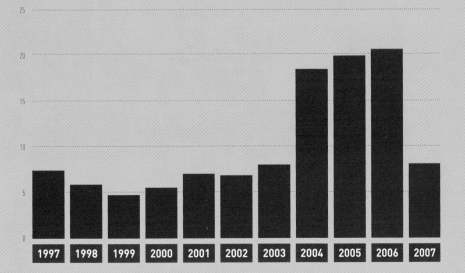

| 1997 | 1998 | 1999 | 2000 | 2001 | 2002 | 2003 | 2004 | 2005 | 2006 | 2007 |

← The global downturn was ushered in by the US subprime mortgage crisis that started in 2007. Subprime mortgages to individuals with low credit ratings and a high chance of default historically made up 8 percent or less of the mortgage market but spiked in the mid-2000s to comprise a fifth. Few analysts predicted the devastating consequences.

For the vast majority of history, the development of money has been slow, occasionally punctuated by developments such as the introduction of cheques and credit cards. However, the revolution that has taken place in the last fifteen years in IT and telecommunications has fundamentally changed the way we look after and spend our money.

THE IMPACT OF TECHNOLOGY

It is a somewhat mind-boggling concept that the vast majority of the money that we have does not exist – at least not in physical form. Most of us are paid directly into our bank accounts, while large regular expenses, such as mortgages, pass silently from one account to another at the beginning or the end of the month. Increasingly even low-value consumer goods are traded online with no physical money actually changing hands. So how has technology changed our day-to-day relationship with money?

Electronic everything

These days most of us take it as a norm that we can bank online as well as buy Christmas presents or do the weekly grocery shop with a few clicks of a mouse. Meanwhile, merchants are increasingly adopting Near Field Communication technologies that allow us to pay for goods and services simply by waving a suitable smartcard or cell phone over a payment module (see pages 80-1 and 247). However, with each new development comes the potential for abuse. As quick

↓

It is estimated that at least half the population of the globe now pays to use a mobile phone. The exponential growth of cellular technology has been particularly prevalent in developing countries, where a lack of effective ommunications infrastructure has traditionally been one of the biggest obstacles to economic growth.

as developers create new applications, a nefarious army springs up looking to exploit weaknesses in security.

Everyone with an email account has at some time received a phishing email – a fraudulent missive designed to coax confidential financial information from the recipient. Pharming scams, on the other hand, attempt to redirect users to fake websites for similarly underhanded purposes. Computers can also be infected by Trojan Horse programs that appear to be useful, but are quite the reverse. Some, for instance, download key scanning programs allowing a third party to read passwords and login information.

Web users can protect themselves to an extent, practicing discretion by protecting their personal information and making sure that their computers have updated security software. But the battle for Internet security is being waged constantly between programmers and hackers, and only time will tell who ultimately wins the war.

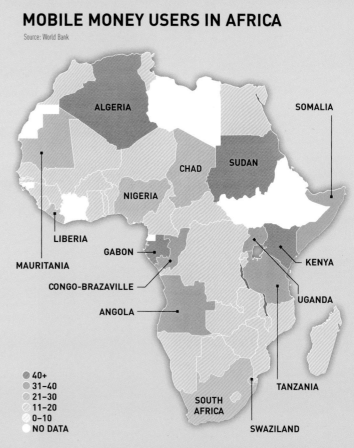

MOBILE MONEY USERS IN AFRICA
Source: World Bank

- 40+
- 31–40
- 21–30
- 11–20
- 0–10
- NO DATA

Financial services for the unbanked

One of the most exciting technological developments of recent years is the growth of "mobile money." It is now possible to undertake a full range of banking functions using a mobile phone, as well as pay bills or make purchases either by sending premium rate text messages or by putting charges directly on to a phone bill. For that large part of the world population that does not have a bank account, mobile money offers access to financial services once beyond their reach.

It is estimated that 50 percent of the world's population is "unbanked," the majority of them in the developing world. A study of 150,000 people in 148 countries conducted by the Gates Foundation, World Bank and Gallup World Poll suggested that the unbanked rate among the world's poor is as high as 75 percent (with women less likely than men to have an account). Yet according to the Mobile Money for the Unbanked Program launched in 2009, a billion people in the developing world who lack a bank account do have access to a cell phone.

In practice, mobile money means, for instance, that a family in a rural area can receive a remittance from abroad without having to travel hundreds of miles to the nearest bank, that a smallholder can obtain insurance against crop failure where once they were excluded, or that a market trader can pay a peasant farmer for a small quantity of a staple crop using a SIM card costing just a few cents.

↑

Africa has been at the forefront of the mobile money revolution. A World Bank survey revealed that of the 20 countries in which more than 10 percent of adults used mobile money in 2011, fifteen of them were in Africa. Kenya is the clear world leader, with 68 percent of adults participating. Somalia, meanwhile, had a participation rate around a third of all adults, a remarkable figure in a country that had been without a functioning government for twenty years.

Just as emerging technologies have redefined the relationship between the individual and money, so they have utterly transformed the nature of financial trading. There was a time when the financial markets were operated by traders barking buy-and-sell orders on the word of all-powerful brokers. But with the introduction of the PC to international trading floors from the mid-1980s, the markets changed forever as their reliance on cutting-edge technology intensified.

ELECTRONIC TRADING

Among the most profound effects of the computer revolution was the leap in the quantity of trades that could be carried out. The London Stock Exchange, for instance, carried out 20,000 daily trades prior to the introduction of automated trading in 1986. Within a year that figure had tripled, and today there are in excess of half a million trades a day.

The ability to do business via the computer has led to a democratization of the financial world, allowing new participants into the markets, regardless of their physical location or the absence of traditional connections with the investment world. It is also a considerably cheaper activity than it once was, since brokers and floor traders are often cut out of the loop altogether.

This technological blossoming has, though, brought into focus the issue of cyber security. The markets are prime targets not only for criminals intent on self-enrichment, but also for those who want to disrupt the system for other reasons (e.g. as an act of terrorism or war). Many of the world's big players – including the US and China – have established state-sponsored cyber defence organizations, raising the prospect that wars in the future could be decided not with bombs and guns but with computer wizards fighting for control of the markets.

↑

The Internet has opened up the markets to new customers by making investment in stocks, commodities, futures and forex easier. All you need is a computer and an online trading account. Among other benefits, online trading helps participants save time and money.

Algo trading

With more trades than can be physically transacted by humans, the markets are increasingly reliant on algorithmic trading (algo trading) – computer programs that buy and sell automatically when certain pre-ordained conditions are met. It is believed that at least half of all trades are now generated in this way.

THE GROWTH OF ALGO TRADING IN ASIA

Algorithmic trading as percentage of all trades

Source: CELENT Group

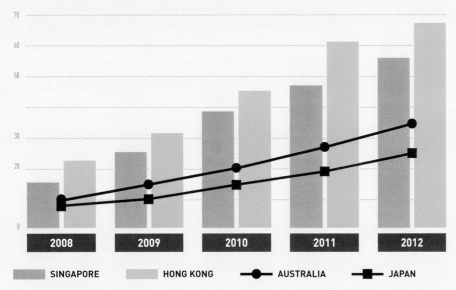

Though Europe and the US lead the way in algo trading, with up to half of all trades now done in this way, it is on the rise in Asia. With a chance to learn from the mistakes of others, like the Knight Capital Group (see below), plus the expertise of some of the world's top mathematicians and software engineers, it seems likely that the Asian markets will develop some of the best electronic platforms for algorithmic trading in the world.

SINGAPORE   HONG KONG   AUSTRALIA   JAPAN

Modelled by mathematicians, these programs work on formulae that predict future market movements based on the statistical analysis of past trends and patterns. A few even have elements of artificial intelligence written into them to allow for adaptive strategies.

Such systems are not without their critics. As many observers have pointed out, markets are complex animals, driven by irrational human behavior that mathematical programming simply does not recognize. Furthermore, there is the threat of a phenomenon known as self-reinforcing feedback loops. In short, it is feared that algo trading can turn a crisis into a disaster. Imagine, for instance, that a stock drops in value and so is automatically sold by one algo trading program. The price is thus pushed down farther, prompting another program to sell, and then another, until a full domino effect is in evidence.

One particular type of algo trade – High Frequency Trading (HFT) in which holdings are bought and sold on within a few seconds – has come under particular scrutiny, particularly after its involvement in the US Flash Crash of 2010 (see page 119), when a technology issue caused a surge of volatile trading, resulting in $440 million being lost. As Australia, Canada and the EU all surged ahead with plans for increased regulation of HFT, the US nonetheless showed no great desire to follow the same path.

THE INTERNET HAS ACCELERATED THE PACE OF STOCK TRANSACTIONS WORLDWIDE, BY SPEEDING UP THE EXCHANGE OF INFORMATION AND PROVIDING ACCESS TO GLOBAL INVESTORS

Driving the markets is information. It allows traders to predict trends, establish price and decide exactly when they should buy and sell. Data also serves as the fuel for all the algorithmic trading models. Information has always been the most valuable currency in the market place, but the rise of new technology has forced markets to adapt to cope with unprecedented volumes of data flashing around the world at once and with unimaginable speeds.

THE DATA EXPLOSION

The world's first exchange as we would recognize it today appeared in Bruges in the early 1300s, centered around a family-run inn called Ter Beurze. From this institution we derive the modern word *Bourse* for an exchange. Conveniently located on a large square where traders could carry out business, one of the inn's other great advantages was that it provided accommodation to travelers who passed on news of goings-on across the continent – wars, births, deaths, political machinations, sunken ships – such information oiled the wheels of the Bruges market.

Getting the gossip first

Now as it was then, traders strive to get the gossip first. Once horses were the fastest way to communicate news, then carrier pigeons (an innovation adopted by the founders of Reuters), before the emergence of the telegraph and the telephone in the 19th century transformed the scene. Meanwhile, newspapers printed once or twice a day kept everyone in the loop. But today, advanced telecommunications means that we can witness the news in real time – on the TV, over the Internet, even via our cell phones.

As for the market, its hunger for up-to-the-minute news is sated. But this flood of information brings its own challenges. Firstly, there is the possibility of data-overload. Indeed, one of the motivations for developing algorithmic trading models is that they can analyze data sources far more quickly than the human brain. Then there is the danger that news broadcasters do not merely serve as purveyors of information, but actively influence the story. A rolling 24-hour news service was first provided by Ted Turner's CNN network in 1980. Subsequently, the "CNN effect" has become a widely discussed phenomenon: just how much does the intense spotlight of real-time news coverage affect the decision-making processes of those featured in the news? In August

EVERYWHERE YOU LOOK, THE QUANTITY OF INFORMATION IN THE WORLD IS SOARING. THE TERM "BIG DATA" HAS EMERGED TO DESCRIBE THIS MONSTROUS GROWTH IN VOLUME. BIG DATA COMPRISES DATA SETS OF BETWEEN 3 AND 10 TERABYTES (3 AND 10 TRILLION BYTES) IN SIZE

2011, for instance, the Dow Jones fell 500 points in a single day. As the collapse played out over the course of the day, the leading news networks disrupted their normal coverage to focus on the story. Did this attention, some asked, exacerbate investor nervousness, fuelling still greater losses?

Many argue not, highlighting the sophistication of professional investors as well as the presence of computer-driven trading. They may be right and the question might be imponderable, but it is nonetheless one worth asking.

THE BLOOMBERG STORY

Among the biggest winners of the data boom is Bloomberg LP, founded in 1981 by Michael Bloomberg. He had just been fired from Salomon Brothers, a Wall Street investment bank. Leaving with a $10 million severance package, he was keen to invest. In 1982 he secured a further $30 million funding for his new enterprise from Merrill Lynch. Today Bloomberg has over 200 offices and 13,000 staff around the globe, compiling and distributing raw financial data, news and analysis via a combination of specialist software packages and broadcasting, publishing and online platforms.

The jewel in the Bloomberg crown is the Bloomberg Terminal, a computer system that allows users to monitor the latest market movements, analyze data and place trades on an electronic platform. An industry standard package, the Bloomberg Terminal boasts over 300,000 subscribers worldwide.

Bloomberg is estimated to have around a third of the multi-billion dollar international financial data market, about the same as its chief rival, Thomson Reuters. As for Michael Bloomberg (estimated wealth: $25 billion), he gave up his executive role in the company to become mayor of New York City in 2001.

← Michael Bloomberg's foresight in designing a financial investment system to house and analyze huge amounts of data played a major part in amassing his personal fortune. Today, the Bloomberg Terminal, which provides 24-hour financial information and news, is an essential tool for traders throughout the world, with over 300,000 in operation each day.

9 MONEY AND THE LAW

↑
The statue of Lady Justice on top of the Old Bailey in London carries the scales of truth and justice. It stands as a mark of society's never-ending fight against dishonesty, much of it in the criminal pursuit of other people's money.

It is often said that money is the root of all evil. In fact, in the Bible, when Paul wrote his first epistle to Timothy he declared that the "love of money is the root of all evil." A subtle difference, but one with enormous implications because the problem is not money itself, but our unending desire to possess it. Wherever money exists, there are those who want to procure it dishonestly.

From the pickpocket to the bank robber, the accountant gently cooking the books to the CEO plundering the pension pot, criminals have never ceased attempting to get their hands on filthy lucre. In response, society has striven to counter them, either through prevention or apprehension and punishment.

Is it worth the risk?

So why do criminals consider it worth the risk to seek out money that isn't theirs? Because, quite simply, they make a couple of simple economic calculations. Firstly, they evaluate that the reward they might receive (the stolen wealth) outweighs the trouble in which they could find themselves (e.g. with a criminal record, facing jail time or even, in some cultures, suffering corporal or capital punishment). Secondly, they calculate that criminal activity is a more profitable use of their time and labor than any other economic activity that they might reasonably undertake.

While criminal enterprise may be profitable for the individuals involved, it is entirely detrimental to society at large. The cost of financial crime is never restricted to the capital sum stolen. For example, a theft may incur some or all of the following supplementary expenses: the replacement of the capital sum (e.g. in an insurance payout), increased insurance premiums, disruption to the normal economic activity of the victim (e.g. a business having to close for repairs), installation of additional security precautions, policing costs, justice system costs, lost resources for socially productive economic activity (e.g. the criminal's time, labor and other resources) and lost tax revenues, with the stolen capital sum going "underground."

Today, the law fights battles on two distinct fronts: against the traditional criminal underclass (for instance, muggers and armed robbers) and against "white-collar crime." White-collar crime, an expression originated by the sociologist Edwin Sutherland in 1939, refers to financial crime, usually non-violent, perpetrated by an individual or group in the course of their otherwise legal occupations.

↑ Police chase an armed bank robber along the freeway in Palmdale, California in late 2012. Despite increasingly sophisticated technology and strenuous efforts by law enforcement officers in the fight against this kind of activity, the FBI recorded over 5,000 bank crimes in 2011, which netted over $38 million.

Robbery – the process of unlawfully taking property by force or threat of force – is a statutory offence throughout the world. It is a crime with a clear victim and often immensely disruptive repercussions, with punishments to match (including, historically, measures as draconian as transportation and execution). Yet our relationship with the robber is a complicated one, with numerous examples of thieves venerated as folk heroes.

ROBBERY

There are always people prepared to thieve, in good times and bad. Nor is robbery the chosen vocation of a certain personality type or the result of a particular background. Nonetheless, it appears a logical assumption that crime will peak during economic downturns. With less money to go round and more people out of work, it seems natural that people in desperate circumstances will look to dishonest ways to overcome financial shortages.

However, the evidence to prove this thesis is scant. For instance, at the end of December 2008, CNN reported that bank robberies in New York had risen by 54 percent on the previous year, prompting them to pose the predictable question: "Is recession behind the spike in bank robberies?" Yet just over a year later, *USA Today* put out a story under the headline "Despite recession, bank robberies dropped in 2009," reporting a nationwide fall of 20 percent to the lowest rate in a decade.

In fact, most academic studies into the relationship between crime and recession find no direct correlation, despite widespread statistical evidence of higher crime rates in areas of steep unemployment. One explanation is that crime is more likely to be the result of long-term unemployment. A short-term dip in the economy is less likely to breed a crime wave, so the theory goes, than an expectation of persistent joblessness.

↓

This graph, plotting FBI data on property crime against the seven recessions identified by the US National Bureau of Economic Research between 1960 and 2010, shows an inconsistent relationship between crime and the state of the economy.

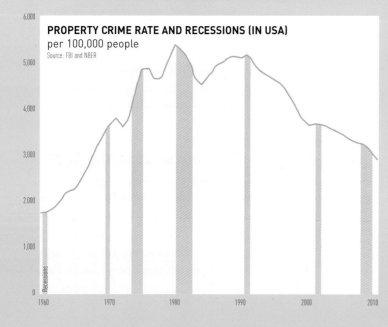

PROPERTY CRIME RATE AND RECESSIONS (IN USA)
per 100,000 people
Source: FBI and NBER

The Robin Hood phenomenon

While robbery is almost universally accepted as socially destructive and undesirable, a few protagonists have been reconfigured as popular champions. Most famous and enduring of these is Robin Hood. Despite a distinctly hazy historical provenance, legend has it that Robin pranced through the forests of 13th-century England stealing from the rich to give to the poor. Cast against the misrule of bad King John, he is the archetypal

little guy striking back at an unfair system on behalf of his fellow oppressed citizens. His legend became a David and Goliath tale for the economically deprived of the medieval age, and of all the ages that followed it.

Others have emerged more recently to fulfil a similar role. In Australian culture, for instance, Ned Kelly was elevated from robber and cold-blooded killer to rebel against the Anglo-Australian ruling class. A little later in the USA, John Dillinger and Bonnie and Clyde emerged from the Great Depression as popular heroes, despite all of them having the blood of innocents on their hands. At times of highly visible economic inequality, it seems that the robber can become an icon of the have-nots against the haves (even if in reality they seek to join the haves via ruthlessness and dishonesty, rarely showing much regard for other have-nots who happen to get in their way).

↑
Robin Hood is the archetypal noble outlaw. Along with others of his kind, like Dick Turpin, Ned Kelly and Bonnie and Clyde, his crimes have taken on their own morality as he fought the injustice of King John's corrupt governance.

THE BIGGEST BANK HEIST OF ALL TIME

History is littered with tales of audacious and outrageous robberies, yet the single largest bank job ever was committed not by an armed man wearing a balaclava, but by a world figure (albeit a much reviled one). In March 2003, Saddam Hussein's world was collapsing around him as US-led forces bore down on Baghdad. Over a period of several days he authorized his henchman to raid the country's central bank and seize an estimated one billion dollars, much of it earmarked for his son, Qusay. US forces subsequently recovered most of the money, including $650 million hidden in Saddam's abandoned palace.

■ Fraud is an act of deception for personal gain. A broad banner, at the lower level it might be an individual attempting to use a credit card that doesn't belong to them or collecting for a charity that doesn't exist. At the top end, many of the really big frauds – the ones that rake in millions and even billions – are perpetrated by large organizations or renegade individuals working within them.

FRAUD

↓

Sophisticated, trusted, highly regarded and already running a successful and legitimate business, Bernard Madoff was the ultimate fraudster. He ran the largest Ponzi scheme in history, making millions of dollars for more than ten years undetected by the authorities. The success of such a fraud depends on an infinite supply of new investors, whose money is used to pay existing investors. Madoff's scheme began to unravel as the market declined in 2008 and investors wanted to withdraw their money. Even then it took a confession to reveal the true extent of his crimes.

Virtually every country has at least one financial regulatory authority to keep an eye on the integrity of its businesses and financial institutions. Often there will be more than one, each concentrating on a particular business sector. They go under an array of names and include such giants as the Federal Reserve System and the Securities and Exchange Commission in the US, the Financial Services Authority in the UK, the Federal Financial Supervisory Authority in Germany and the China Banking Regulatory Commission. Their success is, in some respects, immeasurable, since when things are going well we hear little of their activities. Nonetheless, a steady trickle of reports of major corporate frauds from around the world suggest there is much work still to be done.

At its worst, white-collar fraud can threaten the very stability of a country. Take the case of Ramón Báez Figueroa, president of Banco Intercontinental in the Dominican Republic. Government officials claim that, under his governance,

as much as two-thirds of customer deposits were funnelled away from the official books. The bank collapsed in 2003 with a deficit of $2.2 billion, equivalent to two-thirds of the national budget, and had to be bailed out with public money. Subsequently, inflation exploded, poverty increased and the currency was devalued. As for Báez Figueroa, he was eventually sentenced to ten years in prison.

MADOFF MONEY

If a single case of fraud came to symbolize the global economic turmoil of the late 2000s, it could be argued that it was that concerning Bernard Madoff's wealth management business. A former chairman of the NASDAQ exchange, Madoff set up an investment firm in 1960, running it until his arrest in 2008. By then, his hedge fund operations had run up losses of some $40 billion, but hid this fact by paying its earlier investors with money taken from those who joined later. This sort of operation is known as a Ponzi scheme (named after Charles Ponzi, an arch exponent of the model in the early 1900s). In March 2009 Madoff admitted 11 federal felonies and was sentenced to a 150-year prison term.

The Enron moment

A watershed moment in the history of corporate fraud came with the 2001 collapse of Enron, a Houston-based energy giant with annual revenues in excess of $100 billion. Through a combination of exploiting accounting loopholes, setting up special purpose entities (separate legal companies) and misreporting the company finances, executives systematically managed to hide losses of billions of dollars for years on end.

When Enron filed for bankruptcy in December 2001, it was the largest corporate bankruptcy in US history. Several executives were subsequently convicted of assorted charges, including its founder, Kenneth Lay, who was found guilty on six fraud and conspiracy charges (though he died of a heart attack a few months before he could be sentenced).

Responsibility for auditing Enron rested with Arthur Andersen, at the time one of the world's Big Five auditing firms. It was found not to have fulfilled its professional responsibilities and was also convicted of obstruction of justice after shredding documents relevant to the case, although that conviction was later overturned by the Supreme Court of the United States. Another of Andersen's clients, WorldCom, was soon caught up in an accounting fraud of its own and filed for bankruptcy in July 2002, supplanting Enron as the US' biggest bankruptcy. These were just two of a spate of accounting scandals that caused the largest economy in the world to question severely some of its fundamental practices. Meanwhile, Andersen, founded in 1913, sold its practices to other firms, though a skeleton staff continues to deal with the legal fallout.

Insider trading

Another form of fraud linked to the corporate world is insider trading – the dealing of a security by someone with access to non-public information about that security. Think Gordon

↓

From this building in Houston, Texas, executives built Enron into America's seventh largest company. Their greed knew no bounds as they systematically cooked the books, sold their own stock and made millions before the company went bankrupt.

> "INSIDERS MIGHT SELL THEIR SHARES FOR ANY NUMBER OF REASONS, BUT THEY BUY THEM FOR ONLY ONE: THEY THINK THE PRICE WILL RISE."
> PETER LYNCH (B. 1944), RENOWNED US INVESTOR

Gekko in the movie *Wall Street*. Nor does the individual making the trade have to be an employee of the company involved to be guilty of the crime – anyone benefitting from the receipt of the non-public knowledge is culpable.

Among the most notable figures to be convicted of insider trading in recent times is the American business magnate, lifestyle guru and television personality, Martha Stewart. With a personal fortune estimated at a billion dollars, she was accused of selling her holding (worth just over $45,000) in ImClone Systems in December 2001 after allegedly receiving a tip-off from her Merrill Lynch broker that the company was about to find itself on the receiving end of a detrimental Food and Drug Administration ruling. Criminal proceedings ensued and Stewart was given a five-month prison sentence in 2004. The affair threatened to derail the career of a figure that *New York* magazine had described in 1995 as "the definitive American woman of our time."

However, Stewart might consider herself lucky by comparison with Raj Rajaratnam, who once headed up the Galleon Group hedge fund. As the focal point of an extensive insider-dealing network, he was convicted by US courts in 2011 and ordered to serve eleven years in jail and pay $10 million in fines – the longest ever prison sentence for insider dealing in recent memory.

Yet there are those that argue that insider trading might actually be beneficial to the markets. Milton Friedman said in 2003: "You want more insider trading, not less. You want to give the people most likely to have knowledge about deficiencies of the company an incentive to make the public aware of that."

INSIDER DEALING

1 Employee A tells Employee B he has seen a document detailing a proposed buyout of the Red Company by the Blue Company at above market price.

2 Employee B tells Person C about the gossip.

3 Person C buys 1,000 shares in the Red Company for $10,000.

4 The Red Company announces a takeover by the Blue Company. The stock price rises to $15 a share.

5 Person C sells their shares for $15,000, making a 50 percent profit from insider dealing.

There is no single, standard definition of what constitutes organized crime, though in 1988 Interpol agreed on the following description: "Any group having a corporate structure whose primary objective is to obtain money through illegal activities, often surviving on fear and corruption."

ORGANIZED CRIME

A non-exhaustive list of the activities undertaken by organized crime includes extortion, theft, fraud, trafficking (of, for instance, narcotics, weapons and people), prostitution, illegal gambling, protection rackets, counterfeiting, bid-rigging and contract killing. In addition, many organized crime outfits run ostensibly legal businesses both as a front for their illegal activities and as a way of laundering money.

Organized crime in the modern sense is generally considered to have its roots with the Mafia families of Italy, who exported their particular brand of criminality to the United States in the early years of the 20th century. And while the American-Italian Mafia has arguably had its wings clipped in recent decades, organized crime as a transnational phenomenon continues to boom. In particular, the 1991 collapse of the Soviet Union gave criminal enterprises the opportunity to establish themselves throughout Eastern Europe and Central Asia. Today, the reach of organized crime extends to virtually every corner of the world.

↓

Organized crime remains a major problem for police forces all over the world. Central America is currently the world's hot spot for drug trafficking, with 90 percent of the cocaine supply bound for the US passing through the area. Gang wars for control of the trade have been raging here since 2006. It is estimated that there have been 33,000 homicides in Central America since 2010. Here members of the Mara Salvatrucha gang are arrested on homicide charges in the suburbs of San Salvador in El Salvador.

GLOBAL CONTRABAND

Major trade routes for drugs, people and counterfeit goods
Source: UNODC

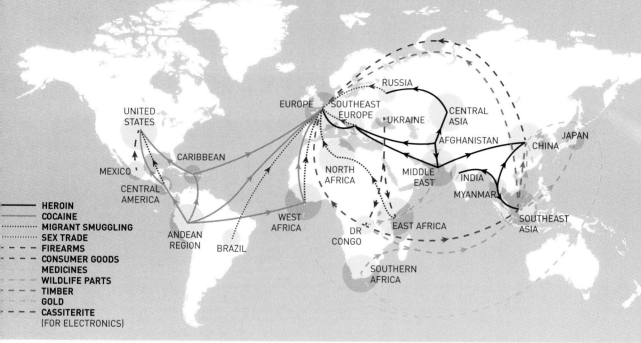

HEROIN
COCAINE
MIGRANT SMUGGLING
SEX TRADE
FIREARMS
CONSUMER GOODS
MEDICINES
WILDLIFE PARTS
TIMBER
GOLD
CASSITERITE
(FOR ELECTRONICS)

↑

Transnational organized
crime, including trafficking
in drugs, firearms and
people, has reached macroeconomic proportions
with illicit goods sourced
from one continent,
trafficked across another
and marketed in a third.
Organized crime is not
stagnant, but adapts as
new crimes emerge and
as relationships between
criminal networks become
both more flexible and
more sophisticated.

Global reach

In 2012 the UN Office on Drugs and Crime estimated that organized crime
generated $870 billion per year globally. That roughly equated to 7 percent of
world exports and 1.5 percent of the entire planet's GDP. Meanwhile, Misha
Glenny in his 2008 work, *McMafia*, suggested that international organized crime
accounted for as much as 15 percent of the global economy, concluding that
organized transnational crime represents a bigger threat to global stability than
international terrorism.

Certainly, Mafia enterprises reconfigured the economic landscape of Russia
after the fall of communism. The Global Organized Crime Project of the Center
for Strategic & International Studies estimated the existence of 6,000 organized
crime groups within Russia's borders by 2000. Other academics posited that
40 percent of the economy was in criminal hands, while money funnelled out
of the country in the late 1990s was put at almost $20 billion per year.

The global economic crisis of the late 2000s provided international criminal
enterprises with further opportunities for expansion. The Italian Mafia has been
particularly effective at bucking general global trends, heavily investing their
necessarily liquid funds in areas where others feared to tread at the time, notably
real estate and the credit markets. The Italian Mafia enjoyed an estimated
8 percent profit growth in 2009, raking in $104 billion on revenues of $180 billion.
Producing imitation money and then laundering it has long been a staple activity

THE NOBLE EXPERIMENT

When the 18th Amendment to the US Constitution was ratified in January 1919, it appeared to be a triumph for the prohibitionists as it saw a ban on the commercial production and distribution of alcohol. But while they might have stemmed supply, they couldn't stop demand. So it was that organized crime stepped in to fill the gap. The most famous Mafia figure of the era was Al Capone, whose operation by the late 1920s was raking in at least $60 million a year from illegal hooch. However, prohibition also had devastating effects on legitimate business and furthermore a thousand Americans were dying each year from drinking illegal alcohol. In 1928, President Hoover spoke of the 18th Amendment as "a great social and economic experiment, noble in motive and far reaching in purpose." It was repealed in 1933.

of organized criminal gangs. When counterfeit money enters the economy, it effectively reduces the value of real money by increasing supply. Furthermore, businesses that accept counterfeit currency at face value often go uncompensated for their direct loss.

From the 1980s until at least 2000 the USA was plagued by "superdollars" – fake US$100 bills so effectively forged that they were all but undetectable. It was suggested by Washington that they derived from North Korea, which was said to have laundered the fake cash in order to bolster its coffers with genuine dollar currency.

However, the effects of funny money at the macroeconomic level should not be over-estimated. With the majority of money now existing in electronic form, an influx of fake cash is unlikely to have a significant impact on, for instance, inflation.

↓

A police officer presents a sample of nearly two million confiscated dollars in counterfeit US$100 bills during a news conference in Lima, Peru, in 2011. Police discovered the phony bills when they raided a restaurant that had a printing machine. Authorities discovered that the restaurant was part of a sophisticated counterfeiting ring operating in the Andean capital.

The informal economy exists in something of a legal gray area, comprising that unofficial part of the economy that goes unregulated, untaxed, unmonitored and largely unreported in official statistics. It goes under an array of different names, including the shadow or underground economy, the black market and System D (derived from the phrase *l'economie de la débrouillardise* – the name used for this sector in French-speaking Africa and the Caribbean).

THE INFORMAL ECONOMY

While informal economies are by their nature not legal, they are not considered in terms of organized crime. A World Bank policy research paper published in 2010 defined it thus: The shadow economy includes all market-based legal production of goods and services that are deliberately concealed from public authorities for any of the following reasons: to avoid payment of income, value added or other taxes, to avoid payment of social security contributions, to avoid having to meet certain legal labor market standards, such as minimum wages, maximum working hours, safety standards, etc., and to avoid complying with certain administrative procedures, such as completing statistical questionnaires or other administrative forms.

↓

A market stall holder waits for customers on her stall in Kota Bahru, Malaysia. Estimates are that by the year 2020 two-thirds of the world's workforce will earn their living through the informal economy.

The sector encompasses a vast number of different business models, from sole traders working as street vendors or rubbish recyclers to much bigger and more organized businesses involved in, for instance, manufacturing and transportation.

Typically, employees earn low wages and have little or no job security. Nonetheless, the shadow economy commonly offers rare opportunities for employment in areas where the formal economy lags behind. The informal sector is likely to thrive where institutions are weak, where there are significant barriers to entry into the formal economy, and where there is rising demand for low-cost goods and services.

An unofficial powerhouse

The informal economy is unequivocally vital to the global economic system, particularly in the developing world. In 2009 the OECD estimated that 1.8 billion people were employed in the shadow economy, and it is expected to account for two-thirds of the planet's workforce by 2020. Academics have put the value of the global informal economy at 17 percent of total official world GDP, with the figure rising to 38 percent in sub-Saharan Africa. By contrast, among high-income nations of the Organization for Economic Co-operation and Development (OECD), it falls to 13 percent. Worth some $10 trillion per year, if the sector were a nation, it would be the world's second largest economy behind the USA.

While the emergence of an informal economy is generally indicative of failings in its formal counterpart, were it not to exist the results would be calamitous.

↓

According to World Bank figures based on data for the first decade of the 21st century, there were 13 nations in which the shadow economy made up over half of the entire economy.

THE SHADOW OF INFORMALITY
1999–2007
Source: World Bank, 2010

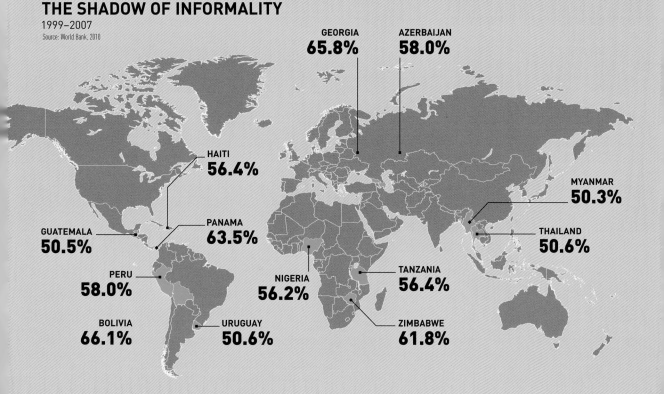

GEORGIA
65.8%

AZERBAIJAN
58.0%

HAITI
56.4%

MYANMAR
50.3%

PANAMA
63.5%

GUATEMALA
50.5%

THAILAND
50.6%

PERU
58.0%

NIGERIA
56.2%

TANZANIA
56.4%

BOLIVIA
66.1%

URUGUAY
50.6%

ZIMBABWE
61.8%

Tax evasion is the term used for the avoidance of paying due taxes by illegal means, usually by a conscious misrepresentation or concealment of genuine financial circumstances. It should be seen as distinct from tax avoidance, where legal – though sometimes morally dubious – methods (such as the exploitation of tax loopholes) are employed in order to pay a reduced level of tax. Tax evasion is practiced both by individuals and by organizations and in most jurisdictions is punishable by fines and, in certain circumstances, incarceration.

TAX EVASION

> **"THE DIFFERENCE BETWEEN TAX AVOIDANCE AND TAX EVASION IS THE THICKNESS OF A PRISON WALL."**
> DENIS HEALEY (B. 1917), BRITISH POLITICIAN

Tax evasion is a headache for governments who must eternally contend with the tax gap – the difference between the tax that is owed across an economy and the amount that is actually collected. This can significantly impact on governmental revenues. For instance, unofficial estimates of the US tax gap in 2008 put it at up to $500 million, a sum that would have proved a useful stimulant to the federal reserves as the country entered a notably turbulent economic period.

Tax avoidance takes a number of forms, including: withholding payment of tax owed, non-submission of a tax return, misreporting on a tax return, typically by underestimating income or overestimating expenses, misreporting employee details in order to pay lower employer taxes, covertly importing or exporting (in other words, smuggling) to avoid payment of customs duties and hiding funds, for instance in an offshore account (see p. 51).

THE GREEK DEFICIT
as percentage of GDP
Source: OECD

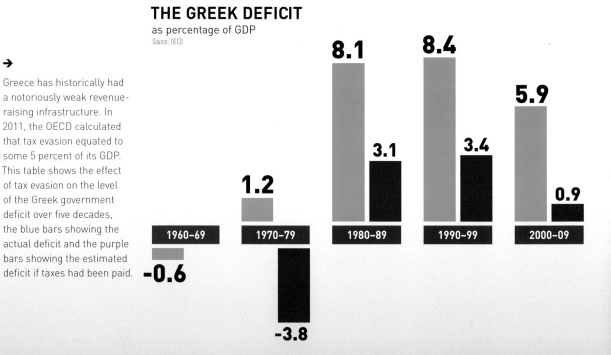

→

Greece has historically had a notoriously weak revenue-raising infrastructure. In 2011, the OECD calculated that tax evasion equated to some 5 percent of its GDP. This table shows the effect of tax evasion on the level of the Greek government deficit over five decades, the blue bars showing the actual deficit and the purple bars showing the estimated deficit if taxes had been paid.

1960–69	1970–79	1980–89	1990–99	2000–09
-0.6	1.2	8.1	8.4	5.9
	-3.8	3.1	3.4	0.9

The harder they come

Tax evasion has been the downfall of many notable historical figures, from businessmen and politicians to sports stars and film idols. It also proved to be the Achilles' heel of Al Capone, that gangster of gangsters. From his Chicago base, Capone marshalled a ruthless criminal network, earning vast profits from illegal gaming, extortion, prostitution and moonshine liquor. He was also widely held to be behind the nadir of 1920s Mob violence, the St Valentine's Day Massacre of 1929.

Yet, unable to finger him for any of these activities, in 1931 the authorities decided to go after him on tax evasion charges instead. He was found guilty and sentenced to eleven years, ordered to pay $215,000 in taxes due plus interest, $50,000 as a fine and $7,962 for court costs. He served seven years, much of it in Alcatraz, before being released suffering from syphilis. The illness curtailed his mental faculties, ruling out a return to the criminal underworld, and he died in 1947.

However, even Capone looks a little lightweight, at least in tax evasion terms, when compared with the crimes perpetrated by Walter Anderson, a telecommunications entrepreneur who dodged paying what he owed in the 1990s via an intricate web of offshore tax havens, shell companies and aliases. In 2005 he was arrested and pleaded guilty to concealing $365 million in earnings. Spectacularly, in 1998 he declared an income of $68,000, when the real figure was $126 million. He paid just $495 in tax at the time. But the taxman was not to be cheated for good. In 2011 Anderson was ordered to pay $250 million to cover back taxes and fines. He was additionally sentenced to nine years in prison to mull over his misdemeanors. At the taxpayer's expense, of course.

↑
A smiling Al Capone (center) with his attorneys in the Chicago courtroom where he was found guilty of tax evasion in 1931. He served seven years in prison, five of which were spent in cells 433 and 181 at Alcatraz (below).

The rogue state is a somewhat controversial concept given the flexibility of its interpretation. The term is used broadly for countries deemed a threat to the security of the international community by the breaking of international law (typically, through human rights abuses, sponsorship of terrorism or proliferation of weapons of mass destruction). Aside from questions about which nations deserve to qualify for the list, discussions on how to undermine such regimes generally include a financial aspect.

ROGUE STATES

↓
Currently among the most unpopular members of the Axis of Evil are Iranian President Ahmadinejad (foreground) and Supreme Leader Ali Khamenei. Iran has been subject to both unilateral and supranational sanctions since the Islamic Revolution in 1979 and because of its alleged nuclear weapons program.

The designation of the rogue state label is an informal affair and has historically relied on the political positioning of the White House at any given time. The phrase was actually phased out of US State Department use in 2000, with expressions such as "states of concern" taking its place. However, with the terrorist attacks of September 11, 2001, the Bush administration began talking of an Axis of Evil (comprising Iraq, Iran and North Korea), ensuring the idea of the rogue state remained alive. The cast of rogue nations changes with time, though Iran and North Korea have proved long-term members of this unpopular gang.

In dealing with them, the international community has three broad strategies: diplomatic negotiation, economic sanctions and armed engagement.

Clearly, the first two options are by far the most desirable, and it is often argued that sanctions grant diplomats greater leverage. These may be imposed unilaterally (i.e. by one nation against another) or by supranational bodies, such as the UN and the EU. By imposing them, the sanctioning body: highlights the unacceptable actions of the sanctioned regime, ensures that the sanctioning body's finances are not available to the rogue regime (e.g. for civil rights abuses or nuclear weapons development), thus establishing a degree of moral authority and squeezes the finances of the sanctioned regime, making it more difficult for it to operate. Sanctions may also increase popular discontent within a country that can lead to changes in policy or even in government.

"I USED TO HAVE A JOB ASSEMBLING MERCEDES-BENZ CARS, BUT NOW, BECAUSE OF THE SANCTIONS, DAIMLER HAS CUT ITS TIES WITH IRAN AND AS A CONSEQUENCE I LOST MY JOB. I'M SELF EMPLOYED NOW, BUT I'M STRUGGLING TO PUT FOOD ON THE TABLE."
FEREYDOUN, CAR-MAKER, KARAJ, IRAN

Cutting off the finances

For sanctions to have any chance of effectiveness, it is vital that they are properly implemented. Partly for this reason, there has been a concerted international drive to reform the offshore banking sector in recent decades. Offshore banking allows depositors to locate their money outside their domestic borders, often in institutions in tax havens offering high levels of secrecy.

The use of offshore banking services does not inherently indicate any criminal wrongdoing on the part of the depositor, but the sector has long been associated with tax evasion and money laundering, particularly for organized crime. It also offers laundering opportunities for rogue nations as well as assisting companies to hide potentially sanction-breaking business dealings. In the aftermath of the 9/11 attacks, there has been particular scrutiny of how offshore banks are used to channel funds to terrorist organizations.

The members of the G7 group established a Financial Action Task Force in 1989 to combat money laundering, and from 2001 its remit was extended to include a focus on the international financing of terrorism. Certainly, many traditional tax havens, including Switzerland, have agreed to greater cooperation with the international community in rooting out all forms of criminal activity.

↓

Regarded with similar suspicion, North Korea is also subject to military and economic sanctions imposed by the UN. Described as a secret state, the country remains strictly quarantined from outside influences. Little information emanates from Pyongyang apart from images of a powerful military and a developing nuclear capability.

ROOM 39

North Korea is widely believed by foreign intelligence organizations to run an outfit known as Room 39 or Bureau 39. It is suspected of raising government funds by a combination of legal and illegal enterprises, many of which operate abroad. Estimated to make between half a billion and a billion dollars each year from its illegal enterprises, Room 39 is accused of involvement in banknote counterfeiting (including the superdollars mentioned on page 183), money laundering, insurance frauds, counterfeit cigarettes and pharmaceuticals, and narcotics smuggling. The White House has long striven to undermine its operations, for instance forcing the closure of a number of international banks suspected of laundering money for the pariah regime in Pyongyang.

선군혁명총진

The emergence of the Internet created a new Wild West for criminals, an environment where the law struggles to keep up with those who want to breach it. Cybercrime encompasses any illegal activity undertaken with the use of computers and the Internet, a great deal of which is financially motivated. From clumsily worded emails offering vast lottery payouts (for a small administrative fee, naturally) to complex bank frauds, the cyber-world is a panacea for everyone from cheeky chancers to the most organized of criminal enterprises. And we all pay the price.

CYBERCRIME HAS 556 MILLION VICTIMS PER YEAR, 1.5 MILLION VICTIMS PER DAY AND 18 VICTIMS PER SECOND. THE FIGURES ARE EXPECTED TO RISE

CYBERCRIME

The cyber-criminal is a wily creature constantly looking for new ways to infiltrate hi-tech security. In 2012 the Norton Cybercrime Report put the global costs of cybercrime for 2011 at $110 billion. Add in the costs to victims of time lost as a result of the index crime, and the bill was more than tripled.

Broadband pirates

Then there is the murky world of Internet piracy, in which music, films, books and images are illegally shared between users on the Internet. For some, this free cultural exchange is the height of Internet liberty, but for others (notably the copyright holders and sellers being bypassed), it amounts to little more

Data from the 2012 Norton Cybercrime Survey gives a taste of the economic impact of computer-based crime.

THE COST OF CYBERCRIME
in US dollars
Source: NORTON CYBERCRIME REPORT

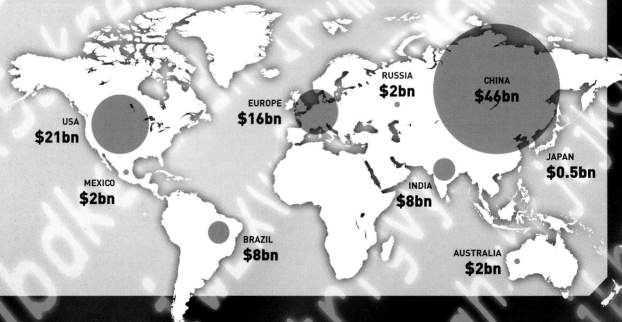

RUSSIA **$2bn**

CHINA **$46bn**

EUROPE **$16bn**

USA **$21bn**

JAPAN **$0.5bn**

MEXICO **$2bn**

INDIA **$8bn**

BRAZIL **$8bn**

AUSTRALIA **$2bn**

than theft. To determine an accurate estimate of the losses attributable to Internet piracy is all but impossible. Nonetheless, market research conducted by the NPD market research group in 2009 found that, for instance, only 37 percent of music acquired by US consumers that year was paid for. Certainly the music industry has felt the squeeze, with its US revenues more than halving between 2000 and 2011.

Another area of increasing concern is the threat posed by cyber warfare. Among the most notorious cases of a concerted cyber attack was that which befell Estonia in late April 2007, when its electronic infrastructure was temporarily paralyzed. Occurring as a dispute raged with Russia over the relocation of a Soviet-era war memorial, many pointed the finger at Russian agents, though this has been denied by the Moscow authorities. Whoever the perpetrators were, Estonia's banks, public services, media organizations and government ministries all suffered distributed denial of service attacks, bringing about a temporary Internet blackout. As well as the obvious threats to national security, the financial costs of government-sponsored transnational attacks in the future are almost limitless. Yet attempts to put in place a Geneva Convention-style legal framework for conduct in this new domain of war have so far stuttered.

WANTED BY THE FBI

Federal Cyber Crime Charges

Kristina Izvekova

Sofya Dikova

Artem Tsygankov

Marina Oprea

Ion Volosciuc

Artem Semenov

Catalina Cortac

Maxim Panferov

↑
This poster, issued by the FBI in 2010, shows photos of Eastern European cyber criminals wanted on a variety of federal charges stemming from illegal activities including money laundering, bank fraud, passport fraud and identity theft in New York. The Computer Crime Unit reported over 15,000 cybercrimes in the New York metropolitan area that year.

OPERATION HIGH ROLLER

In June 2012 news emerged of a massive cyber bank heist known as Operation High Roller. Though the exact extent of the thefts is not known, it was thought that its masterminds could have stolen up to $2.5 billion dollars from banks around the world. The fraud, which was fully automated and did not require human participation in the transfer of funds, targeted high-value accounts and demonstrated a meticulous knowledge of banking transaction systems. Nonetheless, the crime started with a classic scam email to customers – an email that appeared to be a bona fide bank notification but which, when clicked on, downloaded malware to the victim's machine. This then moved funds from the victim's account to a prepaid debit card, which was then promptly and anonymously drained. First witnessed in Italy, the fraud soon spread to Germany, the UK, Latin America and then the USA. From where the criminals themselves originated was not clear, though several servers automating the thefts were traced to Russia.

10 LIFE STAGES

↑

As life expectancy increases, it is beholden upon us to plan our personal finances to meet the various challenges we can expect to face at different points in our lives.

These days we might talk about the various phases of life in terms of newborns, toddlers, tweens, teens, young adults, twenty-thirty-somethings, the middle-aged, senior citizens, the third age, and no doubt a great many other buzz phrases besides.

However we choose to divide it up, our average lifespan is getting longer. Life expectancy globally is around 65 for men and 70 for women, according to UN statistics. When you consider that during the period of the Roman Empire it was no more than 25 years and stood at only 30 as recently as 1900, we who are alive today have much to be grateful for. The news is especially good for women who, in all but a handful of countries, can rely on a good year or two longer than the male of the species.

Correspondingly, our relationship with money goes through a great many phases as we reach the various milestones along the ever-lengthening road between our hatching and dispatching. Nor should it be supposed that the answer to all our problems is having more money (see Can Money Buy

AGEING POPULATION

Source: Population Division of the Department of Economic and Social Affairs of the United Nations Secretariat

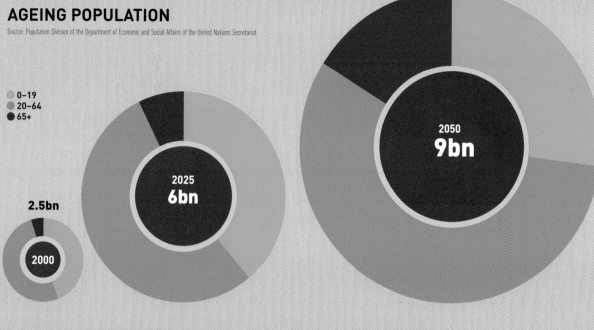

- ⬤ 0–19
- ⬤ 20–64
- ⬤ 65+

2.5bn
2000

2025
6bn

2050
9bn

"MONEY CAN'T BUY HAPPINESS, BUT IT CAN MAKE YOU AWFULLY COMFORTABLE WHILE YOU'RE BEING MISERABLE."
CLAIRE BOOTHE LUCE (1903–87), EDITOR, PLAYWRIGHT, POLITICIAN, JOURNALIST, DIPLOMAT

↑
The world is ageing rapidly. The number of people aged 65 and over will double as a proportion of the global population, from 7 percent in 2000 to 16 percent in 2050. By then, there will be more older people than children (aged 0–14 years) in the population for the first time in human history.

Happiness? on page 35). Certainly, having too little money makes life more of a struggle, but once a certain level of income has been achieved, enjoying life is more a question of successfully managing your finances rather than vastly expanding them.

For instance, a 2012 *New York Times* article by two academics, Elizabeth Dunn and Michael Norton, suggested that once a comfortable living standard had been achieved (around $75,000 per annum for Americans, apparently), the beneficial effects of earning more were fairly minimal. There are several reasons for this including the fact that extra income may well mean longer working hours, increased job stress and less time with the family. And intriguingly, while we may dream about being able to buy whatever we want when we want it, it is actually a recipe for overindulgence that can leave us feeling discontented. In the words of food writer Michael Pollen: "The banquet is in the first bite."

So the following pages look at how economics impacts on us at various points throughout our lives. From the child looking toward their next comic book purchase, to the student funding books and nights out, into the working world and supporting a family of one's own, through to old age and, ultimately, planning for what happens when we die.

Once upon a time Saturday morning meant pocket money and a trip to the sweet shop or a look in the toy shop window before deciding how to spend it. Today, young consumers are faced with much more complicated choices as the world's businesses and their marketing departments come up with ever more sophisticated products and strategies to get their share of the spoils.

It is sometimes said that youth is wasted on the young. In financial terms at least, life is unlikely to get much simpler. No mortgage to pay or job to hold down, car to insure or holiday to pay for – for the average kid in the developed world, dealing with money is most likely to revolve around the question of how best to spend their pocket money.

CHILDHOOD

But before romanticizing childhood too much, it is worth remembering that in relatively recent history (largely in the post-Second World War period), children have been developed as consumers like never before.

The child as consumer

By 2002, for instance, children in the USA between the ages of 4 and 12 directly spent $30 billion. In 2003, the expenditure of American 12- to 17-year-olds was a mighty $112.5 billion. That is significant spending power, financed in large part by kindly parents and, for older teens, with part-time jobs.

Furthermore, children are key to the ways in which the broader family budget is spent. Purchases of food, cars, holidays and even homes are all likely to be heavily influenced by the foibles of Junior. In 2008, it was estimated that America's 2- to 14-year-olds influenced household purchasing to the tune of over half a trillion dollars.

None of this has escaped the attention of the world's businesses, which increasingly target their attentions on the young. After all, if they can't get the young to part with their pocket money directly, they can try to ensure that the parents make the purchase instead to satisfy their children's desires. Marketing expenditure on products aimed at children in the US in 2004 amounted to a cool $15 billion, with the average child exposed to 40,000 ads a year (well over a hundred per day). It is money that the commercial brains believe is well spent, since it not only generates direct sales, but can help establish brand loyalty in customers with decades of buying ahead of them.

CHILD LABOR

While material conditions for most children in the developed world have been on an upward trajectory for many decades, the picture in the developing world is very different. A billion of the world's children are living in poverty.

A potent symbol of the planet's economic imbalances, child labor is endemic in many parts of the globe. According to the International Labour Organization (ILO): "The term 'child labor' is often defined as work that deprives children of their childhood, their potential and their dignity, and that is harmful to physical and mental development."

The ILO estimated that there were some 215 million child laborers in 2008, 115 million of whom were in hazardous work. Most child labor is in rural areas, with the agriculture sector the chief employer, accounting for 60 percent of workers. Only 20 percent of child laborers receive any form of financial recompense, often working for nothing within family enterprises instead.

Though the number of child workers is in decline, it is a slow process, the figure dropping only 3 percent between 2004 and 2008. Meanwhile, a third of children live in countries yet to ratify key ILO conventions, including those concerning the worst forms of child labor.

WORKING CHILDREN AGED 5–14
percentage (in selected countries)
Source: UNICEF

Central and Eastern Europe
5

Latin America and the Caribbean
8

Middle East and North Africa
10

East Asia and Pacific (excluding China)
10

South Asia
13

Sub-Saharan Africa
32

Eastern and Southern Africa
33

West and Central Africa
34

Developing countries (excluding China)
17

Least developed countries
29

World (excluding China)
17

Preparing young minds

Learning to be a consumer is all practice for later life. Despite objections about the over-commercialization of childhood, many parents feel a duty to nurture their children's development as consumers on the basis that they need to learn the skills for adulthood. Where once a child's economic education amounted to learning the need to save, it increasingly encompasses teaching the skills to spend as well.

In respect of savings and investments, financial institutions offer an ever-expanding range of products designed specifically for children, often accompanied by supplementary resources such as online games. While fostering an interest in finance among the young, banks are also taking the opportunity to establish a relationship with customers that they hope will stay with them into adulthood.

Meanwhile, operations such as Child and Youth Finance International seek to assist parents in providing financial education to the young. Established in 2011, it aims to help the 99+ percent of children it says lack "access to financial education and financial inclusion." Its ultimate aim is to provide every child with "access to financial services, financial awareness through education, a reliable source of income and the will to save and build assets to promote their future stability."

Gone, it seems, are the days when a child need only worry about which comic or candy to spend their pocket money on.

↑
One in six children between the ages of 5 and 14 – about 16 percent of all children in this age group – are engaged in child labor in developing countries. The highest proportion is in sub-Saharan Africa where an estimated 49 million children are involved in this kind of work.

There is much to envy in the life of the student. They get up late, are positively encouraged to spend their days sitting around reading books and spend most evenings drinking excessively, while sporadically mulling over the big questions of life. At least, that is what they do in the popular imagination.

STUDENT YEARS

But the question of whether to go to college or university is increasingly one of raw economics for young people around the world. The students of tomorrow have two fundamental quandaries to contemplate: can they afford to carry on their education and can they afford not to?

What a degree is worth

Apart from the intellectual and experiential benefits of going to college or university, there are clear financial advantages too. According to the OECD, citizens of its member countries who graduate from tertiary education can expect to earn on average 55 percent more than those who do not. Furthermore, graduates are more likely to be employed than non-graduates. A graduate with the right degree can potentially earn several hundred thousand dollars more over a lifetime than one who has not completed his or her tertiary education.

The value of a university education is undeniable from an economic point of view. It is widely understood that expense is an increasingly prohibitive barrier to entry for many from low-income backgrounds. The damage done to the wider economy by letting these people slip through the net is, by its nature, incalculable.

There are significant benefits for wider society too. In the first decade of the 21st century, over half of GPD growth in OECD countries was linked to income-growth amongst graduates. According to research by PayScale Inc., a US salary information company, the most valuable degrees in terms of future salary were in engineering, computers, mathematics and statistics. It should perhaps come as little surprise that a liberal arts degree is yet to make it on to the list.

What a degree costs

While education up to the age of 18 is generally provided free of charge in the developed world (and in much of the developing world for that matter), there is significant variation in what students are required to pay for higher education.

Across OECD countries they can expect to say goodbye to an average of $55,000 dollars in total, which includes tuition fees, other expenses and indirect costs such as potential earnings lost while studying.

However, where a student goes to study is key to cost. For instance, tuition fees for 2008-09 were negligible in much of Scandinavia, the Czech Republic, Mexico and Ireland. By comparison, US students at public institutions paid more than in any other country, being required to find over $6,000 per year. The next most expensive countries were South Korea, the UK, Japan, Australia, Canada and New Zealand, all of which exceeded $3,000 per year.

Other estimates suggest that the real total cost of a four-year undergraduate course at a leading American institution is nearer $200,000, while UK undergraduates can expect to pay $120,000 over the duration of their studies. As of 2012, total student debt in the US alone amounted to a trillion dollars.

With graduate employment having been squeezed by the global economic crisis, armies of potential students have been forced to weigh the initial cost of higher education against its potential benefits over a lifetime. While scholarships, bursaries, grants and loans of varying value are available in many countries, few cover all expenses. Most students ultimately rely on a source of private income (more often than not in the shape of Mum and Dad) to pay their way.

QUICK
REFERENCE

The cost of learning

While the first three items on the list below are likely to be the most significant, the others cannot be ignored and will vary greatly depending of the character of the student concerned!

University fees
Accommodation
Food
Toiletries
Books and stationery
Clothing
Telephone/Internet
Leisure

THE BEST YEARS OF YOUR LIFE?

Some people find it all but impossible to leave the student life behind. Among them must be counted Benjamin Bolger, a native of Michigan, who since 1992 has acquired 13 university degrees. Others may have earned a greater number of qualifications – for instance, Dr Hardial Singh Sainbhy, an Indian, has accumulated 35 degrees, of which 20 are at post-graduate level. But few can match Bolger's list of alma maters, which includes the universities of Oxford and Cambridge in the UK, and Harvard, Stanford, Columbia, Dartmouth and Brown in the USA. He now runs Bolger Strategic, a boutique admissions consulting practice.

Earning your first paycheck marks the start of what might be five decades or more in the working world. Unless you are lucky enough to marry or be born into money or else benefit from a lucky windfall, your choice of career will be the most influential factor in deciding the economic destiny of your life.

ENTERING THE JOB MARKET

The value of all incomes across the world is about $70 trillion per year, with the annual salary for each worker – according to a complex model devised by the International Labour Organization – coming to $18,000 (in purchasing power parity dollars). However, the global spread is striking. Coming at the top of the list is Luxembourg (average salary: $48,000) while at the bottom is Tajikistan ($2,700). Clearly, these figures fail to reflect the extremes of earning power, with a lucky few earning billions a year and a far greater number earning less than a dollar a day.

Once you have gained sufficient qualifications, which careers are going to earn you the biggest bucks? According to the US Department of Labor, the highest paid occupations by median hourly wage are: dental and medical professional, engineer, legal professional, IT manager, air traffic controller and pharmacist.

↓

This graph compares earnings between three different levels of educational attainment amongst 25-64 year olds from a selected group of OECD countries.

RELATIVE EARNING CAPACITY
in terms of quality of education
Source: OECD

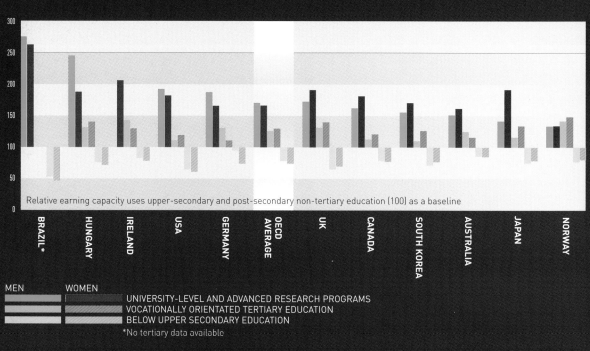

Relative earning capacity uses upper-secondary and post-secondary non-tertiary education (100) as a baseline

BRAZIL* · HUNGARY · IRELAND · USA · GERMANY · OECD AVERAGE · UK · CANADA · SOUTH KOREA · AUSTRALIA · JAPAN · NORWAY

MEN   WOMEN
UNIVERSITY-LEVEL AND ADVANCED RESEARCH PROGRAMS
VOCATIONALLY ORIENTATED TERTIARY EDUCATION
BELOW UPPER SECONDARY EDUCATION
*No tertiary data available

Global patterns

Many of the countries with the lowest unemployment rates are situated in southeast Asia, reflecting prolonged economic growth and international investment in that region. Thailand, Singapore, Vietnam, Malaysia, South Korea and Hong Kong all appeared among the ten countries with lowest unemployment in 2011. Qatar and Thailand were the world leaders, each recording only 0.5 percent. Zimbabwe, on the other hand, had a rate that some estimates put as high as 95 percent. The USA, meanwhile, was distinctly mid-table, recording a rate of 9 percent, while Spain was the worst performing EU nation at over 21 percent.

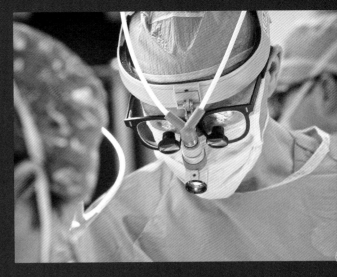

In terms of how hard employees work, there is a pattern of shorter working hours and longer holidays in the developed world. Though the economically advanced South Koreans work hardest, putting in an average of 2,193 hours per year, the next longest hours were in Chile, while Asian nations including Bangladesh, Malaysia, Thailand and Sri Lanka also featured prominently.

So how is it that some of the hardest working people are the least well paid on the global scale? At root, it comes down to productivity – workers in developed economies have the skills and the tools to achieve more in less time; in developing economies, workers need to work longer to reach their productivity targets either because they lack skills or access to suitable technology. Stereotypically efficient Germans, it is worth noting, come almost   the bottom of the international working hours league, putting in just 1,408 hours per year (a total beaten only by the Netherlands).

↑
Right at the top of the list of well-paid careers is that of a surgeon. It is well paid, has a high level of job security and provides a challenging and rewarding career. However, the education and training requirements of physicians are amongst the most demanding of any occupation and it is unlikely that you would actually start performing operations for at least sixteen years from the start of your training. Your reward – an average annual salary of $250,000, though a specialist brain surgeon or a plastic surgeon in Beverly Hills would all earn much more.

THE MINIMUM WAGE

The minimum wage is a legally defined lowest wage that workers must be paid. Initiated in New Zealand in 1894, today around 90 percent of countries have at least some minimum wage provision. Devised with the intention of improving the living standards of the lowest paid workers, its effectiveness is highly contested among economists. Opponents suggest that it increases unemployment as employers reduce the workforce to compensate for the higher wages they must pay. They also argue that small businesses suffer most and that it effectively encourages the exclusion of the lowest skilled and most vulnerable workers from employment. However, defenders of the minimum wage argue that such criticisms lack the support of empirical evidence. Indeed, many advocate for its replacement with the even higher living wage – a wage sufficient to maintain a decent standard of living within a given community.

↓

Planning a wedding is a difficult task, made harder by an industry primed to try to make you spend as much money as possible. The list below illustrates the sort of expenditure an average western wedding is likely to entail.

The happiest day of your life is also likely to be the most expensive. Unless the happy couple is content with a low-key ceremony followed by a sandwich and half a glass of bubbly for a select few guests, they can expect to see their finances take a hit. If you are thinking of saying "I do," it's worth remembering that you'll need to save up first.

GETTING MARRIED

The average cost of a wedding is a notoriously difficult statistic to establish, particularly because many of those who offer estimates are wedding suppliers with a vested interest in persuading brides, and grooms-to-be that they should be spending big. The wedding business is an important sector of the economy in many countries. In the USA, for instance, the IBISWorld market research organization reported industry revenues of almost $43 billion in 2009, down from a high of $67.5 billion in 2005.

It is generally fair to assume that the three most expensive items on the wedding balance sheet will be venue hire and catering costs for the reception, followed by the honeymoon and the bride's outfit.

According to Reuters in 2012, the average cost of an American wedding was $27,000, while *Which?* magazine had put the average price of UK nuptials at $32,000 a year earlier. Elsewhere, the *Australian* quoted $50,000 for a wedding Down Under in 2009 and the *Christian Science Monitor* suggested as long ago as 2005 a price of $34,000 for a middle-class wedding in India.

TIM AND SALLIE'S WEDDING BILL

Item	Av. cost (in US dollars)	Av. %
Insurance	$170	0.6%
The service	$800	2.8%
Reception (venue, food and drinks)	$6,200	21.5%
Evening reception (venue, food and drinks)	$2,670	9.2%
Entertainment	$1,335	4.6%
Flowers	$1,075	3.7%
Balloons and decorations	$725	2.5%
The bride's outfit	$2,500	8.6%
Hair and beauty	$267	0.9%
The groom's outfit	$350	1.1%
Attendants' outfits	$900	3.1%
Photography	$1,420	4.9%
Videography	$1,420	4.9%
Transport	$750	2.6%
Stationery	$730	2.5%
The wedding cake	$580	2.0%
Wedding rings	$990	3.4%
Gifts	$320	1.1%
Stag and doe nights	$440	1.5%
Honeymoon and first night hotel	$5,350	18.5%
Total	**$28,992**	

CELEBRATING IN STYLE

If the wedding of the UK's Prince William to Katherine Middleton was the most scrutinized of recent history, it was not the most expensive. Despite an estimated cost of $34 million (including $800,000 on flowers alone), their bill is dwarfed by the $60 million plus paid in 2004 to celebrate the union of Amit Bhatia to Vanisha Mittal, daughter of Indian steel magnate Lakshmi Mittal.

The wedding was held over six days at venues in and around Paris, including Louis XIV's palace at Versailles. A thousand guests received their invitations in the form of silver books and were treated to lavish banquets (including over $1.5 million worth of Mouton Rothschild wine), fireworks over the Eiffel Tower and even a performance from pop princess Kylie Minogue.

The dowry system

In certain cultures, notably in South Asia, the cost of a wedding for the bride's family is inflated by the need to fund a dowry – that is to say, property or a sum of money that the bride brings into the marriage. In India, for instance, the dowry system has been implicated in the skewing of the sex ratio, with some parents choosing elective abortions to avoid the financial strain of having a daughter. India has passed several laws since the 1960s seeking to outlaw the payment of dowry but it nonetheless carries on to a significant extent.

Another shocking consequence of the system is an increase in the number of dowry killings in recent decades. In such cases, a groom's family typically murders a wife (often by burning) either because her family fails to pay the full extent of a demanded dowry or as an alternative to returning an "unsatisfactory" bride to her own family, since this would also require the repayment of the dowry. The number of such crimes recorded in India alone in 2010 was 8,391.

↓

Amit Bhatia (second from left) and Vanisha Mittal (second from right) were married on June 22, 2004, racking up a $60 million bill for their thousand-guest wedding in the process. After a six-day celebration, which included a re-enactment of the couple's courtship, as well as an engagement ceremony at the Palace of Versailles, the wedding was held at a 17th-century French chateau.

Many of us spend years dreaming of owning our own homes, and then when we have them we dream of owning somewhere bigger with a south-facing garden. As we chase this dream, buying a house is likely to be the largest financial commitment most of us will ever make.

THE HOUSING LADDER

While home-ownership is the Holy Grail for many in the world's richest nations, Germany is a notable exception. In Europe's leading economy, renting is the norm, with home ownership hovering around 42 percent. Indeed, in Berlin rental property makes up fully 90 percent of the entire residential market. Reasons for this cultural inclination include difficulties in getting mortgages (deposits of 20 percent and proof of consistently high earnings are common) and the absence of a house price bubble in the recent past. While in other countries property ownership has seemed like a shortcut to generating personal wealth through house price inflation, Germans simply have not experienced the phenomenon. And having seen the fallout from property price bubbles bursting in Japan in the 1990s and in the USA and much of Europe in the 21st century, it is unlikely that there will be a surge to buy any time soon.

To buy or not to buy

Few homebuyers are in the position to purchase a property outright. Most need to secure a mortgage instead. A mortgage is a loan from a financial institution paid back over a long period (typically 20 or 25 years), using the property being bought as collateral. Should the homebuyer fail to keep up their mortgage payments, the lender may foreclose on the collateral, which is a slightly opaque way of saying they can repossess the property and sell it to pay off the outstanding debt on the loan.

→

This graph illustrates the disparity in home-ownership even among the world's richest nations. Most notably, such a beacon of affluence as Germany clearly does not prize home-ownership as a goal in the same way as, say, the more troubled economy of Spain.

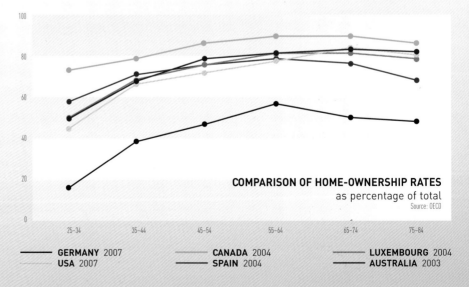

COMPARISON OF HOME-OWNERSHIP RATES
as percentage of total
Source: OECD

GERMANY 2007
USA 2007
CANADA 2004
SPAIN 2004
LUXEMBOURG 2004
AUSTRALIA 2003

A mortgage borrower eventually pays back the full value of the capital sum borrowed plus interest. Most mortgages require the gradual repayment of the capital sum and the interest over the period of the loan. However, there are alternatives. For instance, with interest-only mortgages, the capital sum is not paid off until the end of the loan term. An example of an interest-only mortgage is the endowment mortgage, where the capital sum is paid off using money accumulated by an endowment insurance policy.

Other less common mortgage forms include lifetime (or equity release) mortgages, typically offered to older people. The borrower is allowed to retain their property while receiving a lump sum or regular income stream from the lender. In return, the lender must eventually be paid back, usually on the death of the borrower and financed by the sale of the property.

TOP OF THE MARKET

According to the Global Property Guide, the 10 most expensive cities in the world for buying property (with 2011 prices per square meter) were:

1. Monaco ($53,000)
2. London, UK ($25,000)
3. Hong Kong, China ($19,000)
4. Paris, France ($18,000)
5. Singapore ($17,000)
6. Moscow, Russia ($14,000)
7. Tokyo, Japan ($14,000)
8. New York, USA ($13,500)
9. Mumbai, India ($13,000)
10. Geneva, Switzerland ($12,000)

The subprime crisis

In 2011 the Ambani family moved into their new 27-storey home, which boasts a library, ballroom, spa and theater. Just what Mumbai's millions of slum-dwellers make of it can only be imagined.

The global economic crisis of the late 2000s was signposted by the subprime meltdown that befell America in 2007. After years of signing up higher-interest mortgages to increasing numbers of applicants with poor credit histories and low incomes, the housing market price bubble burst and borrowers began to default in ever-greater numbers. Financial institutions that had made easy money by bundling together subprime loans and trading them on the markets suddenly found themselves burdened with toxic assets and huge losses. Meanwhile, countless ordinary families were forced to give up their homes, prompting the appearance across the country of tent cities more usually associated with developing nations.

In contrast the house widely heralded as the world's most expensive is to be found on Altamont Road in Mumbai. Named Antilia, after a mythical island, the house was built by Mukesh Ambani and is said to have cost over a billion dollars. Nonetheless, his bank account should be able to take it; the business magnate is rated by *Forbes* magazine as India's richest man with a fortune of $22 billion.

Having a child might complete your life, your offspring's innocent smile filling your heart with joy. All of that comes free. But the reality is that raising a family is a massive financial drain as well. While your heart will no doubt feel fuller, your wallet will more than likely feel just the opposite.

RAISING A FAMILY

Across the globe, the average fertility rate (the number of live births per thousand woman of childbearing age) in 2010 was just under 2.5. Somewhat counter-intuitively, the rate is highest in the developing world, in areas that seem least well-equipped to sustain more children economically. However, there are a number of well-established reasons for this trend: a higher birth rate is needed to compensate for a higher rate of infant mortality, there are less effective educational and birth control programs, along with an expectation that children will work for family enterprises and so increase family income and that children will look after parents in old age where state care is limited.

"THREE GROUPS SPEND OTHER PEOPLE'S MONEY: CHILDREN, THIEVES, POLITICIANS. ALL THREE NEED SUPERVISION."
DICK ARMERY (B. 1940), US POLITICIAN

The cost of bringing up baby

Clearly, there are major differences between the costs of child rearing in different countries, and even within a country itself. In 2011, the US Department of Agriculture's Center for Nutrition Policy and Promotion put the price of raising a child from birth to 17 years of age at $235,000. For low-income families, the total figure was lower, but accounted for 25 percent of total income. Middle-income families could expect to part with 16 percent of their income, while for high-income families the figure was 12 percent.

Parents in every industrialized country benefit from various packages of tax concessions, subsidies and services in kind. In many places, legislation also exists obliging employers to grant a prolonged period of absence for new parents, often with at least part of it paid. However, there are no recognized standards so provision among countries is variable.

Sweden, for instance, is widely regarded as the world leader in the field, allowing parents to take up to 480 days leave per child, of which 420 days are paid at 80 percent of salary. By comparison, US employers are only legally required to provide qualifying parents with a maximum of 12 weeks unpaid leave – an entitlement that lags behind such nations as Bangladesh, Somalia and Ecuador. Australia, Canada and Singapore, meanwhile, all operate variations on a "Baby Bonus" scheme, so that parents of newborns receive a one-off government payment.

THE CHUKWU OCTUPLETS

If having one or two babies is going to leave you short of cash, a really rare multiple birth is full of financial promise. In December 1998 Nkem Chukwu gave birth at St Luke's Episcopal Hospital in Houston, Texas, to octuplets (six girls and two boys) amid much media excitement. Alas, one of the babies died at a week old but the other seven survived. Mrs Chukwu and her husband, Iyke Louis Udobi, were inundated with offers of gifts and assistance from both individuals and corporations. This included a six-bedroom house donated to the family by a mortgage firm.

HOW MUCH DOES A CHILD COST?
in US dollars
Source: US Department of Agriculture

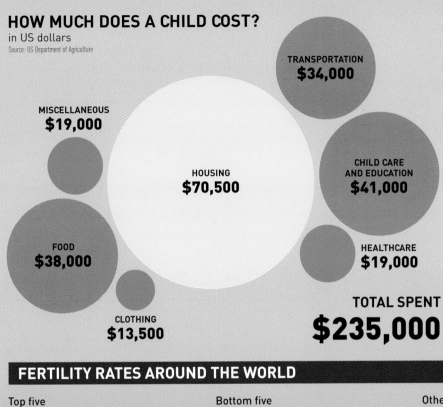

TRANSPORTATION
$34,000

MISCELLANEOUS
$19,000

HOUSING
$70,500

CHILD CARE
AND EDUCATION
$41,000

FOOD
$38,000

HEALTHCARE
$19,000

CLOTHING
$13,500

TOTAL SPENT
$235,000

← These figures represent the estimated child rearing expenses by category from birth to 17 years of age for a middle-income American family.

↓ Despite falling fertility rates, a huge increase in the population base means that the world's population is growing faster than ever before. The next 35 years are projected to add another 2.5 billion people – 90 percent of them in developing countries like Niger and Somalia.

FERTILITY RATES AROUND THE WORLD

Top five		Bottom five		Other selected nations	
Niger	7.06	South Korea	1.22	Australia	1.92
Somalia	6.34	Andorra	1.22	China	1.60
Mali	6.29	Latvia	1.17	Germany	1.39
Afghanistan	6.29	Singapore	1.15	India	2.62
Zambia	6.26	Bosnia and Herzegovina	1.15	UK	1.94
				USA	2.10

Source: World Bank, 2010

Those in middle age – specifically, people in their 40s and 50s – have traditionally been the biggest consumer spenders, reflecting their prominent financial muscle. Workers tend to be at the peak of their earning power in this period and move into the most expensive homes they will ever own, while at the same time paying out to provide for their growing children.

THE MIDLIFE YEARS

If the average professional uses their 20s to get a foothold on the career ladder and their 30s to make some steady progress up the rungs, it is in middle age that they are likely to reach senior positions that command the biggest salaries. And a good thing it is too, for this is also the period when the strains on personal finances are likely to be their worst. There may well be a mortgage to meet, kids to pay for (up to 87 percent of US pre-teen money is supplied by parents), cars and holidays to finance, and perhaps even divorces to fund. Not to mention a burgeoning taste for some of the finer things in life.

↓

With their earning capacity at its peak, middle-aged men walk a fine line between good sense and bad taste. For them the question is whether to spend wisely and save the excess for old age, or to splash out on that sports car they've always dreamed of. Sadly, many choose the wrong option.

MIDLIFE IS A KEY TRANSITION POINT FROM EGO DEVELOPMENT TO EGO TRANSCENDENCE. IT'S A TIME WHEN THE HUMAN BRAIN IS ACTUALLY AT ITS PEAK

MIDLIFE CRISIS

"Midlife crisis" was a term coined by the Canadian psychoanalyst, Dr Elliott Jaques, in 1965 to describe the emotional crisis that some people seem to suffer in middle age as that sense of immortality gifted to the young fades. A much-debated phenomenon, some argue that it is merely a construction of Western culture's obsession with youth, while others hold that it is a genuine psychological condition that manifests itself in erratic and damaging behavior. One large study in the 1990s found 46 to be the most likely year for individuals to succumb to the condition.

In the popular imagination, the classic midlife crisis case is a man of a certain age with a paunch and an identity crisis squeezing himself into inappropriately youthful clothes, splurging on a motorbike or a little red sports car, buying rounds of drinks for his new friends in expensive bars, and forking out for all the latest gadgets. While trying to put the price on a midlife crisis is a fool's errand, it is widely acknowledged that a prolonged bout can have a significant impact on personal finances, with sufferers turning to their savings or credit to fund their excesses.

A time to save

The years of middle age are also traditionally a period when individuals sharpen their focus on saving. With the clock of life ticking a little quicker, people become aware of the need to prepare for their old age by making sure their pension pot is in good shape. In addition, they may have the formidable specter of their children's college and university fees bearing down on them. On top of that, many strive for a readily accessible slush fund to cope with those life emergencies that inevitably crop up and to pay for the odd indulgence like a new car or an exotic holiday for the whole family.

With all this financial pressure, it should perhaps come as no surprise that while middle-age incomes are high, this is not always reflected in their personal happiness. Although experts disagree about when middle age officially starts – some say 36, others as old as 60 and some even claim it's nothing but a state of mind – academics have discovered that globally our self-reported sense of psychological well-being is at its lowest ebb at the age of 46, before beginning an upward arc that thankfully continues into old age.

Nonetheless, statistics suggest that the middle-aged are the best equipped to put money away for a rainy day. In much of the developed world, the early- to mid-50s are the peak savings years. In contrast to earlier life phases when a greater proportion of one's income went to meet obligations such as mortgages, the middle-aged man or woman is likely to have greater financial flexibility that allows them to develop a balanced portfolio of savings and investments. That is to say, a spread of different investment and savings types giving the best opportunity to maximize returns while minimizing the fallout should any individual investment fail.

↓

The years 45 to 54 tend to be the most bountiful for working people, if not always the happiest.

HOW AGE AND INCOME RELATE IN THE USA
IN 2011
average salaries in US dollars
Source: US Census Bureau

Age	Average salary
15–24	$30,460
25–34	$50,774
35–44	$61,916
45–54	$63,861
55–64	$55,937
65+	$33,118

Never before has the world hosted such a wealthy, healthy, active and long-living older generation. Whereas there were 200 million over-60s in the world in 1950, by 2050 it is predicted there will be two billion, by which stage there will be more people in that age group than under 15.

RETIREMENT

The economic power of this "silver army" is mighty. For example, it is believed that the over-60s will have a 23.6 percent share of US national income by 2020, while the figure for Swedish over-60s in the same time scale is put at 34.3 percent.

The silver economy

The "silver economy" is an informal term referring to the financial activity of the older generation, a consumer group increasingly valuable to marketeers. It is estimated that consumers over the age of 60 spent some $8 trillion in 2010. The Daiichi Life Research Institute reported in 2012 that 40 percent of Japan's consumer spending already came from the over-60s, while the Boston Consulting Group has predicted that over-55s will be responsible for more than half of consumer spending in the developed world in the period to 2030.

In the years to come, retailers will sell products increasingly targeted at older people. US food manufacturers, for instance, are already designing Mexican

↓

The gross pension replacement rate refers to the level of pension in retirement relative to working-life earnings.

PENSIONS: A GLOBAL COMPARISON
as percentage of salary
Source: OECD pension models, 2010

AUSTRALIA
47.3

CHINA
77.9

EU27
61.6

GERMANY
42

GREECE
96.7

ICELAND
96.9

IRELAND
29

RUSSIA
62.7

SAUDI ARABIA
100

UK
31.9

USA
39.4

THE PENSIONS CRISIS

With more people living longer, more money needs to be found to pay their pensions. The gap between the funding of the world's various pension schemes and their future obligations is at the heart of a global pensions crisis that weighs heavily on the shoulders of economists and governments everywhere. In 2008, for instance, some estimates put underfunding of the US pension program at a trillion dollars.

Part of the problem is that there are simply not enough working people to support those no longer working. Across OECD nations in 1950, there were 7.2 people between the ages of 20 and 64 for every one aged 65 or over. By 2010, that figure was 4.1 and was expected to fall to 2.1 by 2050.

Three basic solutions have been suggested to solve the crisis: firstly increasing the ratio of workers to the retired by, for instance, tweaking employment policy, raising the retirement age and increasing working-age immigration; secondly by moving from the defined benefit model to the defined contribution model (see Jargon Buster above) and capping entitlements or, finally, by raising taxes and increasing contribution demands to meet obligations.

The answer no doubt lies in finding a balance between these three strategies. But whatever the solution proves to be, getting there is certain to be a painful process.

dishes with the elderly in mind, having discovered that hot and spicy food is particularly popular amongst a generation whose age has reduced the sensitivity of its taste buds.

Similarly, marketeers will no doubt seek to address the common complaint from older people that advertising is too fixated on the young and patronizes the elderly. The entire shopping experience will likely reflect this demographic shift in consumerism too, with predictions that shopping aisles will widen, seating provision will improve, shelving will be more accessible, and labelling will be clearer.

Planning for retirement

This economic clout does not happen by itself, but is a result of long-term progress in retirement financial planning. The most common type of retirement plan is a pension payable as a regular fixed sum after an individual has given up work. These come in several major forms.

Many countries offer a state pension paid to individuals above a certain age who have made qualifying contributions during their working life (typically via the tax system). Depending on the country, state pensions may or may not be means-tested.

Occupational (or employer) pensions can either be contributory or non-contributory. In the first case, both employer and employee contribute, while in the latter only the employer contributes. The amount paid to the employee on retirement depends on a variety of factors such as scale of contribution, length of service and average or final salary.

With a private (or personal) pension, individuals (e.g. the self-employed) arrange their own pension provision, for instance by paying into a pension scheme run by a financial institution that invests the pot to provide an income in due course.

✳ JARGON BUSTER

Defined benefit pension: in which an employer guarantees a level of payment related to the employees salary and employment history.
Defined contribution pension: in which payment level depends on the extent of employee contributions and the investment performance of the pension pot.

↓

The "silver army" have never had it so good: wealthy, healthy and active, but they have a rough ride ahead because of the global pensions crisis.

However much we accept Benjamin Franklin's assertion that the only certainties in life are death and taxes, it does not make it any less galling to think that when we finally shuffle off this mortal coil, we are expected to pay for the privilege. Yet, just as life is an expensive business, so is death.

DEATH

Taxes incurred as a result of death are termed as death duties. Given the widespread unpopularity of paying tax at a time of personal loss, many countries choose not to charge such taxes at all. However, such taxes have their defenders too. Winston Churchill, for one, argued in favor of death duties in 1924 as "a certain corrective against the development of a race of idle rich" – that is to say, as a way to curb people relying on inheriting their wealth rather than earning it. The two most common types of death duties are estate taxes: levied against the estate of the deceased before it is dispersed, the rate depends on the value of the entire estate above a minimum threshold, and inheritance taxes, payable by an heir at a rate determined by the value of what they inherit. This is sometimes known as "the last twist of the taxman's knife."

↓

Many countries do not charge death duties. But for citizens of those that do, death does not mean that they automatically stop paying their debts. Funerals can rank among the most expensive purchases people will ever make, and the burden of payment often falls on the grieving family.

Funeral costs

The other great cost resulting from death is that of the funeral. Even in the hardest of economic times, the funeral business is, of course, the one trade that can rely on keeping its customer numbers up.

For the bereaved, the logistics and cost of arranging a funeral can come as a nasty surprise. As a result, many people make some provision in life to arrange for what happens to them after their death. This might include setting out their desired funereal order of service in a will (for more detailed information about wills, see page 231) to arranging an insurance policy that will cover the costs.

An average funeral in the US in 2008 cost between $7,000 and $10,000. However, there are ways to keep the expense down. While it might seem an unpalatable way of going about things, in most countries there is no legal requirement to use a funeral director, so the deceased's family could theoretically arrange everything themselves. In many jurisdictions it is even possible to be granted permission for a burial in the back garden. The environmentally concerned could also look to save on the casket by buying a bargain-priced, fully biodegradable cardboard coffin. And for those with a particularly tight grip on the purse strings, you can choose to donate your cadaver to science, with the institution to which you bequeath yourself responsible for picking up the tab.

QUICK REFERENCE

Expenses for a cremation

Estimating the likely costs of a cremation before the event will lighten the load for those who suffer a bereavement. You should consider budgeting for the following items:

Funeral director's fee
Announcements in newspapers
Casket/coffin
Vehicle hire
Suit hire
Flowers
Funeral service costs
Urn
Disposal of ashes
Memorial
Post-funeral reception

GOING OUT WITH A BANG

History has given us some pretty spectacular "going away" parties, from the extravagant burials of the Egyptian pharaohs through to the state funeral of Britain's Queen Victoria and the sad farewells to JFK, Elvis Presley and Diana, Princess of Wales.

In terms of straightforward funeral costs, the ceremony for Pope John Paul II in 2005 was perhaps the most expensive of the modern era, costing the Vatican some $9 million. However, the funeral of former US President Ronald Reagan a year earlier arguably cost much more.

Lying in state in Washington for several days before the funeral, Reagan's body received hundreds of thousands of visitors, with the expense to the District of Columbia put at several million dollars. However, the real cost came when George W. Bush, the president at the time, announced a day of national mourning. Wall Street closed, government workers had the day off and trade across the country was sluggish, all of which cost the taxpayer upward of $400 million according to some commentators.

Yet it is the great Macedonian empire-builder, Alexander the Great, who is said to have had the most expensive send-off of all time after his death in Babylon in 323 BC. His funeral is estimated to have cost around $600 million in today's money. His body, preserved in honey, was supposedly interred in a solid gold sarcophagus inside a golden casket, which then set off for Macedonia in the company of a large funeral party, which included sixty horses. Some accounts even suggest a new road was carved out in order to support the weight and size of the procession on its journey. The funeral convoy was ultimately redirected to Egypt, where Alexander was buried in Alexandria. Somewhat ironically, given all the expense, the exact location of his resting place has been lost in the mists of time.

"THERE IS ONLY ONE BOSS. THE CUSTOMER.
AND HE CAN FIRE EVERYBODY IN THE COMPANY
FROM THE CHAIRMAN ON DOWN, SIMPLY BY
SPENDING HIS MONEY SOMEWHERE ELSE."
SAM WALTON (1918–92),
FOUNDER OF WALMART

11 SAVING, SPENDING AND GIVING

↑

Once you have been able to earn money, basic personal finance comprises three essential areas: saving, spending and giving. Research suggests that teaching young children about this will help them to deal with the financial challenges and temptations they'll face when they become adults.

If money seems like an unendingly complex subject, it is worth remembering that when all is said and done you can only do a few things with it: keep hold of it, spend it or give it away. In this chapter we look in a little more detail at each of these options.

The conundrum for most of us is to decide in what proportions we should do each of these. We have no choice but to spend a certain amount on life's necessities, like food, water, clothing and shelter, but few of us manage to keep our spending only to that. Saving, on the other hand, requires us to buy into the theory of deferred gratification – that having money to spend later on will be more satisfying than blowing it all now.

"RESOLVE NOT TO BE POOR: WHATEVER YOU HAVE, SPEND LESS."
SAMUEL JOHNSON (1709–84), ESSAYIST, LEXICOGRAPHER,
BIOGRAPHER, POET

There's no logic in it

Savings rates tend to be in constant flux, but it is interesting to note that they are often higher in hard times, when logic would suggest that saving is tougher to do. In the developed world, for instance, saving fell off in the 1990s and into the 2000s when economic growth seemed like it would go on forever. Come the global crisis, though, and the rate went up as people worried about what the future held.

Giving, meanwhile, not only affects our finances but also reflects how we see our place in the world. Why we choose to give, to whom and how we expect our gift to be used are all highly personal choices. This helps to explain why patterns of giving are so difficult to predict.

Take the US Bureau of Labor statistics on giving for 2007. Across the country, people gave an average of 2.2 percent of their income to charity. The rate among the country's highest earners was just below that at 2.1 percent, while among the lowest paid it was over twice that at 4.3 percent. Furthermore, while generosity traditionally declines in periods of downturn, it does so least among the poorest. Perhaps it is the case that those nearest to the economic precipice themselves have greater empathy for those in need.

↓

There is, of course, no one-size-fits-all spending plan. How a household disposes of its income depends on the extent of income, the specific needs of the household and a multitude of personal preferences. This chart is an example of a non-specific but commonly used "rule of thumb" guide to personal expenditure.

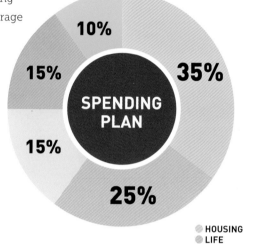

SPENDING PLAN

10%
35%
15%
15%
25%

- HOUSING
- LIFE
- TRANSPORTATION
- DEBT REPAYMENT
- SAVINGS

MADAME DEFICIT

Despite fierce competition, Marie Antoinette – wife of the 18th-century French king, Louis XVI – emerges as one of history's most notorious spendthrifts. Marie, something of a tomboy as a child, soon developed decadent tastes after marrying into the French court. She ordered 300 outfits a year from the esteemed fashion designer Rose Bertin, commissioned specially created perfumes and spent untold francs on hosting lavish parties – all at a time when Louis was piling up debt in support of his foreign policy. Hence Marie soon earned the nickname "Madame Deficit." To cap it all, her name became embroiled in scandal when a diamond necklace worth $100 million in modern times was smuggled out of the country. Despite her almost certain ignorance of the scam, her reputation for excess was sealed. In the end, her love of spending was a passion for which she would pay with her head in the French Revolution.

However hard we try to be sensible with our money, sometimes it just seems to burn a hole in our pocket. Of course, humans have always gone about buying and selling, but consumerism began to accelerate exponentially as a result of the Industrial Revolution. Industrialization brought about the production of more, better and cheaper goods that could be sold to work forces gradually finding themselves in possession of higher wages and more leisure time. Nor does the consumer growth spurt show any signs of slowing over the long term.

CONSUMER SPENDING

In economic terms, consumer spending refers to the money spent by households to meet their needs and wants. It includes: durable goods (those with a long lifespan, such as televisions and kitchen equipment); non-durables (items with a short lifespan, such as food and drink); semi-durables (goods – such as clothes – that can be used continuously or repeatedly over a reasonably long lifetime, though for a shorter time than durable goods) and services (such as travel and entertainment).

Global patterns

The US is by far the world's largest consumer market. In 2009, for instance, total global consumption was put at $34.6 trillion, of which the USA accounted for just under 30 percent. The next biggest consumer spender, Japan, contributed less than 9 percent to the global total.

Consumer spending in 2009 accounted for over 70 percent of American GDP, significantly higher than other major economies, including China (37 percent), Japan (58 percent), Germany (59 percent), and the UK (65 percent). Nonetheless, it is in some of the world's poorest countries that consumer spending takes up most of GDP, with Liberia running the highest rate at 184 percent. In the world's poorest countries, though, consumer spending is concentrated on essentials – notably food – while in the developed world a much greater proportion goes on what we might regard as luxury goods and services.

Retail therapy

Retail therapy is a term used to describe shopping undertaken with the principal purpose of improving the shopper's mood. It specifically does not refer to the purchasing of essential items but to the buying of non-essential treats, or comfort buys. It is often unclear whether the "therapy" results from the pleasure derived from the item bought or from the very process of making the purchase.

Closely associated with rich societies and the phenomenon of materialism (an unrestrained desire to acquire and consume), there are serious sides to unfettered consumerism. A survey by the European Union in 2001 found that 33 percent

⬇

A.T. Kearney's Global Consumer Institute carried out a study of global spending patterns from 1990 until 2020, looking at over 70 product categories across 86 countries. Their results suggest we are not going to stop spending anytime soon.

SPEND, SPEND, SPEND
in trillions of US dollars
Source: Euromonitor; A.T. Kearney analysis

1990
$18

2000
$22

2010
$28 +43%

(ESTIMATE) 2020
$40

of respondents demonstrated a "high level of addiction to rash or unnecessary consumption," while some psychologists now recognize oniomania, or compulsive shopping syndrome. Beyond debate is the fact that many consumers find their unbridled spending leading them into serious financial problems, particularly in societies where credit is readily available.

SHOPPER'S PARADISE

The jet-setting shopaholic could do much worse than head to downtown Dubai, where they will find the Dubai Mall. The world's largest shopping mall by area at 12 million square feet (equating to about 50 soccer pitches), it is located over six floors of the towering Burj Khalifa complex.

Opened in 2008, it boasts over 1,200 stores, including many of the foremost names in international retail. Offering car parking space for 14,000 vehicles, in 2011 it was the world's most visited shopping destination, with 54 million people coming through the doors. There is as especially good reason for the sweet-toothed to book a trip, as the Dubai Mall is also home to Candylicious, the world's largest sweet shop.

↓

The jewel in the crown of Asia's retail shopping centers is Hong Kong. Famed for its favorable tax rates, the city's traditional markets, like Stanley Street and the Temple Street night market, combine with state-of-the-art malls and department stores to provide retail therapy for even the most demanding shopaholics.

"Neither a borrower, nor a lender be." So said Polonius in *Hamlet*, yet it is a warning largely ignored in the modern credit-hungry world — almost one in ten adults across the world takes out a formal loan from a financial institution in any given year.

BORROWING

When you get a loan, the interest rate you see advertised is not necessarily the one that you will get. The exact terms that you are offered will depend upon your credit rating. This is a score that takes into account your assets and liabilities, as well as your borrowing and repayment history. Credit reports can be sourced from an array of credit bureaus operating throughout the world. The better your credit rating, the better loan deal you'll secure. It is also worth remembering that a lack of credit history can work against you. However, they can be built up by managing, for instance, a series of low-level direct debits. If you are new to the credit game, it could be worth using such a measure to grow your credit score ahead of seeking out more significant credit.

Multiple options

For those considering borrowing, there are a multitude of options available, some more attractive than others. A fixed rate loan provides a borrower with a set sum repayable at a fixed interest rate over a defined period of time. This is the classic bank loan model. An authorized overdraft is a pre-arranged agreement between a bank and an existing customer allowing the customer to take their bank account balance into the red for a set (and usually short) period of time. There may be an accompanying fee or interest charged, with unauthorized overdrafts attracting significantly higher penalties.

Payday loans are intended to be short-term (they were originally intended to tide the borrower over until payday, hence the name). They often have giant interest rates, with APRs in the thousands not unusual. If paid off quickly, they can be useful, but if not, they can become enormously burdensome.

Installment plans (or installment-plan agreements) are normally arranged directly with a retailer. Typically, the customer pays a deposit on a purchase and is allowed to take away the item immediately. The remainder of the cost, along with interest and administration fees, is paid off via a series of regular payments. The buyer does not actually own the good until full payment is made. In-store credit has similarities with installment

↓
Whichever borrowing option you choose, the bottom line with all loans is that the quicker you pay it back the less you will pay.

plans in that it is a "buy now, pay later" scheme with a credit line directly between retailer and purchaser. Some deals offer 0 percent interest, making this an attractive way to pay for big-ticket items over a longer period of time. However, some in-store credit schemes charge high interest, often comparable with credit cards.

Peer-to-peer lending has become increasingly popular with the rise of the Internet (see page 41). Credit unions are cooperative financial institutions, owned and run by their members. Only members may make deposits or take out loans, which are usually cheaper than commercial lenders as a result of lower administration costs and their not-for-profit status.

Pawnbrokers lend money in return for goods pledged as security and do not consider the borrower's credit rating. The security is retained for a fixed period and is returned to the borrower on full repayment of the loan plus interest and fees. If the loan is not repaid, the security is sold to cover the cost. Loan sharks are exponents of predatory lending. To make matters worse the loan usually comes with a fat interest rate and failure to make repayments might be met by intimidation, violence or blackmail. The best advice is never to swim with sharks.

UNAUTHORIZED AND UNREGULATED, LOAN SHARKS OFFER LOANS TO THOSE WHO PERHAPS CAN'T GET CREDIT ELSEWHERE

The APR

The annual percentage rate (APR) is a figure that expresses the annual interest rate as an easily comparable percentage. However, it is only a baseline guide and the small print surrounding it will describe exactly what will have to be paid back. Loans are usually paid back on a more regular basis than annually. For example, if a loan is taken out that is payable in a year over 12 monthly instalments, with each payment, the size of debt reduces so the amount of interest payable (though not the rate at which it has been borrowed) correspondingly reduces. Thus, if a $100 loan is taken out for a year at a 10 percent interest rate, the final payment will not be $110 but, in fact, only $105.50.

JARGON BUSTER

Unsecured loan: a loan in which the lender has no claim on any of the borrower's assets. As such, they are considered more risky for the lender than a secured loan and so usually command a higher interest rate.

Secured loan: a loan backed by some part of the borrowers assets, such as property or a car. In the event of the borrower defaulting, the lender has a claim on the specified assets.

WHAT A LOAN WILL COST

This table shows how the size of monthly instalments and the total sum payable vary over the duration of a loan if borrowing $1,000 at 7 percent APR.

Loan period	Monthly payment	Total repaid
6 months	$170.09	$1,020.52
12 months	$86.53	$1,038.32
24 months	$44.77	$1,074.54
36 months	$30.88	$1,111.58
48 months	$23.95	$1,149.42
60 months	$19.80	$1,188.07

A credit card allows its holder to buy goods and services on the promise that they will subsequently repay the card issuer. It is different from a debit card, which can be used for purchases only if there are sufficient funds in the holder's account at the time of the purchase (though some debit cards will guarantee purchases up to a certain value).

CREDIT CARDS

Credit cards are an example of revolving credit. With revolving credit, the borrower may borrow any amount up to a pre-agreed credit limit, with the amount of credit available changing as money is borrowed and repaid. It also allows borrowers to use credit repeatedly and to pay back the debt (plus interest, administrative charges and any penalty fees) either over a period of time – credit cards typically demand a monthly minimum repayment – or in full at any time. The great advantage of revolving credit is its flexibility though, as anyone who has ever spent on a credit card will tell, keeping a grip on your spending and subsequent repayment obligations can be difficult.

↓
While the majority of people pay off their credit cards before accruing interest and penalties, a significant minority carry onerous debts.

● FULL BALANCES PAID EACH MONTH
● BALANCES UP TO $10,000 (MEDIAN $2,554)
● BALANCES OVER $10,000 (MEDIAN $17,336)

BY PAYING JUST THE MINIMUM MONTHLY PAYMENT ON THE AVERAGE CREDIT CARD, A $1,000 SPENDING SPREE TAKES OVER 20 YEARS AND $3,300 TO CLEAR

13%

CREDIT CARD DEBT IN THE USA

54%

33%

Addicted to credit?

Credit cards have a habit of making us feel richer than we actually are. Understandably, then, it is hard to say no to them. Yet it has long been a concern that as credit becomes more freely available, our hunger for it continues to grow unabated.

Consider some of the figures. Half of all adults in high-income countries have a credit card (compared to a figure of 7 percent in developing economies). This reflects a love of credit not merely restricted to credit cards – in the developed world, a quarter of adults have an outstanding loan on a property purchase, while the figure for the developing world is just 3 percent.

In practice, the credit frenzy means that there were 686 million credit cards in circulation in the US (over two for every single person) as of 2009. In China, the figure was a comparatively low 199 million, though credit card growth between 2003 and 2007 reached 23 percent suggesting that a booming economy has fed credit lust there too.

In the US, each household carries an average of over $15,000 in credit card debt. Below is a comparison of outstanding national credit card balances across four major economies in 2009 (in billions of US dollars):

■ **US $775** ■ **UK $87.5** ■ **Canada $73.9** ■ **Australia $40.4**

PUT IT ON THE CARD

Edward Bellamy's 1888 novel, *Looking Backward: 2000–1887*, tells the story of a man who awakes from 133 years in a coma at the start of the third millennium. One of the features of the futuristic world that Bellamy depicted was the credit card, a full sixty years before it was actually invented.

Its real world creator, however, was Frank McNamara. While having lunch with a business colleague in the autumn of 1949 at Majors Cabin Grill in New York, McNamara was about to pay when he was horrified to discover that he had forgotten his wallet. While a quick phone call saw his wife come to the rescue on that occasion, the incident played on his mind for several weeks.

After chatting with his lawyer, Frank Schneider, he hit upon an idea for a club whose members could eat at specific restaurants, sign for their meals on the spot and then pay up within a specified time period. By February 1950, the Diners Club opened for business with some 200 invited cardholders joining up for a $3 fee. Unlike most modern cards, any outstanding balance was to be paid by the end of each calendar month. While no interest was charged, participating establishments agreed to pay a 7 percent transaction fee to Diners Club.

Majors
CABIN
GRILL
33 W. 33rd Street
New York City

"*Fine food*
IN A
friendly
atmosphere"

← Majors Cabin Grill on Manhattan's West Side is the birthplace of the credit card. Businessman Frank McNamara set up his diners' club to facilitate payment for eating out in particular restaurants around New York, within a year his club boasted 20,000 members and the age of the credit card had begun.

Retailers constantly strive to secure the loyalty of their customers, so ensuring for themselves repeat sales and a consistent market share. And as history has proven time and again, one of the surest ways to secure loyalty is to buy it. While not yet ubiquitous, loyalty cards are a common part of the modern shopping experience, going under a series of names including advantage cards, club cards, points cards or reward cards.

LOYALTY CARDS

Loyalty programs are based on the idea that shoppers get rewarded for their repeat business. Typically, customers who complete a free application process are issued with a card that is swiped each time they make a purchase, with a number of points automatically added to their account. The types of reward on offer can include: cash back on the current purchase, vouchers for use against future purchases, access to exclusive products or invitations to special shopping events.

Mutual benefits

For the retailer, loyalty programs not only encourage brand loyalty but provide an opportunity to accumulate information on the individual buying habits of customers. Sellers can use their consumer data to, for instance, build up a vast

→

In Europe and the USA it is estimated that an average of over 80 percent of adults own at least one loyalty card, with 25 percent owing five or more, with an average annual saving of $150. These cards have proved invaluable for retailers who are putting ever more effort into marketing them. While members benefit in kind, in return the retailers are able to compile huge amounts of information about their customers' shopping habits.

TRADING STAMPS

One of the earliest organized loyalty programs was started in the USA in 1896 by the Sperry & Hutchinson Company. S&H sold perforated, gummed, trading stamps with a nominal value of 1, 10 or 50 points, to retailers including corner shops, department stores and, later, gas stations. Retailers then passed on the stamps to customers as a reward, the amount depending on the value of the purchase. Customers stuck the stamps in a book that they received for free and on reaching a certain value of points, exchanged them for any number of goods available via a local store or through a catalogue. The stamps, commonly known as Green Shield Stamps, became a feature of American (and, in the 1960s and 1970s, British) life. They were so popular, it is said that by the 1960s the company was distributing three times more stamps than the US Postal Service.

mailing list and target advertising. It can even influence store layout. If customers are shown to commonly buy certain products together, then a wily store manager will make sure these products are stocked close to each other.

Loyalty schemes have taken root throughout North America, Europe, Oceania and large parts of Asia too. Almost 90 percent of Americans are involved in at least one loyalty program, with the average household signed up to 14 schemes.

One of the pioneering, company-specific loyalty schemes of the modern era was the frequent flyer program launched by American Airlines in the early 1980s. Under its terms, members received "air miles" each time they booked a flight, which can later be redeemed against the cost of a future booking. It is a model that has been widely copied across the travel industry.

Criticisms

Critics argue that loyalty programs have numerous downsides. They are expensive to operate and in many instances do not result in increased business, since the customers who sign up may well be loyal patrons already. From the shopper's point of view, there are those who have misgivings that the consumer information gathered infringes upon personal privacy. One has the right to shop, they argue, without having all of one's purchases analyzed by a faceless enterprise.

Another accusation is that such schemes necessarily put at advantage large businesses with the resources to fund them while undermining small business. Some local traders have tried to hit back by issuing disloyalty cards. In 2011, for instance, it was reported that a number of independently-run coffee shops in Boston, Massachusetts, had joined together to set up just such a scheme, with customers rewarded for visiting any of the participating businesses rather than one of the monolithic international chains.

A 2009 SURVEY OF MEMBERSHIP IN LOYALTY PROGRAMS BY INDUSTRY IN THE US REVEALED THAT THE MARKET LEADERS ARE FINANCIAL SERVICES (WITH 422 MILLION MEMBERS), AIRLINES (277 MILLION) AND RETAIL (191 MILLION)

If it is true that there is safety in numbers, group buying (also known as collective buying) should be good news for consumers around the world. Reliant on the ability of the Internet to connect people, group buying offers the promise of low prices as long as there are enough of you who want to buy.

GROUP BUYING

It has always been the case that buying in bulk tends to lower the price of a product. Traditionally, this has been a strategy employed by traders buying from wholesalers, the traders then selling their goods to individual purchasers for a higher price per unit. Until recently, practicalities have ensured that end buyers have largely been unable to organize themselves into buying groups to take similar advantage of bulk buying.

How it works

While there are minor variations between the leading group buying sites, the basic models are similar. Typically, the consumer signs up to a website for free, specifying the locale in which they reside. They then regularly receive an email from the website, offering products or services available in their local area at a significantly reduced price (for instance, 50 percent off theater tickets or 80 percent off a spa treatment). However, the reduction is only applicable if enough people pay to receive a discount voucher in a specified time. In order to achieve this, customers are encouraged to attract other purchasers through their own social–networking channels.

In theory, all the principal parties benefit. The customer gets a cut-price deal, the group buying website takes a cut of every voucher sold, and cooperating businesses get to expand their customer base and advertise for free. In addition, the website builds up a database of consumers with a value of its own.

→

The Internet and its associated social media has allowed groups of people to organize themselves to take advantage of the sort of bulk buying discounts traditionally associated with wholesalers.

Group coupon

One of the foremost names in the group buying revolution, Groupon, (a contraction of the words "group coupon") began operating in November 2008, initially in Chicago. Its founder, Andrew Mason, persuaded a former employer of his, entrepreneur Eric Lefkofsky, to invest an initial million dollars in the project.

Groupon soon gained a foothold in the market place and in its relative infancy was described by *Forbes* magazine as "the fastest growing company ever." Recalling memories of the heady days of the original dot-com boom, the company attracted enormous interest, reportedly turning down a takeover offer from Google in January 2011 of $6 billion. At the time, some analysts valued the company at over three times that amount. In November of 2011, Groupon made an IPO, offering just under 5 percent of its shares and achieving a share price that valued the company at $23 billion.

Nonetheless, soon after its IPO, the company had recorded losses of several hundred million dollars in its short life. While it subsequently moved into profit, its share price had fallen by around three-quarters within a year.

↑
A form of group buying called *tuango* (store mobbing) originated in China in 2010. A group of people, sometimes friends, sometimes connected via the Internet, would visit a store at an agreed time to buy the same product. They would haggle with the storeowner to get a bulk discount. Today, group buying websites like lashou.com have taken over this growing market.

Saving can be defined as the preservation of money resources set aside for future use. In broad terms, savings tends to denote a low-risk strategy to this end, such as depositing money in a savings account at a bank. Savings are often contrasted against investments, when money is used to buy, say, stocks and shares or works of art. Investments generally offer the promise of higher returns but with additional risk, while savings are safe but have a low return. Nonetheless, savings and investments can both be seen as ways of saving.

SAVING PATTERNS AROUND THE WORLD

According to the World Bank's Global Financial Inclusion Database, over a third of the world's adult population reportedly saved or set aside money in 2011, and around a fifth save in a formal financial institution. As to be expected, saving is far more likely in high-income economies where essential spending takes up a lower proportion of incomes. Within developing countries, those in the top fifth

THE MARSHMALLOW EXPERIMENT

This was a landmark psychological study carried out at Stanford University in 1972 under the supervision of Professor Walter Mischel, a specialist in personality theory and social psychology. Focusing on the idea of deferred gratification – the ability to resist an immediate temptation in return for the promise of a greater reward later on – its results had significant implications for our understanding of why some people are better at saving and investing than others.

The experiment used children aged between four and six years old. They were led into an otherwise empty room where they were presented with a marshmallow. They were told that they could eat the marshmallow immediately or wait 15 minutes, when they would be given an additional one to enjoy. Of the 600 children studied, most attempted to hold out but only a third resisted long enough to receive the extra treat.

Many of the subjects were re-evaluated at various points over the proceeding decades, with the children able to defer gratification in the initial experiment exhibiting a broad spectrum of advantages in later life, from higher academic achievement and sense of self-worth to lower Body Mass Index scores and divorce rates. For economists, the study suggested a psychological imperative that prompts some people to spend money for immediate gratification and others to put it away for a rainy day.

of incomes are three times more likely to save than those with an income in the bottom fifth. In developed economies, meanwhile, the richest 20 percent are twice as likely to save as the poorest 20 percent. Across economies there is also a clear correlation between higher education levels and higher rates of saving. Furthermore, globally men are more likely to save than women.

Informal saving

As the graph below clearly shows, a large number of those who do save are using methods other than formal financial institutions. So where do they put their money? The most common forms of informal saving include depositing with friends or family members or savings clubs – community-based clubs where individuals can pool their money. These are particularly popular in sub-Saharan Africa where nearly one in five people (rising to 44 percent in Nigeria) use them or entrusts their money to similar operations. Others prefer asset accumulation – for instance, buying precious minerals, food commodities or livestock. And, of course, there's always "under the mattress" – simply keeping hold of money without the prospect of increasing its value.

FORMAL AND INFORMAL SAVING

AMONGST ADULTS WORLDWIDE
percentage of total income
Source: Demirguc-Kunt and Klapper

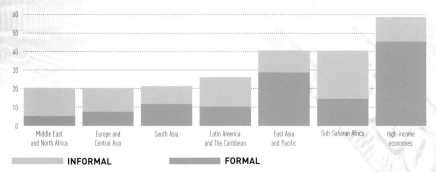

INFORMAL   FORMAL

HOUSEHOLD SAVINGS RATES
percentage of disposable household income
Source: OECD

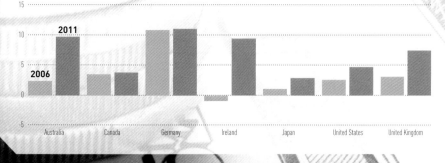

> **"THE ART IS NOT IN MAKING MONEY, BUT IN KEEPING IT."**
> PROVERB

←

Saving to cover future expenses – education, a wedding, a big purchase – or to provide against possible emergencies is a universal tendency. Globally, 36 percent of adults report having saved or set aside money in 2010–11.

←

The amount of household savings is calculated by subtracting household consumption (the value of goods and services bought) from household disposable income.

For those keen to put their money to work for the future, there are a number of options to consider, among them savings accounts, bonds and securities, stocks and shares, property and investment funds.

TYPES OF SAVINGS

To help you choose there are legions of financial advisors attached to banks and other financial institutions. Of course, many of them have vested interests in selling you products and services from which they benefit themselves, so it pays to have a basic knowledge of all the standard types of savings.

Savings accounts usually offer a higher rate of interest than current accounts, but may be less flexible. Depositors may need to give a period of notice before making a withdrawal or must commit to keeping their money in the account for a set period before touching it. Bonds and securities come in a variety of flavors, reflecting differing levels of risk and prospects for returns (see pages 120–1). Government-backed bonds, for instance, are typically low risk and offer suitably low returns, though they may still prove preferable to leaving your money in a savings account. Stocks and shares are investments in companies that can bring rich rewards but can also be risky (see pages 124–5).

Investing in property to rent out (rather than live in) provides a regular revenue source in the short term and a high value asset in the long term. Or you could choose an investment fund, a managed fund that pools together money from multiple investors to create a mixed portfolio of investments.

Compounding the issue

Assuming you keep your money in a savings account for a reasonable length of time, you will feel the benefits of compound interest. Compound interest means that not only do you earn interest on the principal (i.e. your initial investment), but also on the interest it earns. Say a depositor puts $10,000 into a savings account with an annual interest rate of 10 percent, compounded annually. At the end of the first year the $10,000 will have grown to $11,000 (i.e. $10,000 plus 10 percent [$1,000]). At the end of the second year, 10 percent interest is applied to the $11,000 (as opposed to just the original deposit). So after two years, the account balance is $12,100 ($11,000 plus 10 percent [$1,100]). At the end of year three, 10 percent is added to $12,100, giving a new balance of $13,310. And so on for as long as the account is maintained.

YOUR SAVINGS OPTIONS

TIME
▼

INSTANT ACCESS SAVINGS

LIMITED ACCESS SAVINGS

LONG-TERM INVESTMENTS

◀ GROWTH ▶

THE AGE OF AUSTERITY

It is hard enough to save as an individual, but when it is an entire nation that needs to curb its spending, the process can be agonizing. Just such a fate befell numerous countries around the world as a result of the economic crisis of the late 2000s. When a government faces spiralling debts and seeks to cut its spending by a sharp decrease in funding for social welfare and public services, the process is known as austerity.

In 2009, a year before he became the UK's Prime Minister, David Cameron ushered in an Age of Austerity in a speech to his party. In Britain, austerity was hardly a new concept, with an earlier Age of Austerity having stretched from the end of the Second World War into the 1950s, a period in which successive governments sought to repair a war-ravaged economy. The Olympics that were held in London in 1948 were even known as the "Austerity Games," with athletes encouraged to bring their own food since rationing was then in full swing.

While the greatest economic minds of today slug it out as to whether the modern wave of austerity actually works, those living through it have no choice but to put up with the harsh consequences. So prevalent has austerity been in the early stages of the 21st century that it was designated Word of the Year by the Merriam-Webster Dictionary in 2010.

↓

Flat broke after six years of war, London hosted the Olympic Games in 1948. With a budget of £750,000, the athletes were housed in RAF camps and schools and transported around in double-decker buses. The meager diets of the British team were bulked out with whale meat. Despite this, the Austerity Games were considered a remarkable success with athletes such as 30-year-old Dutch runner Fanny Blankers-Koen mesmerizing the huge crowds.

If giving away wealth is a minority sport for most people in life, it takes on major significance in death. A bequest is property, goods or money left either to an individual or to an organization through a will. Strictly speaking, a bequest refers to personal property, while real property (as in bricks and mortar) is covered by the term devise.

BEQUESTS

Whether it is your beloved first born or the cats' home up the road that is destined to benefit, putting in place a legally-binding plan for the dispersal of your estate after you are no more makes the lives of those left behind much simpler.

What is a will?

A will is a legal document written during life to communicate the wishes of a person once they are dead. Typically, a will sets out how the deceased's property should be distributed, how any dependents should be looked after and how any other ongoing concerns should be dealt with. For a will to have legal status it must be written by someone above the age of majority when in sound mind.

It is not necessary to employ a lawyer to oversee the drawing up of a will, but it is more often than not highly advisable.

THE NINA WANG STORY

There's nothing so likely to tear a family apart as a disputed will. At a time when people are raw with grief, the clamor to take possession of the wealth of the dearly departed can result in feuds that never truly end. Someone with an unenviable track record of disputed wills was Nina Wang, once Asia's richest woman. Born in Shanghai, she married Teddy Wang (below left), boss of the hugely successful Hong Kong-based Chinachem

Group. However, Teddy was kidnapped in 1990, never to be seen again, and was declared legally dead in 1999. That prompted a long-running dispute over his estate between Nina and her father-in-law, Wang Din-shin. Both claimed to be sole heirs, with Din-shin accusing her of having had an extra-marital affair and she claiming to be in possession of a will criticizing the extended Wang family. In 2002, after a lengthy courtroom tug-of-war, Din-shin was awarded the estate and charges of forgery were brought against Nina. However, in 2005 the Court of Final Appeal found in favor of the widow and the estate went to her. Nina herself died in 2007, leaving an estimated $4.2 billion. Two wills then made an appearance. The first, written in 2002, left her riches to the Chinachem Charitable Foundation. The second, apparently from 2006, named Tony Chan Chun-chuen, a feng shui expert and Wang's alleged lover, as the beneficiary. In 2010 the Hong Kong High Court found in favor of the Foundation, with Chan subsequently put on trial for forgery, an allegation he denied.

MAKING A WILL

EXECUTOR
Name the person legally responsible for making sure your will is carried out.

GUARDIANS
If you have young children, who is to look after them if you die?

BENEFICIARIES
List the people and institutions you want to leave to, with details of each legacy.

SIGNATURES
Make sure you sign your will and have it witnessed in accordance with the law.

TRUSTEES
If you are setting up a trust, who will administer it?

STORE
Make sure the finished will is locked away somewhere safely, ideally with a lawyer.

The person making the will is called the testator and those parties benefiting from it are known as beneficiaries. Somebody who dies without having made a will is described as intestate. One of the principal functions of a will is to appoint an executor, a personal representative to oversee the administration of the estate and carry out the wishes contained within the will. Bequests given directly may attract death duties (see pages 210–11), but setting up a trust to administer a bequest can reduce and even eliminate tax concerns. In addition, a trust is a good way to look after assets should the beneficiary be very young or otherwise incapable of managing them themselves.

When the testator has died, the executor applies for a legal grant of probate, which confirms the validity of the will. Should a person die intestate, the process is considerably more complicated. The probate court will seek to appoint an administrator (often a close relative or friend of the deceased) to administer the estate. However, if there are legal challenges to the execution of this role, the probate process can be long and drawn out, not to mention ferociously expensive.

Yet wills need not be lengthy affairs. There are several examples in languages other than English that extend to no more than two words, translating roughly as "all to my wife" or similar. The longest will ever, meanwhile, is thought to be that of Frederica Evelyn Stilwell Cook, who died in England in 1925 having set out her wishes over almost a hundred thousand words across four large, bound volumes.

↑
A will is probably the most important document you will ever write. It is your stated wish of what happens to the possessions you leave behind when you die. None of us want to think of our own mortality, but ignoring it is usually even more problematic, especially for those you leave behind.

Etymologically, the word philanthropy comes from Greek and means "the love of mankind." In the modern sense, it is seen as allied to, but distinct from charity. In one sense, the great philanthropic figures and organizations of today are defined by the extent of their charitable work: to give $5 is charity, but to give $5 million is philanthropy. However, that is an over-simplification of a complex subject.

GIVING TO GOOD CAUSES

True charity and philanthropy are both rooted in an altruistic desire to improve the world. However, it has been argued by specialists in the field that there has been a gradual shift from charity (as a tool to tackle the symptoms of a problem) toward philanthropy (as a method to tackle the causes of a problem). Employing a well-established analogy, charity may thus be seen as giving a hungry man a fish while philanthropy sets out to teach him how to catch his own.

Philanthropy or charity?

Many individuals who do not consider themselves philanthropists undertake some sort of charitable giving on a regular or irregular basis. This can range from making a regular financial gift to a favorite charity to putting a few spare coins in

↓

For most of the last twenty years Bill Gates, founder of Microsoft, has been the richest person on Earth. More than a decade ago he decided to start using his wealth – currently estimated at $58 billion – to set up a foundation to promote global health, global development and US education. In 2006, he and his wife Melinda, seen here in Patna, India, decided to dedicate themselves to the work of the foundation that bears both their names.

THE BILL AND MELINDA GATES FOUNDATION

Co-chaired by the Microsoft founder, his wife and his father – this foundation has redefined the philanthropic landscape since its establishment in 1994. With vast resources and an equally impressive public profile, the organization runs three principal programs: Global Development, Global Health and a United States Program. It has endowments in excess of $35 billion and makes annual grants equivalent to 10 percent of the entire US government aid budget. In 2006, Warren Buffett, a trustee, promised to donate shares in his Berkshire Hathaway business over a period of several years. His gift was valued at $31 billion at the time. In 2010 Buffett and Gates announced the Giving Pledge campaign, which they described as "an effort to invite the wealthiest individuals and families in the United States to commit to giving the majority of their wealth to philanthropy." As of 2012, more than 80 billionaires had signed up, potentially securing future philanthropic donations worth hundreds of billions of dollars.

FUNDING BY THE BILL AND MELINDA GATES FOUNDATION 1994–2011

in US dollars
Source: Bill and Melinda Gates Foundation

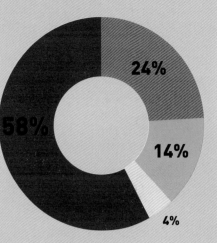

PROGRAM AREAS		
GLOBAL HEALTH	$15,271,000,000	●
UNITED STATES	$6,236,000,000	◕
GLOBAL DEVELOPMENT	$3,613,000,000	◔
NON-PROGRAM GRANTS		○
FAMILY INTEREST GRANTS	$982,000,000	
CHARITABLE SECTOR SUPPORT	$71,000,000	
EMPLOYEE MATCHING GIFTS AND SPONSORSHIP	$21,000,000	
TOTAL GRANTS	**$26,194,000,000**	

a collection box on a store counter. Donations such as these play a vital role in the finances of many charitable and not-for-profit organizations.

For the philanthropist, there are three principal ways of doing good. Firstly, they can make large individual donations to already established charitable organizations. Alternatively, they can make an endowment. This is a gift to a charity or non-profit organization for a stated purpose, such as funding a scholarship. But the most significant donations come in the form of a foundation to oversee specific projects and missions. This was the road taken by some of the great historical philanthropists, with many of their organizations still in operation and highly influential today. Among them are the foundations of the steel magnate Andrew Carnegie, the oil billionaire John D. Rockefeller, the confectioner Joseph Rowntree and the pharmaceutical entrepreneur Henry Wellcome.

↑

Since it was founded in 1994, the Gates' foundation, which is based in Seattle, has spent over $26 billion on good causes, making it the world's biggest private foundation.

The business of giving

Charity is certainly big business. In 2007, the value of donations from individuals giving to tax-deductible charities in the US came to $220 billion. Private charitable giving accounts for around 2.2 percent of US GDP and 1.3 percent in the UK. Charity and philanthropy no doubt have major roles in addressing poverty in the biggest emerging economies too. However, in terms of donations as a proportion of GDP, China and India (where millions live in poverty alongside a significant number of dollar billionaires) both lag behind the US, at well below 1 percent.

In order to make charitable giving more economically appealing, donations attract tax advantages. Writing off charitable gifts against income, for instance, reduces the donor's marginal cost of giving. With the highest earners facing the highest tax rates, tax incentives thus reduce the cost of giving significantly. By offering tax incentives, governments can expect to see greater philanthropy from the richest members of society, aiding a fairer distribution of wealth across society.

"I HAVE FOUND THAT AMONG ITS OTHER BENEFITS, GIVING LIBERATES THE SOUL OF THE GIVER." MAYA ANGELOU (B. 1928), POET, PLAYWRIGHT AND CIVIL RIGHTS ACTIVIST

12 THE FUTURE OF MONEY

↑

From the stone pillars and porticoes of the classical bank, to the skyscrapers of the modern financial districts, the physical landscape of the global economy has changed hugely over the last few hundred years. Though no one can predict for sure how it will develop in the next 50 years, one thing is for certain: the landscape will change.

"This planet has – or rather had – a problem, which was this: most of the people living on it were unhappy for pretty much of the time. Many solutions were suggested for this problem, but most of these were largely concerned with the movement of small green pieces of paper, which was odd because on the whole it wasn't the small green pieces of paper that were unhappy."

So wrote Douglas Adams in the introduction to *The Hitchhiker's Guide to the Galaxy*. While it may be true that money does not hold all the answers to the world's problems (and indeed is the cause of a good number of them), it is nonetheless one of the defining creations of mankind and its role in the future is unlikely to decline. In this chapter we look at how the world of money might be configured in the not too distant future and speculate on some of the questions that may face us. Predicting the future is the perfect recipe for ending up with egg on one's face. Nonetheless, over the next few pages we will attempt to extrapolate from the world as it is today how it might look tomorrow.

THE MIGHTY DOLLAR

By its sheer ubiquity, if nothing else, the American dollar occupies a unique place in the history of money. Today, the one-dollar bill, first issued in 1862, is instantly recognizable. Made from cotton fiber paper, it is also exchangeable in a multitude of countries, including many in which it is not legal tender. With the might of the American economy behind it, the dollar is still the world's principal reserve currency, whether it remains so in the future is open to question.

←

The reverse of the dollar bill shows both sides of America's Great Seal. One side comprises an unfinished pyramid at the base of which is the date 1776 – when America gained independence from Britain – in Roman numerals. There are also the Latin phrases *Annuit Coeptis* ("He [God] favors our undertaking") and *Novus Ordo Seclorum* ("A New Order of the Ages"). The other side has a bald eagle, which holds in its beak a ribbon bearing the motto *E Pluribus Unum* ("Out of many, one"). The motto "In God We Trust," a phrase coined by Salmon P. Chase, Treasury Secretary under President Abraham Lincoln, has appeared on all American banknotes since 1957.

The scourge of income inequality

The chapter starts with a vision of the global economy in 2050 should the general trends evident in the opening part of the 21st century carry on in the same direction. That being the case, it seems a fair assumption that income inequality will remain with us. Identified by some of today's political giants as the single biggest challenge before us, we examine what it is, why it matters, how it's measured and what is being done to deal with it.

One radical suggestion is to reconstruct our fundamental ideas of what a successful economy is. Economic growth is only a good thing, isn't it? So what of the argument that ditching our quest for growth is our best shot at securing the future of the planet? It is doubtless a hard sell, particularly in those places that are only just beginning to reap the rewards of growth, but as the environment becomes an increasingly significant factor in political decision-making, the question may yet force itself on to the agenda.

From there we move on to ask whether the dollar is secure in its role as the world's dominant currency, before considering societies in which money plays no role – barter communities – and where traditional cash has been phased out altogether. Finally, what does the future hold for the academic discipline of economics itself?

In discussing the ideas within this chapter, we make no claim about how money will be in the future, only how it might be. The novelist John Sladek had his own take on what the future holds, which might just prove the most accurate: "The future, according to some scientists, will be exactly like the past, only far more expensive."

> "MONEY PLAYS THE LARGEST PART IN DETERMINING THE COURSE OF HISTORY."
> KARL MARX (1818–83), SOCIOLOGIST AND ECONOMIST

The 21st century has seen the rise of India and, especially, China to the ranks of global economic powerhouses. It has led to fears among the traditional Western powers that the East will dominate the economic picture in the coming century. Certainly, the US and Western Europe face new challenges if their economies are to carry on prospering in the way they have been. But what might the economic landscape of 2050 look like?

THE GLOBAL LANDSCAPE IN 2050

Firstly, economic predictions for decades to come should be accompanied by the caveat that none of us – least of all economists – have crystal balls (see Forecasting on pages 166–7). Predictions are made on the basis of existing evidence – admittedly, a good place to start – but the global economy will inevitably take twists and turns that no one has yet foreseen. Demographic shifts, changes in governance, wars, natural disasters, the environment and technology – all will have their influence.

Chart-toppers

Taking this into account, which nations are likely to be the movers and shakers by mid-century? According to a 2012 report by the global research department of the HSBC banking group, China will swap places with the USA as the planet's foremost economy. (Although, Knight Frank and Citi Private Bank's 2012 Wealth

↓

A building site in Delhi: India looks set to overtake China as the world's biggest economy by 2050. The roots of this development are found in the reforms of the early 1990s when the government adopted free market principles. Since then the economy has seen enormous growth, in its productivity, exports, its working population and its GDP. The government has been careful to invest in the country's infrastructure – thereby increasing long-term growth potential – and been careful to maintain manageable debt burdens.

HSBC'S PREDICTIONS FOR THE WORLD'S BIGGEST ECONOMIES BY GDP IN 2050

in US dollars
Source: HSBC

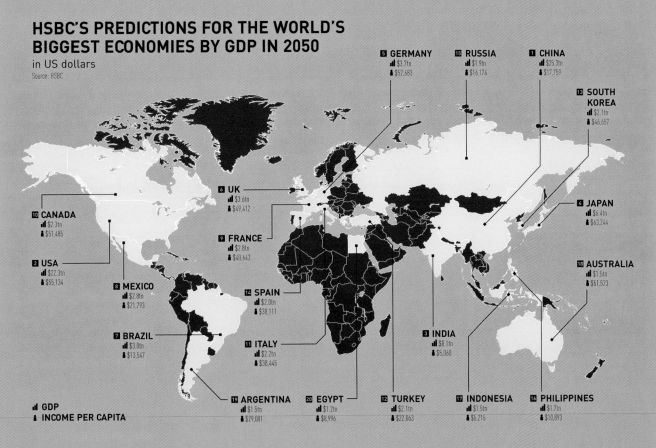

5 GERMANY
$3.7tn
$52,683

15 RUSSIA
$1.9tn
$16,174

1 CHINA
$25.3tn
$17,759

13 SOUTH KOREA
$2.1tn
$46,657

10 CANADA
$2.3tn
$51,485

6 UK
$3.6tn
$49,412

9 FRANCE
$2.8tn
$40,643

4 JAPAN
$6.4tn
$63,244

2 USA
$22.3tn
$55,134

8 MEXICO
$2.8tn
$21,793

14 SPAIN
$2.0tn
$38,111

18 AUSTRALIA
$1.5tn
$51,523

7 BRAZIL
$3.0tn
$13,547

11 ITALY
$2.2tn
$38,445

3 INDIA
$8.1tn
$5,060

GDP
INCOME PER CAPITA

19 ARGENTINA
$1.5tn
$29,001

20 EGYPT
$1.2tn
$8,996

12 TURKEY
$2.1tn
$22,063

17 INDONESIA
$1.5tn
$5,215

16 PHILIPPINES
$1.7tn
$10,893

Report predicted that after China had supplanted the USA in 2020, China itself will be overtaken by India by 2050.) Europe's share of the top ten places in the economic league table, meanwhile, is expected to fall from four to three.

Despite the GDP growth of China and India, both are likely to remain outside the top fifty for income per capita, suggesting that distributing their new wealth to their vast populations will remain an elusive goal. Indeed, by this measure, the traditionally rich nations of Luxembourg, Singapore and Switzerland will top the table, ahead of the USA in eighth, Germany in tenth and the UK in fourteenth place.

The world's fastest growing economies

What is the world's fastest growing economy? China would seem like a good guess. But it would be wrong, although it does make it into the top twenty. The rest of that group, though, is made up of some surprising names. None are in the Western Hemisphere, about half hail from sub-Saharan Africa and most of the rest are Asian nations, many of them severely underdeveloped. This is because it is far easier to grow quickly from a low base of GDP. The country that many analysts believe will grow most quickly over the next few years is São Tomé and Principe, an island state in the Gulf of Guinea with a population of under 200,000. Once reliant on the cocoa trade, it has prospered on the back of oil discoveries as well as a thriving tourism sector. The country is predicted to have a cumulative growth rate in excess of 30 percent in the five years leading up to 2017.

↑

HSBC's predictions for the most improved economies look to be amongst developing nations. Apart from China and India, the Philippines look set to be one of the big winners, climbing into the top twenty from a position in the low forties in the early part of the century. The biggest losers will be in Europe, mainly because of a reduction in the working population.

In 2011, President Obama described income inequality – the unequal distribution of income within individual societies and between nations – as the "defining issue of our time." Although many developing nations have made up ground on the richest countries, a globe no longer divided between the haves and have-nots seems as distant a dream as it ever has. Ensuring that everyone has enough without disrupting the mechanisms of economic growth is perhaps the greatest question economists of future generations face.

↓

Despite Uganda's steady economic growth over the past few years, poverty, particularly among the rural population – some 10 million men, women and children – is described as chronic. The poorest are mainly subsistence farmers whose lives are continually disrupted by civil strife, variable rainfall and poor soil. Even when they are able to produce a good crop, they are unable to get to market because they do not have access to vehicles and roads are poor or non-existent.

ADDRESSING INEQUALITY

There have been few starker examples of income inequality than a 2006 report from the World Institute for Development Economics Research, which concluded that 2 percent of the world adult population own more than 50 percent of household wealth. Even in countries enjoying reasonable rates of expansion, there is no guarantee that levels of inequality will not increase. For instance, the Overseas Development Institute has reported that despite annual growth of 2.5 percent in the period 2000 to 2003, the poverty rate in Uganda actually increased by 3.8 percent. Furthermore, the Asian Development Bank has argued that if income distribution had not declined since the 1990s as economic growth accelerated across the continent, almost an extra quarter of a billion people could have been lifted out of poverty.

Nor is inequality a problem restricted to relatively poorer nations. There was uproar in the USA in 2011 when a report from the US Congressional Budget Office revealed that in the period 1979–2007, growth in real after-tax income grew by 18 percent for the lowest-earning 20 percent, while for the top 1 percent it had increased on average 275 percent. In the same year, the OECD reported that inequality among its member nations was at its highest level for

MILLENNIUM DEVELOPMENT GOALS

One of the great missions of recent times aimed at alleviating the sufferings of the world's poorest people is the Millennium Development Goals initiative. At the turn of the current millennium, the UN set eight goals, with a target date for achieving them of 2015. They are:

- Eradicating extreme poverty and hunger.
- Achieving universal primary education.
- Promoting gender equality and empowering women.
- Reducing child mortality rates.
- Improving maternal health.
- Combating HIV/AIDS, malaria, and other diseases.
- Ensuring environmental sustainability.
- Developing a global partnership for development.

Every member state of the UN plus at least 23 international organizations signed up to them and significant, though by no means comprehensive, progress has been made on many of them. China and India, for instance, have made steps in addressing their poverty rates (each boosted by a decade and more of rapid economic expansion) while other parts of the world – notably sub-Saharan Africa – have recorded much less success.

half a century. Where the richest 10 percent of OECD citizens had incomes seven times as great as the poorest 10 percent in the mid-1980s, by 2011 they were nine times as rich.

The causes and impact of inequality

The major causes of inequality are complex and interwoven. The single biggest cause is wage inequality, which has its own causes: most obviously in gender (even in developed countries like the USA women on average earn 81 percent of male earnings) and in unequal access to education, which impacts directly on future employment prospects. Another important factor is that less progressive tax systems result in a larger tax burden falling on the poor. In addition, it is the rich who are more likely to employ accountants who strive to keep tax bills down through tactics such as tax avoidance. Finally, in countries where governance is poor, corruption and nepotism blooms with the result that money is skimmed o ff the top and retained by those already in positions of relative power and wealth.

The social effects of inequality are well established. By social group, it is the poor that generally have lower life expectancies, lower levels of educational achievement, higher levels of drug use and greater exposure to crime. The economic impacts are less clear though. Many economists argue that inequality holds back growth, weakening demand and leaving economies susceptible to crises.

There are alternative theories, however. Inequality, suggest some schools of economic thought, means the wealthy are more inclined to save and invest their money while the poor work harder to move up the earnings ladder. By contrast, increased equality removes incentives to work and innovate. For many nations, among them China and the USA, equality of opportunity is considered more important than equality of income.

> **"WHILE ECONOMIC GROWTH IS NECESSARY, IT IS NOT SUFFICIENT FOR PROGRESS ON REDUCING POVERTY."**
> BAN KI-MOON (B. 1944), SECRETARY-GENERAL OF THE UN

↓

Oil is the lifeblood of the modern world, and the combustion engine is its indomitable heart. Although arguments rage about how long the planet's oil wells will continue to pump, the fact is that at some point they are very likely to run dry.

Economic growth is an increase in the ability of an economy to produce goods and services over a period of time, and it is commonly measured in terms of GDP. It has long been the orthodoxy that economic growth is necessary for sustained improvement in the quality of life, particularly given the rapid expansion of the global population. But is this an irrefutable truth? Some argue that our attitudes to growth need to change in response to the changing circumstances of the planet.

NEW GROWTH MODELS

The traditional paths to economic growth are well founded: an increase in the working population in turn increases overall productivity while technological innovation allows each worker to increase their personal productivity. The planet, though, faces myriad challenges, among them global warming, declining natural resources and endemic poverty in many of its countries. More than two centuries of post-industrial economic growth, unprecedented in human history, has brought about many benefits but can hardly claim to be a cure-all. So what are the alternatives?

Zero growth

Zero growth is the state of nil economic expansion, with the economy maintaining a state of equilibrium instead. If this happens spontaneously in a poor economy, it is regarded as stagnation and is detrimental to the well-being of those living within that economy. However, there is a small but vociferous army of analysts – among them economists, geographers and environmentalists – who believe that nations with already developed economies should adopt policies specifically to achieve the goal of zero growth.

There are three major reasons. Firstly, economic growth goes hand-in-hand with environmental degradation. If industrialization has been the driver of economic growth for centuries, it has also been responsible for catastrophic environmental damage. Perpetual growth will only exacerbate the problem, the argument goes, until rather than improving our quality of life, growth will render the planet unliveable. Secondly, economic growth relies on the utilization of natural resources. Much of current world industry, for instance, is dependent on oil. Yet, there are only finite stocks of such natural resources. Finally, traditional models of economic growth reinforce inequality and a boom-and-bust cycle that is inherently unstable.

For some, though, not even zero growth goes far enough. Given impetus by the financial crisis of the late 2000s, there have been minority calls for de-growth – that is to say, a policy toward shrinking the global economy.

Alternative thinking

However, opponents of zero growth and de-growth are legion. Basic supply and demand mechanisms, they argue, will protect scarce resources by increasing prices and directing funding toward developing alternative resources. Scientific and technological innovation will, meanwhile, focus on making the achievement of growth more efficient and less energy-intensive. Furthermore, even the most ardent "zero growthers" recognize that it is not a viable option for developing nations in desperate need of economic growth to spur improvements in basic living conditions. Nor does it seem likely that the developed world would agree to such self-sacrifice while developing economies, India and China in particular, continued to use depleting resources to take the competitive advantage away from established industrial nations.

WORLD OIL PRODUCTION BY TYPE

in millions of barrels per day
Source: OECD/IEA

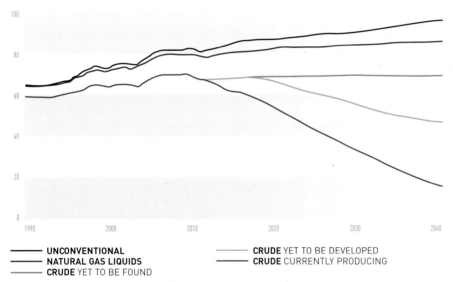

← This graph is based on the International Energy Agency's New Policies Scenario, which takes account of broad international policy commitments from the international community. Though it indicates that currently producing fields have already reached peak oil, oil production in total will continue to grow until at least 2035.

- —— **UNCONVENTIONAL**
- —— **NATURAL GAS LIQUIDS**
- —— **CRUDE** YET TO BE FOUND
- —— **CRUDE** YET TO BE DEVELOPED
- —— **CRUDE** CURRENTLY PRODUCING

PEAK OIL

Peak oil refers to the moment at which the world's production of crude oil reaches its maximum rate before going into decline until all extractable oil resources have been used up. Exactly when peak oil will occur is a source of much debate; with the most pessimistic analysts believing it has already been reached. However, those of a more optimistic outlook predict that any future shortfall in production will be balanced by the discovery of new oil sources.

The implications for the global economy are potentially devastating should oil reserves be depleted before viable alternative energy sources have been adopted. The need to delay the consumption of known reserves is thus a leading argument in favor of pursuing zero growth. Nonetheless, others hold that this would merely put off an inevitable problem and that in reality humanity's ability to adapt and innovate will find a solution instead.

Held toward the end of the Second World War, the Bretton Woods Conference (see pages 66–7) not only established both the IMF and the International Bank for Reconstruction and Development, but effectively elevated the US dollar to the position of de facto global currency.

A SINGLE CURRENCY FOR THE WORLD?

In 2009 a report by the United Nations Conference on Trade and Development (UNCTAD) suggested introducing a new currency to replace the dollar as the reserve currency of choice. So is it possible that a new global currency could be introduced, and if so, why? The idea posited by UNCTAD was not to replace all of the world's sovereign currencies with a new, unified currency in the style of the EU's euro. Instead, it proposed a supranational currency to replace the dollar as a reserve currency. A reserve currency is one held by countries in their foreign exchange reserves that can be used to pay international debt obligations and fund high value international transactions, such as the purchase of oil and gold.

By using a reserve currency, nations do not have to use their own currencies, which are always subject to the vagaries of the international foreign exchange rates, so keeping domestic currencies more stable.

While the US dollar is not the only reserve currency (others include the yen, sterling and the euro), it is by far the most important. It has held its pre-eminent position because of its long-term stability. The US economy has historically been large and strong and not prone to excessive inflation. All of which means, people know where they stand with the dollar.

The dollar's crown is slipping

However, in more recent times, the dollar has not held quite such a steady path, with problems in America's domestic economy impacting at global level. In the 21st century, the country has suffered high unemployment and patchy growth while running up huge debts – the national debt currently standing by some calculations at a little over $16 trillion. Washington has responded by printing new money in a bid to kick start activity, effectively reducing the value of the dollar. Those holding dollars around the world found that their reserves were suddenly worth a little less.

↓

Foreign exchange reserves are stockpiles of foreign currencies held by governments. They are both a major national asset and a crucial tool of monetary and exchange-rate policy, particularly during a financial crisis.

INTERNATIONAL FOREIGN EXCHANGE RESERVES BY CURRENCY

2010 Q2
Source: IMF

3.9%
3.3%
4.2%
26.5%
62.1%

● US DOLLARS
● EUROS
● POUNDS STERLING
● JAPANESE YEN
● OTHER

SPECIAL DRAWING RIGHTS

SDR is an international reserve currency unit established in 1969 by the IMF and was designed as a supplement to existing reserve currencies. An artificial currency, its value is calculated against a basket of currencies made up of the dollar, euro, sterling and yen. IMF member nations can keep reserves of SDRs to settle balance-of-payment disputes between then. For many years, the SDR has had little practical role in the world economy other than as the unit of account for the IMF. Nonetheless, the UNCTAD report of 2009 suggested revitalizing the system as an alternative to the dollar system. Theoretically, the IMF would then be like a global central bank and the stability of the world economy would be less reliant on the economic conditions of any single nation.

Major international players, notably Russia and China, have started to voice the opinion that the global reliance on the dollar is advantageous to the US but less so to other nations. UNCTAD became the first major international organization to add its voice to the argument that a new reserve currency might be desirable. One solution, it suggested, would be to reinvigorate the IMF's existing Special Drawing Rights (SDR) system.

Even this, though, falls short of what is needed for those who advocate a full-scale supranational currency to replace sovereign equivalents. But as the difficulties experienced in the Eurozone attest, developing a single currency that serves the purposes of nations with disparate circumstances and ambitions is no simple task. While a new reserve currency is a distinct possibility, it is by no means a certainty. The chances of a single global currency are much smaller.

↓
Despite the apparent "death" of the euro other groups of countries have seriously considered issuing single currencies of their own. There have been discussions between Australia and New Zealand; various South American countries; eastern and southern African countries about the possibility of such fiscal convergence. Those in favor say it helps integration, brings interdependency, social and cultural integration and therefore peace. Those against think it defeats the purpose of fiscal responsibility, fearing a loss of flexibility and a lack of accountability.

Before there was money, there was barter – the direct exchange of goods and services. Then money came on the scene as a means to measure the value of particular goods and services, gradually subsuming barter in all but a few corners of the world.

RETURN TO BARTER

However, barter has started to make a concerted comeback and, somewhat ironically for such an ancient system, it has been reborn by modern technology. Is it likely to become our standard method of trade? Of course not, but it might just be finding a new place for itself in the world of commerce.

GREECE-ING PALMS

Given years of economic instability, it is perhaps no surprise that faith in the euro has been in short supply in Greece. In the port city of Volos 800 people decided to sidestep the euro entirely, setting up a barter system in mid-2010 that utilizes its own alternative currency, the TEM. With one TEM worth roughly one euro, participants build up their accounts (all stored online and backed up by a voucher system) by exchanging goods and services. For instance, one member might be credited with a certain value of TEMs by clients taking her yoga lessons. She can then use this credit to buy candles from another participant, or language lessons or jam or any other goods or services being offered by participating members. Thus, in this corner of Greece a thriving economy has sprung up with no dependency upon the nation's strained official economy.

HOW THE SYSTEM WORKS

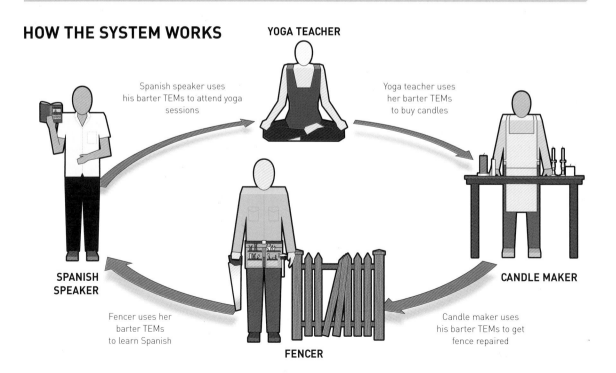

YOGA TEACHER

Spanish speaker uses his barter TEMs to attend yoga sessions

Yoga teacher uses her barter TEMs to buy candles

SPANISH SPEAKER

CANDLE MAKER

Fencer uses her barter TEMs to learn Spanish

Candle maker uses his barter TEMs to get fence repaired

FENCER

A cow, a fence and some bread

The theory behind barter is beautifully simple. Farmer Giles has a broken fence and is worried that his cattle will escape. Handyman Harry has the skills and tools to repair it and gets on the job immediately. When Harry has finished the job, Farmer Giles pays him with a gallon of milk and a side of beef. Harry and his family drink the milk, eat some of the beef and trade some of it with Barry the Baker in return for some bread. And so the system goes on ....

The problem comes in valuing the various goods and services in the system. Is fence-mending worth a side of the biggest cow in the field or the smallest? And how many loaves of bread should Barry give Harry for a cut of meat? Putting a relatively fixed value on each of these things and then exchanging tokens denoting those values is in many ways a cleaner system, hence the rise of money.

But just as the Internet has revolutionized the world of money, so it has transformed bartering. Not so long ago, if you needed a new microwave, you would have to buy one at a shop. Even if you had a chair you no longer needed, it is unlikely you would have persuaded the shop to accept it in a swap. Today, there are countless websites devoted to cyber-barter. Someone with a spare chair can find someone in the next town with a microwave that they no longer want who is willing to take the chair in exchange. They might keep that chair for themselves, or swap it for some beef or as payment for a fence repair. However, it should be noted that for tax purposes many governments treat barter transactions just as they would standard money transactions.

↑
Although barter is said to be making a comeback, it has never really been away. The first ever means of economic exchange, it has remained popular, particularly in low-income economies. During the financial crisis in Argentina in the early 2000s, thousands of people would assemble each week at a barters' square on the outskirts of Buenos Aires in order to exchange goods and services.

▶
See also Alternative Currencies (pages 72–3)

As we have seen elsewhere in this book, technology has gradually eroded the prominence of cash (i.e. notes and coins) in our economies. While no country has yet made the leap to become an entirely cashless society, it seems likely that it is just a matter of time.

THE CASHLESS SOCIETY

IN 2009, AN EU ESTIMATE CALCULATED THAT THE ACTUAL COST OF ALL PAYMENT METHODS, INCLUDING CASH, CHEQUES AND CARDS, WAS SOMEWHERE BETWEEN 2 AND 3 PERCENT OF GDP

Having the technology to do this is one thing but what are the advantages of plastic money and digital wallets over old-fashioned paper and metal? For the financial sector, it is principally a matter of cost. Processing cash transactions is both time-consuming and expensive. Cash is also expensive to move, store and guard. By contrast, the automated transactions on debit and credit cards are more efficient and even make money for the banks when fees are charged.

For governments, the end of cash would see the end of costs associated with printing and minting it. Nor can electronic money be counterfeited as paper money can. It is also argued that cash is favored by criminal enterprises looking to launder their ill-gotten gains since paper money does not leave a paper trail. Electronic money, by contrast, is easier to track and would, the theory goes, make criminal activity harder to conceal. In a similar vein, governments would be able to better ensure tax compliance.

VIRTUAL MONEY

For those generations not raised in the age of the Internet, "virtual money" is one of the more difficult-to-grasp phenomena. Virtual currencies are used in virtual worlds – computer-based worlds inhabited by users who employ avatars to represent them. Many online role-playing games, such as Second Life, allow users to buy, sell and economically interact as they would in the real world. While the currencies used are specially created, in some instances they can be obtained in exchange for real currency. Similarly, many new businesses have been set up to trade virtual goods and services for real money. It has been known for hundreds of dollars to change hands for imaginary real estate in virtual worlds. Facebook issues credits for its users to spend on virtual goods, generating estimated revenues of $1.65 billion for the company in 2012. This interaction between real and virtual economies poses intriguing philosophical questions. Should virtual wealth be taxable if it can potentially be exchanged for real money? Does the prospect of real money profits mean online games should be subject to gambling laws? And if an operator pulls the plug on a game, should they compensate players for the loss of their virtual holdings?

HOW THE VIRTUAL ECONOMY WORKS IN ONLINE VIDEO GAMES

The 'keep cash' camp

However, the dash to ditch cash is not welcomed by everyone. As the debit and credit card revolution has developed a number of disadvantages have come to light. Firstly, there is security. Cash attracts thieves, but plastic cards are regularly stolen and cloned, bank accounts hacked and identities stolen. The cashless society may thus simply see one sort of criminal activity replaced by another. Secondly comes privacy. While it might suit the financial sector and governments to track every transaction within an economy, it may be a trend less attractive to private individuals. But perhaps the most likely problem is digital vulnerability. If all our finances only exist in cyberspace, what if there were to be a devastating accident or cyber attack? Could a blackout across the electrical grid, for instance, render us all technically penniless?

These warning voices may well find themselves drowned out. In many societies cash already seems on borrowed time. Across Europe, only about 9 percent of transactions still include cash and in the USA it's just 7 percent. The country poised to be the first to go cashless is Sweden, where cash transactions make up only 3 percent of the total. Already many businesses (including some bank branches) no longer deal in cash at all, and even some churches have installed card readers to process congregational offerings. The nation has correspondingly seen a steep decline in bank robberies, but a rapid rise in cybercrime (see pages 190–1).

↓

A customer pays for supermarket groceries with a smartphone application in France. The "flash and pay," an application developed by the supermarket, allows customers to manage their shopping list, coupons, loyalty programs, budget and payments with a mobile device in any store offering the service.

It has been said that economics has not come very far since the days of Adam Smith. In his influential 1989 essay, "The End of History?" Francis Fukuyama argued that the passing of the Cold War had secured the ultimate victory of Western liberal democracy. For some economists, that meant the victory of market capitalism too.

THE FUTURE OF ECONOMICS

However, the emergence of China and the shock of the global financial crisis have caused many within the field of economics to question whether they have not grown rather complacent.

No doubt governments and financiers will continue to wrestle with the big economic questions from a broadly neoclassical perspective. But in the future, economics will perhaps make greater room for heterodox schools of thought that attempt to explain economic phenomena using approaches not necessarily considered by mainstream schools.

THE INVESTOR OF THE FUTURE WILL NEED TO POSSESS A SENSE OF THE PAST, AN INTELLIGENT GRASP OF THE PRESENT, AND FORESIGHT FOR THE TRENDS OF THE FUTURE IN NOT JUST ECONOMIC TERMS, BUT CULTURAL, SOCIAL, AND POLITICAL

Heterodox economics

These are likely to include, but are by no means restricted to: environmental economics, which sees economics through the prism of environmental concerns; behavioral economics, which looks at the interaction of economic decision-making and psychology; neuro-economics, which brings together economics,

NOBEL PRIZE FOR ECONOMICS

The single greatest honor that can be bestowed upon an economic thinker is the Nobel Prize for Economics (officially called the Sveriges Riksbank Prize in Economic Sciences in Memory of Alfred Nobel). The youngest of the Nobel prizes, having first been awarded in 1969, it is funded by an endowment from the Swedish central bank and is worth 10 million kroner. It is awarded on the same principals as the other prizes, which means winners have conferred "the greatest benefit on mankind" in the opinion of the Prize Committee. There can be a maximum of three recipients in any one year. The average age of winners is 62 and the vast majority hail from the USA. There has only been one female winner to date, Elinor Ostrom in 2009. Perhaps inevitably for such a politicized discipline as economics, the Prize has attracted considerable controversy over the years. Nonetheless, it reflects a heritage of lively discourse and suggests that economics is not short of big ideas.

psychology and neuroscience and feminist economics, which approaches economics from a female viewpoint.

One potential casualty of such heterodoxy is the "rational actor," a hypothetical figure who has long underpinned orthodox political thought. Rational in the sense of making every decision on the basis of maximizing personal advantage, the model is increasingly seen as a useful but ultimately imperfect caricature. Individuals, it is evident, are driven by mood and circumstances and not always rationality. Neuro-economics and behavioral economics open a new window on how people function as economic participants.

While it is unlikely that economics will undergo a root-and-branch revolution in the years to come, the discipline will inevitably evolve in response to new challenges and circumstances. Clearly history did not end with the fall of the Soviet Union and even if it looked for a short while like the battle for economic orthodoxy had been won, it remains – to a lesser or greater degree – up for grabs.

Only one thing is certain, however, in the words of Ronald Coase, winner of the Nobel Prize for Economics in 1991, who introduced a talk he was giving at the University of Missouri in April 2002 as follows: "What I'm going to talk about today is why economics will change. I talk about it because I don't only think it *will* change. I think it *ought* to change."

↑

Joint winners of the Nobel Prize for Economics in 2012 were American economists Alvin Roth (left) and Lloyd Shapley. Both worked on a central economic problem: how to match different agents as well as possible. For example, students have to be matched with schools of their choice, and donors of human organs with patients in need of a transplant. Their award-winning model has been described as an outstanding example of economic engineering.

GLOSSARY

A

Account – a summary of economic activity over a given period.

Asset – a possession of value.

Austerity – large-scale spending cuts undertaken by a government to address its debts.

B

Bank – a financial institution that borrows and lends money.

Bankruptcy – a legal arrangement deployed when a subject cannot pay their debts.

Bear market – a market in which prices are likely to fall.

Bequest – to leave a gift in a will.

Billion – a thousand million.

Bond – an investor loan to a government or business for a defined time period at a fixed rate of interest.

Boom – a period of strong economic activity.

BRIC(S) nations – acronym referring to the emerging economies of Brazil, Russia, India, China and, latterly, South Africa.

Broker – an individual or company that connects buyers and sellers.

Bubble – a cumulative rise in price driven principally by a belief that the price will rise further.

Budget – a government statement of expenditures and receipts for the coming year(s).

Bull market – a market in which prices are likely to rise.

Business – all forms of commercial activity (also referring to any organization involved therein).

Bust – a sudden economic collapse.

C

Capital – man-made resources used in economic production.

Capitalism – economic system based on the private ownership of property and the means of production.

Cash – money in the form of notes and coins, though sometimes used to refer to money generically.

Central bank – the bank that control's a country's money supply and monetary policy.

Charity – voluntary giving to a good cause (also, an institution administering help to those in need).

Command economy – economy controlled by a centralized decision-making body.

Commodity – raw material that can be traded in bulk.

Competition – the state of individual buyers and sellers having a choice of suppliers and customers.

Consumption – the use of goods and services to satisfy needs and wants.

Cost – the sacrifice resulting from making a particular decision.

Crash – a sudden decline in the value of a market.

Credit – the supply of a good or service for a deferred payment.

Credit rating – an assessment of a subject's ability to pay a debt.

Credit union – a cooperative financial institution.

Currency – the money in general use in a country or regional block.

D

Debt – money owed by one party to another.

Deficit – an excess of liabilities over assets over a set period of time.

Deflation – a progressive fall in price level.

Demand – the wish and ability to acquire a good or service.

Dependant – a person who relies on someone else for economic support.

Depression – an extended period of low economic activity and high unemployment.

Derivative – a tradable security, the value of which is decided by the price of an underlying asset.

Developed economy – an economy with established high levels of economic growth, security and general living standards.

Developing economy – countries with generally lower levels of income, living standards and social indicators.

Dividend – payment by a business to its shareholders, usually on an annual basis.

E

E-commerce – buying and selling using the Internet.

Economic cycle – general pattern of fluctuations in a national economy, such as expansion, peak, recession and recovery.

Economics – social science looking at how individuals and groups use scarce resources to meet their needs and wants.

Economy – system of production, distribution and consumption of goods and services.

Electronic money – money transferred over computer networks.

Employment – service or trade performed for payment under contract of hire.

Equities – stocks and shares in a private company.

EU – European Union, an association currently consisting of 27 European nations, which together form the biggest economy in the world.

Eurozone – comprising those EU member nations who have adopted the euro as their currency

F

Expenditure – spending, either by a consumer, government or investor.

Exports – goods and services sold by one economy to another.

F

Federal Reserve – the system of central banking in the USA.

Finance – the creation, management and study of money (or, alternatively, monetary support for an enterprise).

Financial sector – the part of the economy made up of banks and other financial institutions.

Fiscal policy – government policy on taxation and expenditure.

Foreign exchange – the money of a foreign country.

Fraud – criminal deception to gain an economic advantage.

G

GDP – Gross Domestic Product, a measure of economic activity valuing all the final goods and services produced in an economy over a given time.

GINI coefficient – statistical measure of inequality.

Globalization – the process of worldwide integration of social, cultural and economic systems.

GNP – Gross National Product, a measure of economic activity equivalent to GDP plus net income from abroad.

Gold standard – a system that fixes international exchange rates by making currencies convertible into gold at a fixed price.

Gross – indication of a figure before relevant subtractions have been made.

Growth – increased capacity to produce goods and services within an economy over a given period.

H

Hedge fund – an investment fund that takes speculative market positions in the hope of high returns.

Hyperinflation – rapid inflation that threatens the position of a currency as a means of exchange.

I

ILO – International Labour Organization, a United Nations agency concerned with labour matters and human rights.

IMF – International Monetary Fund, a United Nations agency promoting international monetary cooperation and stability.

Imports – goods and services brought by one economy from another.

Income – money or other assets received.
Inequality – differences in the distribution of money within a given economic system.
Inflation – a persistent trend of rising prices.
Insurance – a contractual agreement to spread and reduce risk.
Interest – payment owed to a lender in excess of the amount borrowed.
International Bank for Reconstruction and Development – *see* World Bank.
Investment – a monetary asset purchased to provide a future income or to be sold for profit.

L

Liability – a legal obligation to make a payment.
Loan – a sum lent and to be returned, usually with interest.
Long position – buying a security in the belief that it will rise in value.
Loss – the outcome when expenditure exceeds income.
Lottery – a game of chance typically offering a significant prize to the winner(s).

M

Macroeconomics – the study of large-scale economic factors.
Market – a forum for buying and selling.
Market economy – an economy in which a significant proportion of goods and services are allocated via the market.
Microeconomics – the study of the behavior of individual consumers and businesses.
Microfinance – banking services provided to those on low incomes who have limited or no access to traditional financial service providers.
Monetary policy – government or central bank policy that manipulates interest rates or money supply to influence the economy.
Money – a medium of exchange and store of value.
Multinational – company operating across more than one country.

N

National debt – the full extent of debt owed by a national government.
Nationalization – the process of bringing a private enterprise under government ownership.
Net – indication of a figure after relevant subtractions have been made.
Not-for-profit – description of an organization where all monies received are reallocated for the pursuance of its objectives and not as profit for its owners.

O

OECD – Organization for Economic Cooperation and Development, a group of 30 free market economies whose mission is to promote policies that will improve the economic and social well-being of people around the world.

Opportunity cost – the opportunity given up by making a particular choice.

P

Per capita – for each person.
Philanthropy – large-scale charity.
Planned economy – an economy in which the majority of goods and services are allocated via a centralized authority.
Plastic money – generic terms for bank cards, credit cards etc.
Poverty – the state of being unable to afford life's essentials.
Price – the amount of money paid for a good or service.
Primary sector – the part of an economy that makes use of natural resources.
Principal – depending on context, the value of a loan without interest or the original value of an investment without earnings.
Private sector – those parts of the economy not under government control.
Privatization – the transfer to private ownership of assets and enterprises formerly under government control.
Profit – the excess of receipts over expenditure for a business over a set period.
Public sector – those parts of the economy not controlled by private individuals or organizations.

R

Recession – a general decline in economic activity, usually observed by successive falls in GDP.
Recovery – the movement of an economy from its lowest point back toward normal levels.
Regulation – rules that individuals or organizations are obliged to observe.
Resources – any assets that can contribute to economic activity.
Return – the proceeds or profit received from an economic undertaking.
Risk – uncertainty over the size of return on an investment.

S

Savings – income not spent on consumption in a given period.
Scarcity – a shortage of something that is in demand.
Secondary sector – that part of an economy encompassing manufacturing, processing and construction.
Security – something pledged to guarantee the fulfilment of an economic undertaking, or a financial instrument representing ownership of a stock, share, bond etc.
Share – a part ownership of an enterprise.
Short selling – selling a borrowed asset or commodity on the assumption that it can be bought back at a lower price.
Single currency – a currency used by more than one country.

State-owned – an entity whose ownership lies with the state, usually represented by the government.
Stock – a synonym for share, or alternatively a store of goods built up by an enterprise.
Stock exchange (or stock market) – an institution where stocks and shares are sold.
Supply – the amount of a good or service on sale.
Supranational – transcending national borders.

T

Taxation – compulsory payments to the government made by individuals and organizations.
Tertiary sector – that part of an economy encompassing service industries.
Trade – the basic act of buying and selling.
Trader – an individual engaged in buying and selling financial assets on behalf of themselves or for someone else.
Treasury – the funds or revenues of a state, or the government department overseeing them.
Trillion – a million million (or thousand billion).

U

UN – United Nations, an organization that aims for international cooperation and peace and which has a membership comprising every recognized nation state with the exception of the Vatican City.
Utility – satisfaction gained by consuming a good or service.

V

Virtual money – money exchanged in computer-generated, simulated environments.

W

Wages – payment for work performed for an employer.
Wealth – total value of assets of an individual, organization or country minus all debts.
World Bank – a supranational body established in 1946 to promote economic cooperation and development.

INDEX

PICTURE CREDITS

The publishers would like to thank the following for providing the photographs included in this book:

Bloomberg/The YGS Group page 93; **Bridgeman Art Library** pages 14 & 15; **Corbis** pages 17, 68, 80 & 106; **Bryan Christie** page 37; **d.light** page 144; **FBI** page 191; **Getty Images** pages 3, 8–9, 11, 13, (bottom), 21, 25, 26, 28, 31, 32, 33, 34, 35, 41, 42, 44, 48, 51, 56, 57, 61, 62–3, 65, 66, 67, 70, 75, 79, 82, 84–5, 88, 94, 95, 99, 101, 102, 103, 107, 108–9, 109, 112–3, 114, 116, 120, 123, 124, 126, 127, 128, 131, 133, 139, 148–9, 154; 159 (bottom), 160–1 (all), 165, 170, 181, 187 (bottom), 188, 189, 192, 205, 206, 212–13, 217, 226, 240, 243 & 247; **Imaginechina** pages 24, 105, 138, 220, 225 & 230; iStockphoto.com/richcano page 90, iStockphoto.com/LockieCurrie page 104; **Louisiana State Museum** page 19; **Opte Project** page 150; **PA Photos** pages 6–7, 20, 23, 39, 45, 52, 53, 54, 55, 58, 60, 64, 68 (bottom), 76, 78, 86, 89, 97 (right), 98 (both); 102–3, 110, 111 (both), 115, 125, 132–3, 142–3, 152–3, 159 (top), 168, 173, 174, 175, 177, 178, 183, 184, 187 (top), 196, 199, 201, 203, 210, 222, 229, 232, 234, 236, 238, 239, 245 & 249 (both); **Portsmouth Museum** page 223; **Rex Features** pages 72 & 73; **Shutterstock** pages 1 & 91 creestee, 40 Vitaly Korovin, 65 (frame) nodff, 97 (left) Ragnarock, 119 (bottom) artjazz, 136 Christian Delbert, 146 Nata-Lia, 156 EDHAR, 159–61 (backgrounds) pashabo/Sergey Nivens, 162 Sklemine Kirill, 164 James Daniels, 166 (both) Thomas Pajot/V.J. Matthew, 172–3 Nicemonkey, 179 Marquisphoto, 190 (background) Balefire, 200 Rudchenko Liliia, 209 Tony Bowler, 214 Orla, 218 (both) photobank.kiev.ua/Uto image, 224–5 Vibrant Image Studio, 226–7 Denis Vrublevski & 248–9 (background) Elnur (name of artist/shutterstock.com); **Wikimedia Commons** pages 10, 12, 18 & 215; **Zildjian** page 134.

While every effort has been made to trace and acknowledge all the copyright holders, the publishers would like to apologize should there have been any errors or omissions. If notified, the publishers will be pleased to rectify these at the earliest opportunity.